Writing Personal Essays:
How to Shape Your Life Experiences for the Page

Writing Personal Essays:

How to Shape Your Life Experiences for the Page

Sheila Bender

WRITER'S DIGEST BOOKS
CINCINNATI, OHIO

This hardcover edition of *Writing Personal Essays* features a "self-jacket" that eliminates the need for a separate dust jacket. It provides sturdy protection for your book while it saves paper, trees and energy.

99 98 97 96 95   5 4 3 2 1

Library of Congress Cataloging in Publication Data

Bender, Sheila
    Writing personal essays: how to shape your life experiences for the
page / by Sheila Bender.—1st ed.
        p.   cm.
    Includes bibliographical references and index.
    ISBN 1-89879-665-2
    1. English language—Rhetoric. 2. Autobiography—Authorship. 3.
    Essay—Authorship. I. Title.
PE1479.A88B46   1995
808'.042—dc20   95-2755
                                                        CIP

Edited by Jack Heffron
Cover and interior design by Sandy Conopeotis Kent

The permissions on page ix constitute an extension of this copyright page.

For my parents Bert and Arline Lillian,
whose story led to mine

ABOUT THE AUTHOR

Sheila Bender lives in Seattle and Port Townsend, Washington, where she writes and teaches writing at colleges and workshops. She has an M.A. in Creative Writing from the University of Washington. Her previous books include a volume of poetry, *Love From the Coastal Route*, (Duckabush Press, 1991) and *Writing in a Convertible With the Top Down: A Unique Guide for Writers*, coauthored with fiction writer Christi Killien (Warner Books, 1992). Her plays have been produced by Youth Theater Northwest on Mercer Island, Washington. She is a regular book review columnist for *Poet Love*, Bethesda, Maryland; *The World*, Boston; and the *Seattle Times*.

PERMISSIONS

ACKNOWLEDGMENTS

A book, like a life, is not created apart from others. There are many people I wish to thank for their support and help.

First and foremost, I wish to thank my husband, Kurt VanderSluis, for his insistence that I remember writing is central in my life. I wish to thank him for his farsighted computer assistance. It began when he weaned me from my typewriter by teaching me my first word processing program and continues now to updating my systems, backing up my hard disk, helping me find documents I've lost inside my computer, and setting up electronic connections for me to use to communicate with other writers and editors. His example of persistence and concentration as he writes his own articles and books is a valuable model for me. His unfailing love, admiration and open heart are the most valuable gifts I have ever received.

Secondly, I want to thank my friends. Poet Paula Jones Gardner was an early and unflagging model of the response method I have written about in the book. Her ability to respond to my work in progress over the years by sharing the feelings aroused in her as she read my words offered the sensitive guidance that helped me grow as a writer. Christi Killien, with whom I coauthored *Writing in a Convertible With the Top Down*, kept my interest in this project alive from the earliest draft. She asked me if there was somewhere she could buy this book. As a result of reading my drafts, Christi made her own foray, after six novels, into essay writing. She told me the ways in which my manuscript helped her and she described the other guidance she wanted to see in it. Also, my thanks to Martha Plotkin for letting me know about Faye Moskowitz's work, to Marilyn Meyer, Betty Ann McCall, Esther Frank, Fran Costigan and Leah Breier for their affirmations of my work, and to Diane Gould, Humanities Division Chair at Shoreline Community College, for supporting me in using early drafts of this book as a teaching text. Thanks also to Jim Guerly, Neile Graham and Brenda Miller for information on computer writing groups and essay markets. Thanks to the Centrum Foundation, Port Townsend, Washington, for the writing residency that allowed me time to synthesize the material in this book. I thank my literary agent, Elizabeth Wales, for seeing me through this project from idea to contract all in the right time, and Jack Heffron, my editor at Writer's Digest Books, for the help he has given me to make this book complete and accessible for the reader. Also, I give thanks to Jeanne Yeasting, past editor at University of Washington Press, and freelance editor Deborah Berger for teaching me how to fine-tune exposition.

And last, but certainly not least, I wish to thank the essayists whose work appears in the book as examples of personal essay writing at its best. They were very generous in allowing me to print their work. I am especially grateful to an honest and open woman, Elizabeth Bamber, whose eight essays and early drafts appear throughout this book, both for her desire to write her way through the passage of her late twenties and her commitment to drafting essays regularly and without procrastination so they could become part of my teaching.

To essay is to attempt, to test, to make a run at something without knowing whether you are going to succeed . . .

One would like to think that the personal essay represents a kind of basic research on the self, in ways that are allied with science and philosophy.
—*Phillip Lopate,* The Art of the Personal Essay

PROLOGUE

At 45

The way I see it, I am at the halfway mark in my life, more or less. Writing this sentence, I suddenly remember my preteen self as I cut through the aquamarine water on swimming race days summers at the Greenwood Swim Club in East Hanover, New Jersey. Midway down the lane and desperate to take a breath, I'd struggle to keep myself from looking around as I opened my mouth for a quick gulp of air. My head back in the water, I'd look to my left and to my right. How far had I come? Were any swimmers behind me in their lanes? How many?

Waiting to hear the names of the winners, I'd stand with the other girls, panting and dripping, self-conscious about the way my ribs and navel showed between the two pieces of my bathing suit. I wasn't exactly a fish in the water, as my parents and their friends would describe other children, but I wanted to be a part of things. I wore the right bathing suit, swam the crawl stroke races, learned to dive from the high dive, and danced with the teenyboppers to rock and roll from the clubhouse jukebox.

I worked so hard to look like the kind of fish everyone else seemed to be that I didn't know what it felt like to be the kind of fish I actually was. All of my growing up, I felt like a hypocrite, a working-hard-to-be-a-part-of-things person on the outside covering up for a sidelines-kind-of-a-girl on the inside. Though I wanted to be sponsored to live on an Indian reservation one summer, I stayed home and enrolled in the shorthand course my mother wanted me to take. Though I longed to go out with our high school's gawky first-chair violinist who enjoyed long walks better than school dances, I dated the president of our youth group. Though the only science facts I could remember vividly were ones like "when you smell manure, you are actually taking particles of the substance into your nose," I declared I would be a science major on my college applications because all the smart kids were going into science. Though I longed to travel and live abroad, I finished college and became a teacher so I had a career I could fall back on, something my mother told me time and again was necessary. She wanted me to have a career that would wait for me when I had children. To have children, I married a guy who was swimming in the same water I was trying so hard to stay in.

While he was in medical school, I directed a day care center. When he became an intern and we had kids, I asked for a leave from my job. I sat in the bleachers during my kids' swimming lesson discussing Volvos and home furnishings with the parents beside me. I chauffeured and shepherded my kids from class to class, playmate's house to playmate's house, preschool potluck to preschool potluck. I was a good wife to my tired and overworked husband. I ran off one evening a week to take a watercolor class at the community center and one day a week to volunteer at the juvenile court. It seemed all right from the outside, but raising my children was rapidly becoming the first job I couldn't succeed at with sheer activity. I loved them too deeply. I knew at my core my hypocrite days were over. Raising them to be happy would mean raising them to be the true people they were inside. How could I do that if I denied them who I was? I would have to shed that person working so hard at swimming to the end of the lane and find the person who was lurking on the sidelines. What was her element?

While I folded clothes from the unending piles of laundry in my life, I began to hear poetic lines inside my head. I had only written in grade school and then once or twice when I was in high school. But since college, poetry books by people I'd never heard of had jumped of their own accord into my hands whenever I visited bookstores. I never spoke of this to anybody, but I had taken to buying them; the books insisted on it. Now that I was hearing these lines, I started to write stanzas during my children's nap time. I felt like a song was there in the sounds I was making, but the words didn't convey much. I had found the tune my inner self sang, but I didn't know the words to it. I continued reading poems voraciously and trying to write them.

The next summer, when I was looking for classes for my children,

I found a catalog from the University of Washington, and I read about poet David Wagoner's Poetry Writing Workshop. I would need to submit poems to be considered for the workshop, so I struggled to rework the few "almost poems" I had managed to pull from myself all those nap times.

The day I was to drop them off at the Creative Writing Office, a good friend and I headed to the campus with our strollers and diaper bags and my envelope of poems.

"Why couldn't I be applying to social work school?" I lamented. "At least then I'd be able to help people when I got my graduate degree."

My friend assured me writing poetry was a humanitarian act.

"Right," I said, "but I really can't shake the idea that I am supposed to do something to serve my country. To be a good citizen."

"It's that Sputnik thing again, isn't it?"

I nodded. When Sputnik was successfully launched by the Russians, our grade school teachers had cried before our eyes telling us our country was now at risk. All classes reported to the auditorium where we were told how important physical fitness, science and math were to be from then on and how art and music were not as important anymore in our battle to regain leadership of the world.

"I had a lot of trouble climbing the thick hairy ropes they suddenly hung from the gym ceiling, but I thought I could help another way. I feel guilty about poetry. People think it's superfluous and dilettantish," I said.

"Learning your own heart is a big contribution," my wise friend said. "Do you know how much better the world would be if more people had true insight?"

Amazingly, David Wagoner accepted me into his class. In September, I began going three times a week. No matter how hard it was to make child care arrangements or how much trouble I had parking or how many times my poems were heavily criticized or how many times not one student in the class seemed to care what I said since I was new and unpublished, I was happy. David Wagoner's class was the first place I had ever congregated where I was completely at peace. I understood the thinking and the ideas. I liked what we talked about and I liked what we did. I knew I would learn how to do it better. It didn't matter if anyone else recognized this about me. It was enough that I recognized it. My classmates could tear into my poems and I never flinched. In class, I never felt time go by. I was never out of breath. I didn't think about where I was or who I was ahead of. It didn't matter how far I had come to get there or how far I would need to go.

As my children grew, I wrote and learned and published. To make a poem sound right and mean right, I had to listen closely to it, check it with my ear and my heart, until all my conscious mind's attempts to short circuit the revelation of truths or supply unearned truths were stopped. Each time I wrote, I had to get beyond what my "good girl, good citizen" self propounded and find the sources of pain and joy in my life, no matter how small or how large, how alike they were to those of others or how different they seemed. My conversations with my children became passageways into my poems. When my daughter told me that when she grew up, I would grow down, I wrote about that, and I shared what I wrote with her. Though she may not have understood the meaning of my words, she learned the sound of her mother's heart and mind. When she told me she dreamed I came out of the sky with the raindrops and opened my umbrella and floated back down to earth watering the flowers, I felt more real than I ever had winning a race or getting a job.

Poetry had taken me to my inner self, and everything I had accumulated with my old outer self fell away, including my marriage. The hardest thing about saying goodbye to my marriage was being unable to explain to my parents and relatives why I was doing it. They had never seen the inside me. They didn't really trust insides or foster recognizing them. They said my divorce was making them sick. The fact that I couldn't be heard no matter what I said allowed me to give up trying. I wasn't going to swim in an element wrong for myself anymore. My children understood me without much explanation. My son would fall asleep nights to the sound of my Olivetti truck of an electric typewriter and report to people that the only problem with having a poet for a mom was hearing the typewriter at night. I became a teacher of writing at community centers and community colleges, a state artist-in-residence and a member of literary project boards. When I was overwhelmed with other people's writing and the administrative details of the projects, my son told me he wanted to build me a house on wheels so he could drive me around and I could be free to write and write.

I am remarried now to a man who found me through my poems.

He was a friend of one of my best friends when my first book of poems, a locally published twenty-page chapbook, came out. He saw it on her coffee table, and he read it while she was on the telephone. Then he asked her how she had found this poet. When she said I was her friend, he insisted on organizing a picnic to meet my children and me. That was almost ten years ago.

There have been many eddies and stagnant pools in the new waters of my life, but always the flow of fresh water, which poetry brings, has cleared me of those spots. This week I am turning forty-five. As my last child prepares to leave the nest this summer, a proposal for my third book is in my agent's enthusiastic hands.

I know how far I have come. I enjoy recognizing myself as someone who has let her true self emerge, who won't need to push herself down the wrong lane anymore, desperate for breath. I think often of my grandfather in summer, the way he would float on his back in the Atlantic Ocean off Coney Island, hands behind his head for a pillow. He was the only person I knew who could float as long as he wanted to without sculling his hands or kicking his legs. There he is, smiling and buoyant, the water glistening with sun.

◆ ◆ ◆

I write this essay and for a moment there is nothing else to be written. Then, the emotional occasion of my birthday is covered by the tide of my life and what it brings to my attention—a colleague's success, my son's fall down concrete steps, the smell of floor cleaner, a new friend telling about refrigerators abandoned in Utah fields with their doors unhinged so children cannot be trapped inside. I am ready to shape more life experience for the page. I started not sure at all where I am going, but I will know my ending when I am more sure where I have been.

What Is a Personal Essay?

Essayists are ambidextrous, not glamorous; switch-hitters going for the single, not the home run. They're character actors, not superstars. They plug along in a modest manner (if any writer can be called modest), piling up masonry incrementally, not trying for the Taj Mahal like an ambitious novelist.

— Edward Hoagland, "To the Point: Truths Only Essays Can Tell,"
Harper's Magazine, *March 1993*

I like to compare the personal essay to a vessel engineered according to the laws of buoyancy and durability and built from raw experience. Some personal essays turn out to be oceangoing cruise ships, some battleships, some tugs, some sailboats and some simple dories, but all of them, when finished, take their authors and readers across waters they might not otherwise have negotiated. It is work to build this kind of craft, but always the finished vessel is useful.

Writer Tobias Wolff says:

> ... the real possibility of the personal essay, which is to catch oneself in the act of being human ... means a willingness to surrender for a time our pose of unshakable rectitude, and to admit that we are, despite our best intentions, subject to all manner of doubt and weakness and foolish wanting.

Novelist and essayist Edward Hoagland says:

> ... when I am miffed with my sister, at sixes and sevens with my mother, groping for an intelligent (as distinct from

blind) empathy with my daughter, or tangling with the woman I presently share my life with, I'd as soon read a first-rate collection of essays for guidance as *Anna Karenina*.

But what is the blueprint for making the sturdy vessel? What is the practice by which one shakes a pose of rectitude or even recognizes it? How does a personal essay tell its author's story intimately and with real meaning for others?

These were the kinds of questions I had when I began teaching composition at colleges fourteen years ago. To answer these questions for myself so I could effectively help my students write essays, I drew on my experience and training in creative writing, particularly the writing of poetry. Foremost, I kept in mind that writers write and rewrite and rewrite and rewrite and rewrite. A revision process does not stop until the writing is fully realized. Most texts I found to use with my students did not represent this rewriting part of the process effectively. They would show a paragraph here and a paragraph there in first draft form and then revised. Sometimes, they would show an essay by one student in first draft and then finished draft and perhaps one more essay by another student in both first and revised drafts. I thought that students would get a lot from following writers over a longer duration to see the writing and rewriting process fully. After all, those who write need to get to know one writer and one writing process very well indeed: their own. So, in the classroom I instituted the following measures: my students could continue to rewrite any or all of their papers from the first due date until the end of the term and they would work in writing groups where they would get to see the work and revisions of their fellow students throughout the term. Their final essays were good. In fact, many of them were later published in anthologies.

Writing Personal Essays: How to Shape Your Life Experiences for the Page captures my approach in a book, apart from the classroom. I offer the blueprint for successful essay writing by exploring eight styles of essay writing, by offering eight questions that help writers figure out which parts of their life experiences are best explored by using each of the eight styles. Next, I offer help for the writers who need to get underneath easy judgment to discover the deeper meaning in a life experience. This help comes in the form of gathering exercises that focus writers on their material, elements of which may be long buried. It comes in the form of sample essays written by people with a variety of personal experience. It also comes in the form of staying with the efforts of one writer, Elizabeth Bamber, throughout the eight styles.

The trappings of Elizabeth's life are those of a single, urban, college-educated, working young woman, but the epiphanies and understandings she comes to are the universal moments from which an inner life is made. You may feel after reading each of Elizabeth's first and final drafts that you never want to think about another cafe, pastry or city outing again. It is difficult sometimes as a reader to follow the developing work of one writer. You must switch hats, though, from reader to writer and realize you are following in order to learn what happens along the way in the writing process. Every writer, including you, has certain personal obsessions, favored images and familiar settings.

Eavesdropping on Elizabeth's efforts will help you develop patience and a respect for your own efforts. Your world, if you keep on exploring it, is made of sameness — same children, neighbors, spouse, job, parents and history as you have always had. You must get past the feeling in developing your essays that what hasn't changed isn't worth using in your writing. Instead, you must write using the images and situations of your life as best you can, finding the meaning.

You will see how by exploring her own life through the eight essay writing styles, Elizabeth brought emotional issues to closure and cleared a way towards new, and perhaps more welcome, life events. By getting to "listen in" on my responses to her work-in-progress, you will develop the ability to respond to your own work and revise more quickly. The more familiar the sound of Elizabeth and I working together becomes for you, the more quickly you will develop the ability to think as a writer revising toward meaning.

Essayist Nancy Mairs says in her book *Ordinary Time*, "It's as though some writers have the sense never to enter the room until they've thrown the switch and flooded it with light, whereas others, like me, insist on entering rooms with burnt-out bulbs or blown fuses or maybe no wiring at all." Elizabeth and I set out on an exploration without knowing what was in the rooms or even which of her life's buildings we'd explore. I am convinced that the best learning and the best teaching takes place that way and I want to share it with you.

I have risked your frustration in being Elizabeth's captive reader. I have done this, however, in the hopes of a fruitful result. Let us go now not only to listen in on Elizabeth's process, but to locate the buildings of your explorations, burnt-out bulbs, miswired outlets and all.

CHAPTER ONE

Empowering Yourself to Write the Personal Essay

The squeaking of the pump sounds as necessary as the music of the spheres.

> — *Henry Thoreau,* The Heart of Thoreau's Journals, *edited by Odell Shepard*

Through the techniques of writing the personal essay, you can recall your experience and release the essence of it in fewer pages than you might imagine. You can write about the time you waited in the car while your father went into his mother's house to receive an "heirloom," came out empty-handed and slammed the driver's side door so hard the car rocked like a boat in tall waves. You can write about the time you walked home from high school on a windy day and your mother told you to look at yourself in the mirror because you were so beautiful in the flush of early spring. You can write about the time the toaster oven you'd received as a wedding gift burnt out and you knew for certain this was a metaphor for your marriage. If you have ever found yourself saying, "If only I could write a book about my life" or "I want to write but I don't know exactly what I want to write," the personal, or first-person, essay is right for you.

The term *essay* may be lumped together in the files of your mind with the dreaded weekly theme and the boring what-I-did-over-my-school-vacation assignments of childhood. If writing was dull, difficult and removed from anything you really felt, it may have been because you felt your life was not important enough to merit words on a page or you "couldn't describe things in words" the way you experienced them in life. Perhaps you felt the teacher wanted to hear something other than what was true for you, or you may have been afraid to put your truths on paper.

In the introduction, I addressed the need for every author of personal essays to acknowledge the elements of their lives, no matter how mundane, in order to draw meaning from them. In each chapter of this book, I offer you exercises to help you gather the words for writing your experiences with fullness and life on the page. Here I would like to address the last two inhibitors to good writing—fear of your audience and fear of your truths.

You have the right to say what you want about your experience. It is, in fact, essential to living your life. Using the personal essay, you have, as book reviewer Joan Frank declares in the July/August 1990 *Utne Reader*, "a two-way mirror, prompting a startling moment wherein writer and reader each recognize some aspect of themselves in the other and come away from that moment transformed."

When you write a personal essay, you write on a topic of your choice, because you want to find the truth in your experience. If you find it, your essay will be interesting to someone else. You and your essay are in charge, not your high school or college English teacher. In fact, as you will find out in the following chapters, the essay itself will be your teacher. This teacher serves you, however, only when you trust in vulnerabilty.

Like the lodgepole pine, which has evolved so that its cones don't open to let seeds drop out until fire has scorched the forest, you can learn to let the world's fire provoke you into bringing forth your voice, rich with human qualities. When you are willing to be vulnerable, your fond memories will be fonder and your humorous moments more humorous. Your defeats will be more deeply felt, but your triumphs, even the smallest, will resound like the Liberty Bell.

SEEK KNOWLEDGE THROUGH WRITING

Getting to the flower of true voice requires work. A seed cannot perform the miracle of growing into a new plant until it is released from what encloses it, and often you must dig deep into the experience of your life to find the seed from which to write. In doing so, you learn something new about yourself and your circumstances.

I may think I have a funny story to tell about the time my sister and I went to New Haven, Connecticut, to visit our great aunt and her two sons. I may think what is important is recounting every detail of the train trip we took between Newark, New Jersey, and New Haven because that was my first train ride. Yet when I write, I remember the new hats my mother insisted we wear for the trip because

"Aunt Bertha is from wealthy New England." I remember how we excitedly put the hats on as the train was pulling into the station. Greeting us, Aunt Bertha insisted we take the hats off immediately "because they looked so silly." When I write about this moment and reexperience Aunt Bertha's comment, I recognize that the deep experience of my train ride is not the ride itself but what it felt like to be a stranger.

How do you get beyond mere recounting of experience and find the wisdom and knowing inside it? I have developed eight "write" questions. These questions, along with exercises I introduce for answering them, help you think of personal experience topics. They help you make discoveries, and they help you write essays readers can follow.

Each of my questions is paired with one of eight essay forms. Using games, I will help you understand the pattern of thinking used in each form. By combining your understanding of the form with your answer to the "write" question, you will achieve essays that release the experience from inside your mind.

Whether you come to this book with a desire to write but no topic in mind, or with a desire to write about specific experiences in your life, the "write" questions and the writing exercises are designed to help you find surprises. You will write the material that comes as you do the exercises in each chapter. You will learn to write from experience even when you don't know exactly what in your experience is significant. Each time you use a chapter and explore one of the forms of essay writing, you will enter a "writing patch" inside yourself, a place where images and details arrive to help you grow the "experience plant" and then see it bloom.

In each chapter, you can read sample essays and follow my discussion of how the writing brought discoveries for the authors. In addition, after you answer the "write" question in each chapter and understand the pattern of the particular essay form, you can read Elizabeth Bamber's draft and follow my comments as I respond to it in a special three-step process. This process gives writers a nonjudgmental report that helps in revision. The three steps cover what is memorable in the work, what readers feel upon reading the work, and what readers are left wondering about. It is like fertilizer. When you learn to respond this way to your own drafts, you will enhance the quick growth of your writing from inception to finished piece.

After my three-step response to Elizabeth's work, you can try your hand at your own draft. Then, putting your draft away for a while, you can read Elizabeth's revised essay and my response to it. Finally, you can revise your first draft into a fully satisfying personal essay.

REALIZE THAT "BAD" WRITING IS THE OPPORTUNITY FOR GOOD WRITING

When you write in the shadows of fear (and most of us have at least some shadows when it comes to writing), your writing may go on and on, like a boring teacher, never distinguishing the important details from the unimportant ones. Or your writing may get so busy screaming like a hysteric about how you think you ought to feel that it can't evoke what you're really feeling. Or your writing may flit from one topic to another like a social butterfly to avoid examining something difficult.

You must accept that sometimes the boring teacher, the hysteric, or the social butterfly will come into your writing. Your job is not to worry about their presence, but to learn to hear them covering or circumventing true experience. Using my three-step response, you will learn to recognize the opportunity to cut away words that distort your true voice. You will honor whatever images and details are most important to your experience.

SAY "I"

You may have had writing teachers who told you never to write "I" in an essay or to keep the number of times you wrote the word to a minimum. If you took that advice to heart, you may have stopped writing. You probably couldn't figure out from whom your writing would originate if not from "I." If you kept on writing, you may have twisted and turned phrases so they appeared as if they were never written by an "I" at all. After all those maneuvers to eradicate any evidence that you actually wrote your material, your meaning was probably quite blurred.

Just as you dream your own dreams, you live your own experiences. You are the filter for what you see, hear, taste, touch and smell in this world. It is not only okay to report, "I watched the leaves of the poplar trees blowing silver side up in the wind as my father told me my grandmother was dying," it is imperative for good writing. You must own your experience, every detail of it, to write well about it.

Each piece of experience builds into a bigger piece of experience. When you report where you are, what you see, taste, touch, feel and smell, you also release what is inside of you, the pattern of what you have learned. It is as if elements of the inside experience attach themselves to specific places on the outer landscape. That the leaves were silver side up as I heard the news of my grandmother's dying leads me as writer to other elements of my experience — the silver of my grandmother's hair and her temper blowing like strong wind. Sensitive to all experience, no matter how small, the writer is more deeply informed, and this information leads to discovery.

When you are writing, do not worry about how often you use the word *I*. Use it as much as you need to. Just as you can weed out other words you no longer need when your work is nearing completion, so you can weed out extra *I*s by combining sentences or editing phrases. It is very easy to take out what is no longer needed at the end. It is much harder to give yourself enough material to work with at the beginning. Say "I." This word lets you speak from your experience.

RECOGNIZE THAT WRITING IS A FORMAL AFFAIR

The essay is a container from which readers will take your insight. The container comes in eight styles: description; narration; how-to; comparison and contrast; division and classification; definition; cause and effect, and, finally, argument and persuasion.

An understanding of each style's structure (its strategies and components) will help you create writing that moves along gracefully — writing that helps you and the reader discover the shape of the experience inside your life events. In your life, things happen and you see and you do and you go. However, recounting what happened, what you saw, where you went and what you did doesn't by itself aid you in discovering and communicating the *experience* you have gained from those happenings. It is the structure of the styles you are using in your work that becomes, both for you and your readers, a bridge to your learning, insight and wisdom.

In this book, essay styles introduced in later chapters make use of styles introduced in earlier ones. The patterns of thinking you engage to use each style are more elaborate as you move through them. However, it's not that you use one style over another to be more profound. The description essay style, which comes first in this book, creates essays that are just as profound as those created using the argument essay style, which comes last. Knowing all the styles gives you the *dexterity* with which to fully find and communicate the *range* of your human experience.

Here is an excerpt from the writing of a man in his mid-thirties who was assessing his life. Since it is written without good use of the styles available in the craft of essay writing, he thwarts his own search for self-discovery:

I am feeling terribly relaxed and thoughtful just now. The sea is rolling slowly toward the gray horizon just after sunset. I stare at it for hours. It is my Mantra. My life has not been a great joy of late. My job is taking more and more and giving me very little nourishment for the spirit. I wander back and forth across the Atlantic in a continuous twilight fog of jet lag with no direction. I can see that now in a moment of clarity.

I have been floating on a ship in the Gulf of Guinea off the Niger Delta for the last five days. Five quiet unhurried days waiting for equipment to be calibrated and parts to arrive. I can understand how a life at sea becomes so addictive to sailors. Such a soothing effect it has. No telephones, no traffic, no panic decisions. Just the rocking of a big cradle.

The seas are very calm today, almost glassy at times, but visibility is very poor. This is the time of year when northeast winds blow down from the Sahara carrying a very fine dust that fills the air. They call it the Harmatten. I like the name. It can last for days and becomes quite distracting, but it does cool down the otherwise steamy temperatures.

Each of the three paragraphs begins with information about being relaxed: he is relaxed and thoughtful; he is floating on a ship; the sea is calm. However, after the first sentence in each paragraph, the author gives information that contrasts with his stated mood. There is fog of jet lag, waiting for equipment, and the presence of dust and heat. The sea has lulled this writer for five days and now that he is writing about it, his first impulse is to gloss over his emotions by glossing over the dangers of being at sea. (Don't sailors make panic decisions and face difficult situations on board?) This writer's easy life is taking place in fog and high temperatures. The writer can't get beyond being stuck in the calm of the sea even as his heart (and ours) is ready to motor into the rolling and difficult waves of life's trials.

If this writer understood the structure of description or narration, comparison and contrast or some of the other essay styles I share in this book, he would be able to use his experience at sea to make a discovery about himself. The reader would experience not only the discovery, but the author's process of uncovering a hidden truth.

GET RESPONSE

Many writers find it helpful to work with a writers group. Having an audience that meets regularly and is committed to writing affirms writers in their work. Everyone in your group does not actually have to be a writer. Anyone truly interested in experience and in responding to writing can be helpful. Although even one person is valuable for getting response to your work, two or more are better since you will get a variety of responses to consider.

Whether you are reading your work to one friend, forming a new writers group, or working with an existing one, you may want to familiarize anyone you trust to listen to your work with the response method I present in this book. I have developed the response method after years of finding out what goes wrong for new writers as they put words together on a page and finding out what goes wrong for writers when others evaluate their work or offer "constructive" criticism. Responding to writing is different from telling someone how to fix writing. No one who wants to write should flounder and fall away because of criticism and old schoolroom jargon.

My three-step response teaches you to talk nurturingly about your writing-in-progress so you can find the opportunities for good writing. When you share your writing with a single friend or in a group, be sure to share only the words on the page. Listen to the response without defending or explaining your work. Don't be tempted to verbally fill in points. If you explain, the response will be to what you have said, not to what you wrote. Your job is to develop your writing, not your explaining.

If you do not have anyone nearby with whom you want to share your writing, there are other ways to get a response. Users of the Internet and other electronic bulletin boards can find writers discussion groups in Usenet newsgroups and listserv subscribers-only mailing lists. Once you make contact with a group, you can pair up with one or more writers and have private "conversations." You can use these conversations to share the three-step response method idea and give each other reports on your writing-in-progress.

If you have a home computer but do not have access to the internet or to electronic bulletin boards, be sure to check with your local or county library. With the help of special grants, more and more libraries are setting up internet sites where interested people can gain access to electronic bulletin boards, to the internet with its news groups and to electronic mail. These sites are known as Freenets. While they are "free," people running the sites encourage interested users to make a nominal donation. Check with local computer users to find out what is available in your community.

There are two internet news groups that are handling creative non-fiction on the internet. They are rec.arts.prose and alt.prose. You can use a pseudonym and you can say whether you want response or not, but you must realize in these groups that once sent over the electronic highway, your work is out there and not protected very well. For something more private, there are listserv groups for writing conversations. You can ask for a pen pal to electronically mail to you, and this way your sharing is private. You can even "interview" potential pen pals. To find the listservs, read "misc.writing" on the usenet or consult a printed directory of listservs and news groups. Two excellent resources are *Internet Worlds' On Internet '94, An International Guide to Electronic Journals, Newsletters, Texts, Discussion Lists and Other Resources on the Internet*, from *Internet World Magazine* (1994, Meckler Media, Westport, Connecticut) and *The Internet Yellow Pages*, written by Harley Hahn and published in 1994 by Osborne McGraw-Hill, Berkeley, California.

One group has advertised manuscript exchange services as well as assistance to writers getting "on-line": The "us" Project BBS, 2104 Anson Road, Wilmington, Delaware 19810.

There are also ways writers work alone without any outside response. They read their work into a tape recorder. After a break of at least an hour, they play the piece back to themselves and take notes to respond to themselves. The response, too, can be tape recorded and listened to before the author attempts revision. Other ways of becoming a better responder include retyping a piece of writing to get a new feel for it, translating it into pig latin and back again, or using a puppet while reading the work aloud so the work seems to be coming from someone else's mouth and mind. Some people mail their manuscript to themselves so that by the time it arrives back in their hands, it seems like something they have never seen before.

Whether you use a group, one trusted listener, pals on the Internet, tape recorders, pig latin, puppets or the U.S. mail, what matters is that you can detach yourself from your own words long enough to see them as someone else might. That allows the writer the opportunity to see what is memorable to the reader, what is felt by the reader and what the reader is curious to know more about. Then the writer is in a good position to begin revisions.

STUDY THE WORK-IN-PROGRESS OFFERED IN THIS BOOK

Writing essays is a lot like hiking unmaintained trails through a wilderness. There is a path you can find if you use the right tools to keep you on track. Just as a compass indicates the direction to travel, your inner voice aided by the response of your listeners indicates the path of your essay. Additionally, you learn to read the essay structure just as you would a map. You do this partly by understanding how memorable images make a reader feel and by hearing what else a reader wants to hear about. Eventually, you will arrive at a place of surprising beauty.

In this book, I show how an essay develops from its first draft to its final form. At first, it might seem boring to read a first draft in its entirety and then read a final draft containing much of the same information. Please do it because you will learn an important lesson about how the process of writing leads a writer to discovery. Getting to discovery requires effort. As a writer developing your own personal essays, you will benefit from witnessing the hard work of someone else's process.

USE WRITING AS A PROCESS

When you read the final drafts of your own essays or someone else's and compare them to the first drafts, you see not only the trail that was found, but how it was uncovered. When you read the work-in-progress offered in this book, listen to yourself responding to the work. Before you know it, you will be able to listen in this same way to your own work-in-progress. Using other people's ears at any stage in the process is always a short cut, though.

IN SUMMARY

An essay helps you learn in a more complete way what it is you have actually experienced. Unlike journal writing done for your eyes only, essay writing forces you to shape your experience until it can be fully understood by others. Only when another can receive the full insight, wisdom and learning of your experiences can you truly see and feel that insight, wisdom and learning. This is the moment of the two-way mirror.

To help you write the personal essay, I will:
- share with you, step by step, writing games to help you research yourself for experiences
- share and discuss finished model essays in each of the eight styles
- introduce and demonstrate the three-step response method
- show you how this response method helps you find your true voice, so you can shape your starts into finished essays.

As you follow the discussions in each chapter:
- pause in your reading to do the games
- write first drafts of your essays
- follow a student through her drafts and my responses to them
- seek responses to your first draft
- use those responses to help you develop your draft.

Now let's get started.

CHAPTER TWO

The Description Essay

Writing About the People, Places, Events and Things

The boundaries of our world shift under our feet and we tremble while waiting to see whether any new form will take the place of the lost boundary or whether we can create out of this chaos some new order.
—*Rollo May*, The Courage to Create

Good essay writing requires good description. How can we hold on to what an author is saying in any piece of writing if we cannot see what the author sees, hear what she hears, taste what she tastes, smell what she smells and touch what she touches? But you might sit down to write and become afraid that you are not up to describing a person, place, event or object so a reader can experience what you experienced. You might even feel your own experience suddenly becoming vague and disappointing compared to the strength of your feelings when you first sat down to write.

You can offer your reader and yourself the experience of whatever person, place, event or object you are remembering by learning and following the elements of the description style essay. This style is especially effective for the personal essay when you want to write about the people, places, events and objects for which you have extremely strong feelings. Once you learn the elements of good description, you will be able to include description as part of the seven other essay styles, all of which require description as a basic ingredient.

I have always succeeded in teaching the description essay by asking my students to answer the question, "For what person, place, event or object involved in my life do I have strong feelings of love or hate?" Why write unless you have strong feelings? If you already have an area of your life you want to write about, you have strong feelings about it. Now is the time to organize the strong feelings around specifics and create a new order out of the chaos. For instance, divorce, parenting, illness, fighting a war or visiting a foreign country may be among your topics of personal interest. Ask: "What do I hate or love about my divorce, parenting, illness, war experiences or visit to a foreign country?" Don't allow yourself to answer with generalities such as loving or hating the freedom of divorce, the magnitude of being responsible for someone, the limits illness creates or the fear of taking orders from an inept sergeant. Answer with something specific. You loved or hated the way your ex-spouse looked when you argued, the way your baby smiled when you tickled him in parent-infant classes, the way your neighbors came through for you, the way a superior gave orders in the army, the way mossy rocks felt in a streambed in France.

"I hate the slippery, mossy rocks and the way they will not allow me a foothold," might be your answer to "What do I hate about my trip to France?" Or if you love your trip to France, you might find yourself saying, "I love the bread everywhere—under the arm of the man returning home by bicycle, on the blue-and-white checkered tablecloth with no plate beneath it, in the windows of the *pâtisseries*."

If you have no particular topic in mind, simply ask, "What do I love or hate?" Suddenly, you may remember the county fair you went to each year as a child, the old Ford pickup still parked in your driveway, your grandmother's jam, your grandfather's woodshop, your first piano teacher or the dune buggies in an Oregon state park.

After you are drawn to a particular topic, you can list the smells, tastes, sounds, sights and textures of the event, place or person you have chosen to describe. In your writing, you will have to smell, taste, hear, see and touch what you are writing about *as if for the first time*. This requires that you avoid *telling* your attitude about your topic and instead let the images and details of the experience speak for themselves.

I remember a little boy who attended one of my Saturday morning writing classes. He wrote, "My teacher is gross." I told him I understood how he felt about his teacher, but I did not get the *picture* of a gross teacher. He then wrote, "When she is angry, my teacher looks like a horse with the reins pulled back." Now there was something for me to see! And there was something for him to see as well. His teacher scared him.

Once you use your senses to "get" the tastes, sounds, smells, feel and look of things, you and your readers will experience the subtle and complex feelings that inspired your interest in your subject.

Before you begin writing a description essay in this chapter, you will look closely at two sample essays, do some exercises to help you gather the sensory images and details you will need for your essay, and observe Elizabeth's drafting process.

When you think about a person, place, event or object you care about, the strong feelings you have can make it hard to figure out what to include and what to leave out. How can you make the person, place, event or object real to the reader? How can you relay what your subject really means to you? When you are "in touch" with your topic through the senses, the images of your description essay begin to add up. They allow the meaning, the feelings, to come through. Also, the spatial organization in the description style essay helps you collect your memories and use them to show your feelings about your subject. Here's how two writers did it:

EXAMPLE: DESCRIPTION ESSAY

While you read the following description essay by F. Jeffrey Calvert, pay attention to what reaches you through your senses—what you see, smell, taste, touch and hear.

After you finish reading the essay, imagine yourself in the place described. Think about why it was important for Jeffrey to revisit this place by writing about it. Think about how the order in which we are introduced to the details helps us "get" the author's experience. Where does the writer enter the essay, where does he travel in it, where does he exit?

THE BEACH CABIN

The beach cabin has stood for thirty years now, hanging over the south shore of Hood Canal. It has survived countless storms, hundreds of guests, gallons of paint, and is built sturdy as a ship. The cabin has been in my family for as long as I can remember. The small house is magical to me, like a neutral zone where time sits still. Everyone visiting becomes a kid again once they step onto the beach and start digging in the sand for clams or searching under rocks for the small crab that live there.

"Great! It looks GREAT!" I think to myself as we wind the last curve of the beach road after the school months. I stop outside the house and take a long look at it amazed at the house's durability after the cruelty of the winter. The newest paint job seems to have lasted, and I laugh to myself remembering the old brown and pink paint — "The *only* brown and pink house on the canal," we used to tell our friends. There it is, the long deck where we spend our leisurely evenings barbecuing the day's catch and stretching out on the worn lounging chairs soaking up the last of the day's sunrays.

"Well, so much for sightseeing," I murmur as I start to figure out that it's not as much fun to unload as to load. I set the first boxes down in the kitchen, still mainly pink, a sort of legacy of the original house. The kitchen is a mere hallway that only one person can fit into, and it becomes very crowded at meal times. The heart of the cabin is part dining room, part living room decorated in garage sale tables, paintings of local artists, and old Sears sofas. I race upstairs to put my summer wardrobe away and see my favorite furniture in the house, the old bunk beds. What fun my brother and I have had on these beds, as late in the night we pretended they were our pirate ship, our houseboat, or G.I. Joe's secret raft.

The beach house *is* summer to me. A special place where I can spend my vacation laughing with my friends, water-skiing, swimming, or diving for the sea's treasures. It is a place to enjoy my family and the secrets of the beach, such as clamming or setting the crab pot. It is a place where I can remember all the past summers, too. Especially those spent with my father. Although he died when I was three, he wanted this funny little house for our family and somehow I know how he felt, for these are memories that I'll always treasure. That in itself is truly magical!

The Discovery in "The Beach Cabin"

Now that you have seen Jeff's rooms with their old Sears sofas, heard Jeff talk to himself, felt the bunk bed as a pirate ship, tasted and smelled the day's barbecued catch, you have experienced Jeff's beach cabin as he experienced it.

In the act of writing, Jeff discovered for himself why he feels so strongly about the cabin and as a reader, by the essay's end, you arrived at that deep moment with him. How does the form of the description essay help Jeff make his discovery?

Jeff brings us along with him in a direct path from the cabin's setting on Hood Canal to a closer view as he approaches from the windy beach road, to the inside as he enters, and then to the upstairs as he unpacks. The arrangement of this description is: 1) the whole house from afar, 2) from close up, and 3) from inside.

Once he gets into the bedroom, the most personal space in the house, Jeff makes a statement: "The beach house *is* summer to me." Then he lists things to do there, including remembering other summers spent there, the earliest when his father was still alive.

"He wanted this funny little house for our family and somehow I know how he felt." When your father dies when you are three, being able to know how he felt takes on a lot of extra resonance. All of Jeff's descriptions led him to this statement. By describing a place that is important to him, Jeff is able to boil his reality down to one very important feeling—the magic of knowing how his father felt. And as the opening paragraph lets us know, this house is a sturdy place. The magic feeling is sturdy, too, something Jeff can trust and hold onto after all the years without his father.

The description form helps Jeff organize his experience so that it is possible to go back and forth between physical space and inner space. It is as if the two kinds of space offer a switchback to reach the peak of his feelings, a peak it would be hard to climb to otherwise.

EXAMPLE: DESCRIPTION ESSAY

In this essay, Roy Nims also describes a place, one he hated, one of great discomfort. Again as you read, note what you see, hear, taste, touch, feel and smell on your trip with Roy. You might even want to make columns on a page for each of the senses and list the images from the essay that employ each sense. Where is Roy when he gives the reader each of the images? This is the spatial order of the essay. When you are finished reading, say how you feel. Why does Roy revisit this place? How might he be helped by doing that? What happens for you as you come along?

THE LOCKER ROOM

I'd entered the locker room through the door marked BOYS ONLY. It was across the narrow hallway from the gymnasium on the east side of the ground floor. Once inside, I'd be surrounded by a constantly present cloud of thick steam; the shower room to the back kept the air hot and humid. Whenever I had a cold, which was often, I found this steam particularly annoying. My already swollen and squinted eyes would swell and squint further. I'd breathe only in short, shallow breaths in order to prevent disruption of whatever quiet my clogged sinuses were managing. Such congestion would make me vertigo stricken whenever I leaned down to the small square compartment which could barely contain my clothing.

My locker was to the far back of the room and to the left. To reach it, I'd walk past five or six aisles of tall rows of small square lockers. These aisles were always filled with long haired, half naked boys constantly sneering and guffawing. Very few seconds passed that there wasn't a shoe, towel or some such item of personal property aloft in the steamy air. The slamming of lockers echoed continuously off of the cement walls which hadn't been painted in so long that their color was indiscernible. It seemed such chaos that I couldn't help but assume the defensive attitude of a trapped mammal anticipating, at any time, an attack from an undetermined direction.

The boys at that age exhibited little in the way of compassion. The zoo of the locker room served as their arena for whatever cruelties they found entertaining. They were fond of carrying switchblades, if for no other purpose, to snap open in front of the faces of those smaller than themselves and see the blade reflected in their eyes.

As ages ranged from about twelve to fifteen, there was quite a span of levels of physical development represented. Thus, those boys not yet honored by puberty received vicious and repeated ridicule.

I recall being one of the unfortunates. My mother had been neurotically puritanical in shaping our family's attitudes toward nudity, and for me to strut about the shower room naked as a jaybird was never a matter of joy. It was certainly less than helpful that the embarrassment be infinitely augmented by the crude jeers from older boys concerning my genital development or seeming lack thereof. I would pretend to ignore it and concentrate on the sound of my wet feet slapping the cold cement floor as I made my way to my locker.

I would usually dress facing the dark corner, as discreetly as possible. On one such occasion, I was targeted for a particular amount of abuse. While still naked, I was too slow to stop a fellow from grabbing my athletic supporter, running off and tossing it out the door into the populated hallway.

Everyone in the locker room roared with laughter as I pulled on my ragged bell bottomed jeans. Dressing as rapidly as possible, I dropped my cotton shirt into a puddle of water on the floor.

When finally dressed, I walked as inconspicuously as possible into the brightly lit hallway. The student body had been transformed to one hundred percent female. A number of boys had raced to the locker room doorway to point and screech and clarify to all confused observers the precise nature of the situation. There was my jockstrap in the middle of the floor. I walked over to it. Hardly breathing, I picked it up, my wet shirt clammily staying to my right side and armpit. I felt feverish. My face was flushed and red hot. My heart was beating inconsistently. The boys at the door were nearly in tears and a few girls were giggling as I crowded my way back into the locker room. When inside, I found that my things had been thrown all about the room, on top of the rows of lockers and in trash cans. My jacket had been thrown in the shower and drenched.

Everyday someone was the victim. If the victimization wasn't physical with bodies or property abused in some fashion, it was verbal and grotesque. There must have been a hundred names for a faggot.

There wasn't a time I was there that my attention wasn't fully bent on getting out as quickly as possible. I welcomed the feeling of finally lacing my shoes snugly around my cold feet, which were probably still wet, as I'd toweled myself hurriedly. This final step of dressing done, I'd get up from the bench and waste no time in reaching the door, usually carting too many things and never stopping to look to the side.

I'd welcome the relative freedom of motion offered by the hallways. The lighting was noticeably better and made me feel as if I'd emerged from an abysmal den of mental illness. It was so unexplainable as to make me feel, in a matter of seconds, that I couldn't possibly be remembering it correctly.

The Discovery in "The Locker Room"

We enter the locker room just as Roy did—through the door marked BOYS ONLY. Once inside the door (located precisely, we are told, on the east side of the ground floor), we experience the interior of the locker room through our nerve endings when the speaker tells us how the humid air affected him.

In the second paragraph, more of our senses are involved. Now we not only see and feel the interior of the locker room, we hear it as well—locker doors slamming against cement walls.

And once we focus on the people in there, we are well into the subtext (the emotional tone) of this essay. Our speaker is among the threatened and is acutely aware of his wet feet slapping the cold cement floor. Say that last phrase. The phrase's rhythm and sound emulate what it is describing: the unrelenting pain of walking in that room before those boys! The writer, in owning and remembering his experience precisely, naturally achieves the sound with which emotional meaning is conveyed. (This happens when you are writing well.)

The painful and helpless vulnerability continues, growing in intensity for two short paragraphs and one long one, until even the speaker's jacket, an article of clothing representative of the world outside the gym and its locker room, is affected.

Having toured the locker room with the author, we learn about the others and the insults they endured. Then, like in a film, we get a shot of the speaker finishing the last detail of dressing—tying his shoes on feet left wet from rushing. We can assume that he rushed every day he was required to use that locker room.

Next we go out into the hallway where the lighting is better and where our speaker can no longer believe that the actions, the fear and the hurt inside the locker room were real. Such putting away of the horror of that room was probably the only way he endured. The lit hallway seems worlds away from the steamy, dangerous locker room. We feel both the truth of the horror and the truth of the need to downplay that horror in order to go on in an environment that demanded the same bad experience day after day. Writing about the horror, Roy no longer has to downplay it; he seeks it out and evokes it with every detail he includes. I believe that pushing the locker room events to the surface of his memory helped Roy work free of the shame and torture embedded in him.

LOCATING YOUR DESCRIPTION MATERIAL

Start by asking the "write" question for beginning a description essay: For what person, place, object or activity do I have strong feelings of love or hate? Search for answers using the exercises that follow.

Clustering

Clustering, as introduced by Gabriel Rico in *Writing the Natural Way*, is a method that can help you come up with some unexpected answers to your question. Let me lead you through a cluster. Begin with one of the following words — "people," "places," "things" or "events" — circled in the center of a blank piece of paper. If, for example, you choose to start with the word "people" in the center, draw lines from that word to the names of particular people you know and have known and about whom you have strong feelings. As each name occurs to you, write it and connect it with a line to the center word. Then circle it. Next draw lines from the name to particular images you associate with that person. Circle each image. Pretty soon you will have a bunch of balloons on your page. If you want, do clusters for each of the other words.

When you feel interest in a particular grouping of the cluster, begin a new cluster and associate images and memories for this new subject. For instance, clustering about places I loved, I remembered my back fence in early spring when the tulips along it were in bloom. Then I clustered around the phrase "vanilla tulips along the back fence" and remembered more and more.

The circling is the major difference between Rico's clustering activity and other prewriting activities you may have come across like mind mapping, brainstorming and branching. The act of circling the associations you make, according to Rico, frees your mind from its usual habits and opens you up as a writer to deeper, more unexpected material. I have experienced this as an extremely productive way to center myself in my chosen material. Circling is a simple act, but it is a physical way of keeping the mind from getting too logical and blocking out useful associations. More than that:

> *Everything*
> *the Power of the World does*
> *is done in a circle.*
>
> — *Black Elk, Oglala Sioux,* Catch the Whisper of the Wind

You may have a hard time thinking in circles instead of in lines. Most of us were taught to brainstorm by listing and that can be useful. But when you are gathering, nothing should seem more or less important than anything else that occurs to you. Lists tend to make things look prioritized or organized. The inventive part of your brain doesn't want to be hemmed in this early. Think of circle making as a way to create a net into which your images will swim. It doesn't matter what order they come into the net. The more you practice this approach, the more images you'll catch. If this method feels uncomfortable, keep practicing. You will be delighted with what swims in when you least expect it.

Here is the sample cluster I did about my back fence, a place I love:

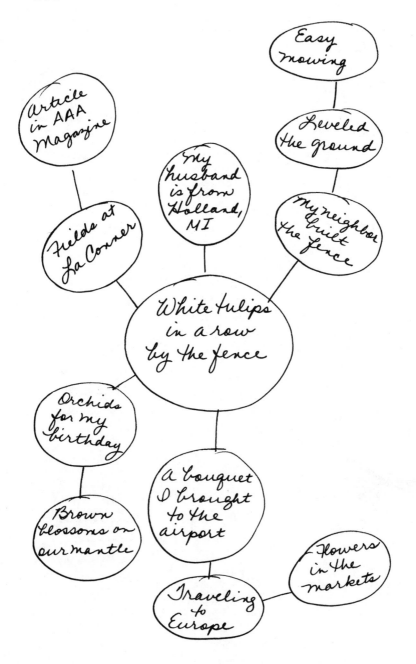

Here is one of the clusters Elizabeth created before she wrote the description essay you will read later in this chapter. After writing a cluster around places she loved and hated, she decided on her beach house as the subject for her next cluster:

Freewriting

After you finish the clustering exercise, a particular person, place, event or object from the circles should draw your attention. If it does, let yourself write for ten minutes without worrying about what you are saying or what you will do with what you are saying. If one particular person, place, event or object doesn't seem more interesting than the others, chose one just for the sake of the exercise. Then write in sentences without erasing or crossing out. Keep your pen moving; keep your fingers on the keyboard. If you can't think what to say next, just repeat what you already said. The idea here is to keep writing. Your mind and memory will eventually jump to a new image. Writing with momentum keeps your writing mind active and noisy rather than inert, overwhelmed and silent. The purpose of the freewrite is to loosen you up, to get some writing out of your fingers and to prove to you that your writing can take on a life of its own. (Peter Elbow has a full discussion of this process in his books, *Writing Without Teachers* and *Writing With Power*.)

Clustering and freewriting create room for the past and the present to intertwine.

SHEILA'S FREEWRITE

Vanilla tulips stand straight against the cedar back fence. Not all of the tulip buds are open, though, and I wonder if the unopened ones might be pink or yellow. And why are they going to bloom later than the white ones? A year and a half ago, I put all the bulbs in and at blooming time, I left to visit my daughter in Europe. When I came home, the tulips were finished. I don't remember now which kinds of tulips I chose or in what pattern I planted them.

So often I change the course I've made or someone else has made for me. My neighbor built the fence and levelled the ground right up to it making an edge for easy lawn mowing. Then I put the bulbs in and now at least in spring, we have to hand trim the grass around the tulips, under the boughs of the cherry trees which blossom then drop their petals like opals over the ground.

When the tulips finish this year, I'll braid their leaves which will make it easier for whomever mows the lawn. But underground, the bulbs will be gathering nutrition for next spring's burst of color, forcing us again away from easy mowing.

ELIZABETH'S FREEWRITE

The last time my mother raised her voice to me was to say, "You know, Lizzie, this is hard for us, too!" They had just informed me they planned to sell the house at the beach come fall. I protested in frustration that I wasn't there in N.J. to help make this decision. I'm 3000 miles away.

I grew up in that house during the summers. Some of the best conversations I have ever had were with friends and family while walking along the edge of the shore while the waves rushed up to greet us.

Falling asleep at night to the waves crashing down always made me dig deeper in my bed to snuggle the linens around my body.

The beach is where friends and family come to visit from miles around. Now, I'm the family that travels by air to return to this special place.

It is hard to let go of a friend that has sheltered you through summers of cleaning guest houses to make money for tuition or holds your secrets like when you sneaked your boyfriend down after your folks had gone back to the city.

Every summer I would plant a garden out front. I'd experiment with different varieties of flowers, geraniums, marigolds, bachelor buttons, salvia. One summer my boyfriend planted flowers with me. It made me very happy as we dug in the dirt together, sipping wine and kissing to celebrate our accomplishments.

I will go back this summer to say goodbye and as always, take this time, for the last time, whatever I need or want.

If you have trouble moving from the cluster to the freewrite, remember to leave the cluster in front of you as you freewrite. Take a second to glance at it if you feel yourself slowing down. Grab whatever image your eye falls on and write it into what you are saying. Don't worry if you contradict yourself or change topics midstream. This is a momentum-building exercise and a way for you to learn to trust the act of writing and how it creates order from chaos by attaching certain images to other images. If freewriting is hard for you, practice just moving the pen with no commitment whatsoever to the sense the freewrite may or may not make. Part of writing is just writing. This is a way to do that much.

This Is a Poem

Now that you have allowed your writing self to write, it is time to think about coaching your writing self to use images that come in through the senses. I have created an exercise to help you gather sensory images about your subject. It comes from a poem by the late Washington State poet, Charles Proctor. The poem may not have as many sensory images as I am going to push you to write, but it has an apparatus, a strategy that lends itself to collecting images. You will see how you can use that strategy to your advantage.

This Is a Poem

This is a poem about going to work.
This is a poem about the floating bridge route.
This is a poem about a reversible lane.
This is a poem about being passed from the right.
This is a poem about being cut in front of.
This is a poem about swerving hard to the left.
This is a poem about a skid.
This is a poem about a roll.
This is a poem about a Renault, without seat belts.
This is a poem about rolling broadside down the highway.
This is a poem about trust.

Notice how the form of this excerpt, the listing and repetition of the phrase, "This is a poem," offers a structure for you. You do not have to worry about where you will start your next sentence; the rhythm of the repetition is like bait, and images and details arrive like fish on the ends of the lines.

Sometimes in working on a This Is a Poem exercise, it takes a little practice to get past general words to the sensory details essential for vivid writing. The first This Is a Poem exercise Elizabeth did wasn't nearly as full of sensory imagery as it could have been:

This Is a Poem

This is a poem about a man.
This is a poem about a handshake.
This is a poem about a conversation about what to do one afternoon.
This is a poem about Granville Island.

This is a poem about a tugboat ride.
This is a poem about looking at art.
This is a poem about strolling side by side telling tales of our lives.
This is a poem about possibilities.
This is a poem about a new friend.

When you read these images, do you see and feel Elizabeth and her friend? Do you want more specificity? Since the poem is about a specific event with another person, it cries out for more imagery. We need details to get a hold on what it feels like to have this new friend.

The words "a man" could become more detailed: This is a poem about a man in khaki shorts and deck shoes.

The words "a handshake" could become more particular. Where was it given? What was the hand like? What else does the speaker remember while the handshake was going on? "A conversation about what to do one afternoon" can be more fully drawn by including the actual suggestions that came up in the conversation. Rowing? Bicycling? Did heads nod or shake no? Did eyes meet? Details! Images!

"A tug boat ride" can be elaborated. Was there a horn bellowing over the salt water? Waves slapping the sides of the boat? Rolling wakes of other boats to cross?

"Looking at art" could include details about the art. Paintings? Sculpture? Name of the artist?

"Telling tales of our lives" must tell more of the tales: i.e., telling the time my cat Fluffy ran into the house with the bird she had caught and killed and dropped it on my prom dress, which was laid out on the bed.

Once Elizabeth got the hang of using details, she wrote:

This Is a Poem

This is a poem about a lunch in a restaurant on Granville Island.
This is a poem about a table for two with white linen cloth.
This is a poem about the view from this table that looked out over the bay.
This is a poem about the boats with red, blue and yellow, framed by the grey rain.
This is a poem about watching the rain drip down the window in front of us.

This is a poem about the noise our stomachs made reminding us
   it was time to eat.
This is a poem about warm pita bread and hummus scooped off
   the plate.
This is a poem about sitting back listening to my friend's story
   about his acting teacher.
This is a poem about how his story became a bridge for me to share
   some of myself.

Compare the last line of Elizabeth's first attempt with the last line of her second try. "This is a poem about a new friend" is general and lacks subtlety of emotion, or what is called subtext. But once Elizabeth put in the precise details of her experience, these details, speaking for themselves, led her to the discovery of what she valued in her experience with a new friend. "This is a poem about how his story became a bridge for me to share some of myself." This is not an abstract new friend she is discussing, but the occasion of her own reawakening.

Now, take the subject you have chosen from your clustering and do a This Is a Poem exercise. Focus on the details that will connect you to your subject.

Comparative Thinking

Another exercise for writing good description is to describe one thing as if it were something else usually thought to be unrelated. In bringing the two together, the reader gets an immediate, refreshed experience of your subject. This kind of thinking helps you describe people, places and events with details that capture the five senses.

Remember how it hit home when the little boy told us his teacher looked like a horse with the reins pulled back? When we use "like," as in the boy's writing, to make a comparison, we make a simile; when we exclude the "like" and say one thing *is* another thing, we make a metaphor. For example, "images and details are fish on a line." Both strategies are examples of comparative thinking.

Describing Birkenstock sandals I wrote, "The straps over your foot are like two highway overpasses." "The meat in oxtail soup looks like already chewed Wrigley's spearmint gum," comments a character in Christi Killien's *All of the Above*. "When I'm in the bathtub, I'm like the seed inside an avocado," a woman said at one of my workshops.

Comparisons come more easily if you practice. Create five to ten a day. Make a game of it with friends or children on car rides.

Start with similes: a window is like, children in a classroom are like, a doorknob is like. . . . Endings will come along in good time: a window is like a movie screen; children in a classroom are like a flower garden; a doorknob is like a knee. This exercise keeps your mind flexible; when you start writing your essay, you will see how comparison pops up into your mind just when you need it to help you fully describe (show through the senses) your subject.

MORE ABOUT DETAIL AND IMAGES

Writing description *requires* that you use images from the five senses. What things taste, smell, feel, sound and look like ultimately tell the story and do the work of describing. To say, "I was always stiff at Grandmother Sarah's house" does not describe rigidity. The following words *show* stiffness:

> I always sat in the red overstuffed mohair sofa, my feet never reaching the floor, watching the white lace of my fancy Sunday anklets above the shiny patent leather of my Mary Janes. The pudgy fingers of my left hand crumpled and uncrumpled the lace that covered the sofa arm I sat against, and I always noticed the dirt under my fingernails, black as my shoes, against the white of Grandmother's lace. I was like a snake without a safe place to molt an ill-fitting skin.

Use sensory details that *show* what you are describing rather than words that merely tell your attitude. Details that are unique to the situation are the basic units of your writing. Ultimately, they are the substance that allows you to gather momentum, to go on, to build a route through your material, to find closure and discovery. You should include them in overabundance in exercises where you seek your material. What did you taste, touch, feel, see and smell in the situation you are describing? Where can a metaphor bring surprise and exactness to your description? If you feel like you are in a detail drought, stop and do a cluster about the particular image.

WRITING YOUR ESSAY

If you haven't done a cluster yet to help you answer the "write" question for description, do it now. Continue with a freewrite for ten minutes on the person, place, object or activity that interests you this time. Do a This Is a Poem if you haven't yet. Practice using some metaphors to describe your subject. Remember the power of detail and images and use them abundantly.

Now, go back and examine how the sample essays begin and are organized. "The Beach Cabin" starts with a statement about the cabin's strength, how long it has survived. "The Locker Room" begins by putting us face to face with an entrance, marked BOYS ONLY, marking an area which, for the writer, is an almost unbelievable "den of mental illness." The organization of "The Beach Cabin" proceeds through the rooms of the house from most public to most private. The organization of "The Locker Room" proceeds from the entrance to the interior of the room to the outside hallway, back into the locker room, and out to the hallway once again

With all your exercise work in front of you, try your hand at a first draft of a description essay. Start with what you see when you think of what you are describing. Or start with why you got to be there.

DEVELOPING THE DRAFT

Put your draft aside for a while as you read Elizabeth's next steps on her description essay. Remember, this is not a finished draft, just a draft as far as Elizabeth could take it on her first try. As you read, note where you feel nicely taken up with the scene she describes and where you feel jarred out of it or confused about what Elizabeth sees or does.

MY HOUSE, THE BEACH COTTAGE

The road sign reads "AVALON, 4 MILES" in bold green letters and my father steers the car towards the exit. I begin to fidget with excitement at the thought of seeing "my house" again. It has been in our family for 15 years, purchased on a whim by my folks who had just come down that day to secure a summer rental. This "L" shaped rancher that sleeps six has seen a lot of life come through her screen doors, family reunions, all night clam bakes for college friends and gatherings with neighbors all red from a day on the beach and strung like wet suits on a clothesline across the front porch. It is times like this when everyone is so full of happiness that I feel the most at home. Time has a way of standing still as if the hourglass has been retired and placed to the side. Days run into night and nights keep fulfilling their promise of returning the day.

I have rolled down the window all the way, and I feel the blast of salt air at my face as our car heads towards the causeway. I remember the year a flash flood almost wiped away the bridge. I worried like a parent with children caught in a storm as to how my house would survive the hurricane. Turning right, up island, I count out loud as the number streets crawl by like the sea turtles that migrate every July three blocks from the bay to the sea. "Thirty-sixth, forty-second, forty-seventh, forty-eighth"; the numbers ring through my teeth like bells announcing a celebration.

The house stands proud just as I left her last year with the faded rainbow-colored wind sock blowing from the flagpole as if to salute me. I inspect her white exterior and freshly painted green trim. I walk over to the rose bushes that have kept her company over the winter, in full bloom now with brilliant red, deep plum, apricot and yellow blossoms. As company arrives mother sends me out with the old, rusty scissors we use for crabbing, to cut a fragrant bouquet to place in their room.

As I expected, I am pulled away from my greeting ritual to help carry things in. I used to curse with great frustration each time we unloaded the trunk because mother insisted on bringing every appliance known to a homemaker from her kitchen, just in case.

I am surprised as I walk in the small, narrow kitchen as mother has replaced the wallpaper with chickens on it with a crisp new striped design. I look over to the wall to double-check that my old fifth-grade bulletin board is still hanging like an honor degree by the phone. Relieved, I see the plastic beach tags, each a slightly different shape, size and color, lined straight like soldiers at attention across the bottom, that help us remember how many years we have been coming back.

The dining room is connected to the living room by a golden, knotted shag carpet that is usually dirty from sandy footprints by our second week down. Both rooms are surrounded by windows and light brown paneling that resembles driftwood. I see my father has added a tan wicker chair in the corner by the front door, his latest bargain from the church rummage sale, I am told. I head for my bedroom in the back of the house, anxious to see what improvements my mother employed in my absence at college. My trundle bed with its new flower-patterned cover takes up most of the room and when it is fully extended you can't move at all. I always slept on the lower bed, close to the floor so that my girlfriends who were scared of the monsters that roamed in the dark would know they'd devour me first and be too full to go on to them. The sound of the distant waves splashing against the surf kept me company at night. I was never scared.

I settle myself on the porch and stretch out my very white legs to rest them on the wrought iron gate. Tomorrow will be a beach day filled with sunbathing, swimming, surfing and hunting for treasures in the sand. For now, I assume this position I will repeat many times over summer as I read from the mystery novel I saved just for vacation or sip wine with my relatives from Florida or coffee with my dad as the hours fade like the sunset into the horizon.

I am so comfortable and at peace at the cottage. She is a special friend that reminds all of us to take time out from our lives to do the simple, pleasurable things that we forget because the tick of the timer is sometimes louder than the voice of our true desire. I always leave my internal watch at the bay as we cross the causeway and pick it up when I head for the city. Until that time, I will walk on the beach, the sound of the fine white sand squishing between my feet, read until the daylight calls it quits and casts a dark shadow over my book, or just hang out on the vast front porch to dry in the company of other "suits on the line."

There are probably parts in this draft you admire and parts that annoy you. Based on your reactions to Elizabeth's drafts, you may be inspired to rewrite your own first draft. Before you do that, though, let's go through the three-step response that will help you revise and develop the draft that you write.

ABOUT THE THREE-STEP RESPONSE

As I explained in chapter one, I respond to work-in-progress in a three-step approach that nurtures the development of writing. This response process emphasizes how the writing makes contact with a reader. To help the writer understand what kind of contact his or her writing makes, my responsibility as a reader of the work is to:

1. report the images and phrases that stick with me
2. monitor the feelings that occur inside me as I read, and report these feelings accurately
3. tell the writer where I want to know more

If you are going to be your own reader, make sure you have managed to take time away from your draft so it will seem like a fresh piece of writing to you and you can be more impartial as you look at it using this response system. If you are going to ask others to respond to your draft, make sure they understand that you want them to respond in the three separate ways I describe below.

Step One: Velcro Words

After I read a draft, I say out loud the phrases and images that stick with me. This method, called "say back" by writing teacher Natalie Goldberg, identifies the details that have jumped off the page and into the reader's mind. One of my students told me she thought of these details as Velcro words.

A note here: Just repeat the words and phrases that stick. Do not tell why they stick. It is important for writers to hear their words back *just as they said them*. To explain why they stick in your mind takes the focus away from the writing.

Step Two: Feelings

Now, as a reader, you're ready to report the feelings you experience from the writing. First, report feelings that seem to be in keeping with the subject and subtext. If someone is writing about being stuck with two two-year-olds in a line of cars at U.S.-Canadian customs and he says he feels like Mt. St. Helens right before she erupted, what do you feel? Bottled anger or almost unbearable frustration may be the feelings you report.

Next, report whatever discomfort occurs from phrasing and details that veer from the writing's subject and subtext. For instance, if the writer above included a detail like, "I was so angry my stomach felt like a pond under a clear blue sky," you might report that the clear blue sky evoked calmness that was annoying in the context of all this frustration.

Peer responses can help you, the writer, identify tailspins and meanderings from your real subjects. If your readers are confused, if they feel ripped off, if they feel batted around in different directions, your words are causing that confusion, that theft, that assault. If such emotional journeys are not in the service of your real subject, you have to change your words.

Step Three: Curiosity

Now it's time to tell the writer where you, the reader, want to know more. Be as specific as possible. Your comments will indicate to the writer where more writing is required.

When, as the writer, you listen to where others want to know more, you recognize your real subject and where and how you have skirted it. You often realize that what you skipped because you thought it might bore a reader is exactly what the reader wants to know.

I will demonstrate this three-step process on Elizabeth's first draft of a description essay. Then, throughout the book, you'll be listening in on my responses to Elizabeth's other drafts. You will be able to use this response method yourself on your own work, but revisions always go a little more quickly if you use someone else's response since you need time and distance to hear your own writing the way someone else hears it. If you develop the habit of relying on trusted readers, make sure they articulate the feelings they get in response to your writing and then leave the fixing to you. If you work alone, make sure you separate the responding from the fixing. Read as a reader would read and do the three response steps. Take notes. Then come to your work as a writer and begin the revisions.

Before we do the three-step response with Elizabeth's first draft, I would like to discuss barriers to using the response method effectively.

About Resistance

Monitoring feelings can be a tiring business. Most of us are not used to paying close attention to what we are feeling as we read let alone what we might name these feelings. Here's an exercise to help:

Fill a piece of paper with the names for feelings: frustration, pleasure, warmth, joy, dislocation, well-grounded, clear, cloudy, disappointed. Go on. Challenge yourself to make a long list. The words will come in handy when you are responding.

As a reader: When you are responding to writing, precision (being "picky") is a virtue. A writer doesn't want anything to get in the way of a reader's full enjoyment. So, to help in the development of those finished pieces, you have to let the writer know what you feel. What enables the writer to really listen to your responses? First, an author enjoys hearing what makes strong contact with others. Second, an author enjoys hearing feelings, not judgments. "I felt confused" is much gentler than "this sounds awkward" or "the writing is disorganized."

As a writer: When a reader labels and judges your writing ("you are being repetitive," "this is wordy" and so on), you may get angry and think, "How do they know anyway?" This reaction can block you from wanting to rework your writing. The three-step response circumvents your natural defend-against-labels attitude and promotes your readiness and enthusiasm for revision. Listening to the results of the three-step response, you learn how your words line up with the content of what you are saying.

I like what Lu Chi, an ancient Chinese poet, said in a long poem about writing:

> *Emotion and reason are not two things:*
> *every shift in feeling must be read.*
> —The Art of Writing, *translated by Sam Hamill*

On Being Wary

Another barrier to using the three-step response method is your own wariness about sharing your writing. You may be sensitive to what people think, afraid others will steal an idea and concerned that exposure will diminish your energy to write.

It is never wholly comfortable listening to people talk about your writing while you are there not saying a word. It is like having people talk in front of you about the clothes you are wearing. Be aware of your sensitivities, but don't let them interfere. The people you have asked to give responses are offering you a gift. Accept the gift. Later you can decide what you are going to do with it.

To work effectively with other writers, you must also understand that cross fertilization is a good thing. Writers are thieves in that they may end up writing about the same subjects as authors they admire. You must believe simultaneously that there are many, many ideas *and* that there is actually nothing new under the sun, only well-wrought tales of the same old same olds. You must understand that your experience, even if similar to someone else's, will be different because it is told in your voice, from your life as only you can write it.

Keep the focus on your writing; when you seek response to your work, concentrate on what is actually written. Let those who respond to your writing respond only to what is on the page. Don't speak but take note of what words and explanations leap to your tongue. Use them in your next draft!

USING THE THREE-STEP RESPONSE ON "MY HOUSE, THE BEACH COTTAGE"

Here is my response to Elizabeth's first draft. As you read my three-step response, note whether the images that kept you in the scene and the ones that jarred or confused you jive with my responses.

Step One: Velcro Words

I would say back: "bold green letters," "L -shaped rancher that sleeps six," "all night clam bakes," "wet suits on a clothesline," "nights keep fulfilling their promise of returning the day," "turtles that migrate every July," "rose bushes," "rusty scissors we use for crabbing," "old fifth-grade bulletin board," "beach tags," "tan wicker chair," "trundle bed," "monsters that would devour me first," "surf keeping me company at night," "sound of the fine white sand squishing between my feet."

Step Two: Feelings

Overall, in reading Elizabeth's beach cottage draft, I can report feelings of anticipation, nostalgia, safety, community, and excitement. When I look at her work sentence by sentence, paragraph by paragraph, I can report my feelings specifically: I like the feeling of being well located that I get when the first sentence places me on the road toward a specific destination. I feel "on my way." The third sentence has me feeling suspicious — would a person who is so excited about seeing her house again stop to give herself the background about how long the house has been there and what style it is? It seems like there would be a flood of memories or concerns in the mind of the fidgeting speaker.

In the next several sentences, I continue to feel outside of the moment. I feel shortchanged and not let in on what the speaker hopes or expects to see when she arrives. When she tells me time stands still like an hourglass placed to the side, I admire the use of comparison, but I remain unconvinced: Time doesn't stand still, I say to myself, just because no one is using an hourglass to measure it.

When I read, "Days run into night and nights keep fulfilling their promise of returning the day," I feel happily lulled, as I would if I were living by the ocean. I like that feeling and I trust it.

In the next paragraph, I enjoy the feeling of the air on my face, though a blast is unexpectedly rough for a place anticipated with such happiness. I am impatient learning how during a storm the author doted on her house as if it were a child because I already know her love for the house. When the speaker counts the streets and they crawl by like sea turtles, I like the introduction of the turtles who live there, but I feel thrust straight out of the essay and into a cartoon where streets form into crawling turtles. Then the numbers, she says, ring through her teeth like bells and I am still in animation land rather than Avalon.

Finally, the house. I doubt if a wind sock would get stiff enough to seem to salute. I feel wary of that image. Next, the speaker makes me feel suddenly very busy without any particular order to the busy-ness: first cutting flowers then unpacking and all the while having started a greeting ritual which is not described. I am feeling jostled from activity to activity.

Next I am inside the house, although I am not sure why I have gone in. I see that Elizabeth has taken the analogy exercise to heart and included some of these comparisons in her images here. I am glad she did that, but I don't like thinking about the bulletin board hanging like an honor degree. I can see the bulletin board well enough without being told it is like an honor degree. Degrees usually hang in offices, not places of leisure. Similarly, I feel spooked by the tags lined up like soldiers because I thought this was a place the author visits to relax.

Analogies make the writer stretch. When they work well they draw the reader further into the experience. When they don't fit quite right into the feeling tones of the writing, they operate as placeholders. The writer can keep working to find more fitting analogies, ones more agreeable to the experience described. Or the writer may find the analogy must give way to more writing, that the comparison was only shorthand for something that will take more words to describe. The analogy, even if not ultimately appropriate for the final draft, helps writers on their way.

Now to the dining room, but why? I feel like a person without my feet on the ground. I get to glance furtively around with not much interesting to note except the wicker chair, and off I go to the bedroom to see what improvements Mother "employed." Whoa! All of a sudden, I feel like I'm in a corporate boardroom where no one is speaking directly anymore. When I get to the trundle bed, though, and hear the images of Elizabeth sleeping on the low bed nearest the monsters so her girlfriends won't be scared, I am delighted to be very much in the childhood moment the author describes. When Elizabeth says the surf kept her company, I immediately remember the lyrical line early in the draft about nights promising to return the day. The sound of that line is like what a little girl might listen to while living at the ocean.

Suddenly, I am off with the speaker to the front porch and ideas of what activities will fill my tomorrow. I don't feel these images as deeply as the little girl's listening.

It is the last paragraph, and I am being told the speaker is comfortable, but I'm not. I haven't been lulled into forgetting the tick of the timer. I don't know from my own five senses the speaker's true desire. I see a huge surreal watch by the bay at the side of the road looming and waiting for the speaker to leave the beach house. I don't feel the peace the speaker says she gets there, but instead, the anxiety of what's waiting for her even as she will walk on the beach and feel the sand. I am uncomfortable thinking of happy people as suits on the line because suits on the line seem stuck in place and pushed around by the weather.

Step Three: Curiosity

In Elizabeth's description draft, I want to know in the first paragraph what the author sees from the car window as her father turns onto the exit. I'd like to know why the author explores the house in the order that she does. I'd like to feel the sand and see and hear from the other people who are comfortable there. What are the reasons for these curiosities? I want to be placed very directly in Elizabeth's experience of the beach house, both her anticipation of getting to it and her being there. I want to feel as if I am there with her, fully in the scene. What exactly is the sound of fine white sand squishing between her toes? What information comes to her through her senses when she hangs out on the porch?

Find your truths in the body, fiction writer Ron Carlson instructs. This is true in the personal essay as well. How is Elizabeth sensing the sand and the conversation? How does she know what she knows about them — through touch, taste, smell, sound or sight?

USING THE RESPONSE

Look for the feeling responses that seem to indicate where the writing is doing its job well. In this case, I have shared with Elizabeth that knowing I'm on the road to Avalon, feeling the salt air on my face, thinking about sea turtles, and experiencing the lyrical quality of the memory of "days running into night and nights fulfilling their promise of the day" make me trust she is at the place being described. Why not do more of a good thing?

Elizabeth's next step in drafting is to do the job of placing herself and her reader ever more in the peaceful place she wants to describe rather than putting us outside of it with huge hourglasses and the language of the corporate boardroom ("employed improvements"). The main vein of gold here is the little girl Elizabeth who took in the sound of the waves, the sight of the sea life and the comradeship of life at the beach.

Using the three steps, you will gain insight into where to "go from here" with your work. As one of my students said, "In college and high school, teachers always told me what was wrong with my work, but not where better work would come from." When we hear how a reader feels about our work—what sticks with them, vaults them out of the experience we are describing, bores them, engages their curiosity—then we are propelled to continue. Using the three-step response helps you move past negative internal chatter like, "I'm such a boring writer," "I don't know enough words to write well," or "Who do I think I am writing this?"

Henriette Klauser, author of *Writing on Both Sides of the Brain*, gives a wonderful example of the difference between nurturing self-talk and paralyzing self-criticism. When her son began to talk, everyone who heard him exclaimed about his "good talking." No one said he pronounced words wrong or used the wrong forms of pronouns and verbs. Who would criticize a child new to speech? But how we say similar things to ourselves when we are starting a new piece of writing! Can you imagine being so hungry you can hardly wait to eat dinner and at the same time talking to yourself about how you hold the fork wrong? Use the three steps of Velcro words, feelings, and curiosity to rethink how you speak to yourself about your writing. Let these steps teach you to become as constructive in evaluating your work as you would like others to be. You can be your own best critic by remembering that there are no wrong ways, only words that stick, feelings that get evoked and places to write more.

THE SECOND DRAFT OF "MY HOUSE, THE BEACH COTTAGE"

Now is a good time to get responses to your draft, but before using it and revising, read Elizabeth's second draft. While you are doing this, you will have some time away from your writing and the response you received. During the time away, your attachment to particular sounds and your certainty that the words communicate what you had in mind will soften. You will become less closely allied with being the inventor of the original and more a reader like everyone else. Then, going back to author, you will be able to demand of yourself what other readers demand. You will be ready to revise.

MY HOUSE, THE BEACH COTTAGE

I have rolled the window down all the way, and the salt air blasts at my face as our car heads toward the causeway past the bridge that was almost wiped away in a flash flood years ago. I call out the names of the numbered streets, thirty-sixth, forty-second, forty-eighth and think about the sea turtles that migrated every July three blocks from the bay to the sea to lay their eggs. This was my least favorite time of the summer because it was the busiest in terms of traffic on the island and so many turtles were killed by cars as they tried to reach their nesting ground. Each time I ventured from the house in the car or on my bike, I would keep a keen eye out for their hard hat shapes struggling across the hot black top so that I might save them from a Goodyear tire across their back. As I carried turtle after turtle to the safety of the grassy sidewalk, I'd be overcome by a sick feeling. How unfair nature could be.

I am sitting in my usual spot now, behind my mother on the passenger side. I learned at a young age to never sit behind my Dad on long drives. My brother and I would resort to hand-slapping games to pass the time and the sharp ringing sounds of our hands engaging in combat would get on his nerves. Within seconds, he'd reach his hand back behind the seat and pinch my calf as hard as he could until I cried and called the game off. Sometimes, if he were really irritated, he would threaten to stop the car and make us walk the remainder of the way unless we found something quiet to do. Within a matter of minutes, mother was reading to us from the pile of books she had checked out from the public library.

It has been two years since my last visit to the beach house. This oasis of relaxation has been in our family for fifteen years, purchased on a whim by my folks who had just gone down to the island for the day to secure another summer's rental. Looking at my mother happily knitting in the seat in front of me, I remember how she used to insist that we leave the rentals cleaner than we had found them to set a good example. It was as if we were scrubbing away any trace that we had been there at all, and when it came time to pack the car at the end of our stay, it always felt that way. I was thrilled by their decision to buy a house which brought with it the promise of many timeless, fun-filled days ahead.

Looking back, I remember the first night we toasted our new home with champagne and sparkling cider the Realtor had given my parents in celebration. I smile to myself as I think of how proud my father looked raising his glass as if to address his fellow West Point classmates on their accomplishments.

We turn up the driveway. The house stands proud and erect, the same faded rainbow-colored wind sock blowing from the flagpole. I inspect the white exterior and green trim. Remembering my old bike, I hurry back to the shed to make sure Dad hasn't sold "the pink queen" at the church rummage sale. As I pull open the door, the sunlight bounces off her rusting yet solid frame. I can still read the bumper sticker, "Bikes Not Bombs," attached to her back fender. I think back to all the trips I have taken to Sylvester's Fish Market on her black leather throne balancing parcels of fresh fish between the handlebars. Just as I reach for the pump to breathe life into her deflated tires, I hear my father calling us to help unload the car. I am pulled away from my greeting ritual to help carry things in.

As I make my way into the back hall, my arms filled with bags of fresh produce, I spot my old fifth grade bulletin board still hanging by the phone. The sun has long ago faded its orange burlap background except where the white plastic beach tags are attached. At the end of August, mother places an honorary tag, each year's a different size and shape, on the board to mark the passing of yet another memorable summer.

The living room looks as comfortable as ever. The beige over-sized pillows where I flop to reread the same short stories each summer rest lazily by the couch. My father's worn, green vinyl chair still stands in the corner where I can always count on finding him Sundays watching golf.

I head for my bedroom. My trundle bed with its mustard yellow cover looks higher than I remember it. It hides a second twin bed underneath which takes up the room when fully extended. I always slept on the lower bed, close to the floor so that my girlfriends, who were scared of the monsters that roamed in the dark, knew they would devour me first and be too full to go on to them. I was never scared. The sound of the distant waves splashing against the surf and the breeze rustling through my curtains kept me company at night. The days ran into night and nights kept fulfilling their promise of returning the day.

I go through each room, opening the shades and windows to invite the salt air and sunshine to bathe my walls once again. The guest bedroom is filled with fresh linen and blankets awaiting the first of countless rounds of company.

The royal blue wallpaper in my parents' room looks especially rich to me just as the sea does the first time it comes into view as I descend from the path to its shore. A doily on mother's dresser cradles the green and aqua blue seaglass we've discovered every summer combing the beach at low tide.

I settle myself on the porch and stretch out my very white legs to rest them on the wrought iron fence. Before I know it, my knee-caps will be bright pink and the hairs on my legs golden blonde from the sun. Tomorrow will be a beach day with sunbathing, swimming, surfing and hunting for treasures in the sand. For now, I assume this position I will repeat many times over summer, reading from the mystery novel I have been saving just for vacation or sipping wine with my relatives from Florida or coffee with my Dad as the hours fade like the sunset into the horizon.

Mother calls to me that company will be arriving shortly. Hearing my cue, I fetch the rusty scissors we use for crabbing out of the shed and walk towards the rose bushes. Ever since I can remember we have greeted friends and family with a generous bouquet of fragrant roses. This year's blossoms — gifts, my mother calls them — are particularly brilliant in color after surviving the heavy spring rains. As I cut a handful of passion pink buds, their petals slightly moist with precipitation, I lose myself in the sweetness of their fragrance. I can really smell how much I love this house and what she gives each of us who pass through her door. Every summer without fail we find relief in her shade and shelter on her porch from the sometimes crazy storm of life.

When the draft is developed, the full effect of life at the beach house is discovered. It successfully shelters Elizabeth from the difficulties of life just as Elizabeth tries to shelter the turtles from harm by car tires. Life at the beach house is more successful at sheltering than Elizabeth can be for the turtles, and Elizabeth relives her good fortune.

You may want to go through the three-step response process again yourself on this draft. I would like to point out two things. First, although the number of comparisons has decreased, the ones that are in this version help express this experience rather than just call attention to themselves. The hard hat shape of the turtles in the road and the blue of the wallpaper like the blue of the sea when first seen each summer help evoke Elizabeth's firsthand experience of the beach house. Second, beach tags lined up like soldiers and the wind sock stiff as an arm saluting have disappeared, but in their place we find out that Elizabeth's father was a West Point-trained officer. It seems the unconscious was trying to advise Elizabeth about how her father felt to her. Elizabeth wasn't ready to attach this information to her concept of her father until she noticed how out of place the military tone was for the wind socks and beach tags in this essay.

When something in your writing gets a negative response, and you feel committed to the image, examine it to discover why it's there. Ask yourself what feeling it evokes. Sometimes messages from the unconscious are delivered to the wrong address. The message is fine, but the image that expresses it needs to be redelivered to another location in the essay.

NURTURE YOUR WRITING AND KEEP DRAFTING

If possible, read each draft of your work aloud to others. While they listen, they can jot down notes if they want, and they can request that you reread parts of your draft. Remember to enjoy the warmth of hearing your own words come back to you. Remember that no one needs to love the whole draft to be able to offer a valuable response. And no one needs to be an expert on writing! If you need some immediate response and don't have a writing group available, a neighbor or even a child can provide reactions with much to teach you.

Write through as many drafts as it takes until you are satisfied that the subject is fully experienced by your readers.

In writing description always remind yourself to:

- Stay with the senses.
- Make comparisons in order to share the experience as it was in the very moment you had it.
- Stay in those moments that interest you.
- Present experience itself. Your images have authority. They say, "This is how it was for me."

Doing these four things, you will discover why you were compelled to relive being with a particular person or being at a particular place or event.

CHAPTER THREE

The Narration Essay

Writing About What You've Lost and What You've Found

The myth of the Fall portrays us all as exiles from the full human potential.... History is the story of our efforts ... to recover a unity we have intuited only in the fragments.
— *Sam Keen*, The Passionate Life: Stages of Loving

Often things happen to you that seem like a story out of a book or film and you want to write the story down in a way that will amuse or affect other people emotionally. Telling a story is called narration. Narration-style essays require the arrangement of life experiences in chronological order, but you must use the chronological order for the purpose of coming to new insight. When you sit down to tell a story, you will not know the whole nature of the insight. You will only know you want to tell about the "time when . . ." But if you examine the reason you want to tell a story, it is usually because during the situation you are telling about, you found or lost someone, something, or some opportunity and writing about it leads you to new understanding. That is why I have my students start finding a topic for a narration essay with the question, "When have I lost or found someone, something or some opportunity?"

A narration essay uses the chronological organization of events to make a point. Like every essay style, it encompasses the sensory detail of good description, which creates a picture. These two elements allow you to build personal narration essays that explore meaningful times by both evoking the times and relating the knowledge learned during them. When you begin to write a personal story, however, you may find that the emotion seems to have skipped town. You may find yourself left with just a string of events on the page and feel your writing doesn't do justice to your experience. You can overcome this problem by using the exercises from the description chapter before you write or by using the exercise I introduce in this chapter.

How do you know where to start and where to stop your story? Writing a good story requires more than stringing events together in the order they happened, even though that is narration's basic organizational feature. Have you ever listened to children five or under tell you about their day? First this happened, then that, then this, then that and on and on. "Where is the story in the story?" you may ask. Telling a good story requires that there be a point to the story and in writing from personal experience, that point is — you've got it — the writer's discovered insight. The trip toward that insight dictates where you will start and where you will end your narration and how much time you will spend with accounts of events in-between.

The "write" question introduced in this chapter allows you to use your personal experience in a narration-style essay to find this insight. If you have no particular topic in mind, simply ask yourself, "When have I lost or found something, someone or some opportunity? You will remember things like losing your first job as a paperboy because someone invited you in for cookies and your cart rolled away or losing the chance to be Homecoming Queen because of being caught drinking while in high school. You may find yourself remembering a friend you lost as you grew older or the time you lost a piece of jewelry in the back seat of a boy's car.

If you do have a topic you are exploring, insert it into the question. For instance, using the example topics from chapter two, you could ask, "When in my divorce, parenting, illness, war experience or visiting another country did I lose or find something, someone or some opportunity?" You might remember losing your home or a particular friend in a divorce. You might remember losing your way on a bicycle trip through the Netherlands and being rescued by a paraplegic with a ham radio. You might remember losing a fellow soldier, finding a ring on a battleground, missing a chance to be stationed at a site that was bombed and finding yourself alive because of that. Losing and finding go hand in hand. When something is lost, something else is usually found and when something is found, something is usually lost. You can start with either the finding or the losing. However, losing seems to have the most memories and feelings attached, and those feelings help you as a writer.

Before I share the new exercise for gathering story material, let's turn to sample essays that explore the memories and feelings of times of loss.

EXAMPLE: NARRATION ESSAY

The first example essay was written by Yvonne Crain. She lost her husband to cancer. In narrating the story of losing him, Yvonne discovers what she gained from her husband and the way the two of them handled his dying. After you read this essay, think about why it starts as it does and why it ends as it does. Think about why the author has given more time to certain events and less to others in her descriptions.

THE PROMISE

Playing house was an important role for me as a child. My sister and I would switch roles of mother and daughter, and if we could sucker my brother into playing the father, we had a whole family. Mrs. Cleaver would have been proud. This is how life was supposed to be. When I got married, it was a picture perfect life; I was playing house again. I followed my husband Mark to Norfolk, Virginia, to live as a Navy wife. We dreamed of taking the conventional steps, first buying a house, second having children and third, growing old together. Little did both of us know "til death do us part" would come so soon.

Nine months into our marriage, Mark was told he had a tumor in his right sinus cavity. Mark's reaction was not of concern, but of naive uncertainty. "Does this mean cancer, or is it just a tumor that can be removed easily?" We didn't know it at the time, but this was the first day of the end. Mark was a strong athlete and kept very active, and when he had to go through radiation and chemotherapy, it was very wearing for him emotionally and physically. His weight dropped to one hundred pounds, and he had no energy.

I was working full-time and trying to support him mentally as well as physically, and little did I know, I was becoming a victim of the situation, also. I had an annoying pressure on my neck and chest. It felt as if I had a neck brace on much too tight; something had a hold of me. I was seeing just as many doctors as my husband. "If only I felt better, I could put all my efforts towards my husband." Finally, a doctor diagnosed me as depressed and prescribed me an antidepressant. After two weeks of medication, the physical symptoms ceased, and I was able to support Mark to the best of my ability.

It was a roller coaster with Mark's illness. We were told biopsy after biopsy that the cancer was gone, but after his third session of chemotherapy, the cancer reappeared. Mark was told he must have major surgery to remove his eye and cheekbone, and he was told his sense of taste and smell would be mortally damaged. I woke up the next morning with Mark sobbing in the shower. Running into the bathroom, I found Mark huddled in the fetal position with his eyes covered by the palms of his hands, whimpering, "I have a bad feeling about this." The collar got much tighter.

Two days later, Mark came out of the seventeen-hour surgery surprisingly well, and after a couple of weeks in the hospital, he was able to come home. Cancer has a muffled sour stench. As designated house nurse, I cleansed his eye socket twice a day, and the gruesome odor overwhelmed me to gagging. Mark was very sensitive about his hygiene, and it was all I could do to hide the spasms pulsating in my throat. Since Mark had no sense of smell, I felt for his sake he need not know the odor that followed him.

After a month at home, it was confirmed the cancer was back and that Mark had two months to live. Mark looked straight ahead and did not blink while receiving the gloomy news from the doctors. Then with a sudden look of desperation, he asked, "Is that it?" The doctor confirmed solemnly. Life isn't supposed to be this way.

Mark and I made a promise to each other that day. I would be with him at the time of his death, and when his spirit rose from his body, he would look down at me and wave goodbye, and I would look up at him and wave goodbye. Mark and I waved goodbye on July 31, 1985.

When Mark died, he took a part of me with him, but I'm one of the few that can say I saw where that part went. Mark had chosen to spend his final days with his family in Lawndale, California, and shortly after we arrived some mystical occurrences happened. Mark would extend his arm and open and close his hand as if to grab on to something, but grasped nothing but air. I would ask him what he was reaching for, but with cancer now taking over his teeth and tongue, all that came out was a nasal sound with no consonants or vowels, but a definite tone of confidence and vigor was there. He knew what he was saying, and that's what counted. After asking him repeatedly what it was that he wanted, I finally asked others in the household if they might know what he was saying. No one knew.

A hospice nurse would come by daily to check his blood pressure, and I mentioned the mysterious movement to her. She gave me a comforting grin and replied, "Someone was reaching out His hand for him." I broke down and wept. Mark and I were not avid church participants, but we did have a strong belief in God, and this clinched our beliefs.

I had stayed up all night with Mark wrestling him to the couch because of uncontrollable seizures; he finally became unconscious in the early morning hours. Exhausted, I fell asleep on the floor next to him. I was in and out of shallow sleep all day, but awoke suddenly. Without hesitation, I rose and went by Mark's side to give him my daily hug and assurance that I loved him. Mark suddenly jolted his arm in the air and as fast as it jolted up, it came down striking my shoulder and landing on his lap for its last destination. He then squirmed in slow motion as if something was being pulled from his thin skeletal body. Mark was gone, and as I watched his spirit leave, a blanket of relief fell over me, and with it something was opening up for me.

Mark's death was spiritually fulfilling for me. It was Mark's turn to take care of me, and through his strength I could and would become stronger.

Mrs. Cleaver is now also a widow, but one thing has changed since the black-and-white days: Mrs. Cleaver is a woman of the nineties. She is strong, proud and would leap over any mountain that got in her way. My fantasy is again a reality.

The Discovery in "The Promise"

Yvonne evokes two stories for her readers when she relives the sad nine months leading up to the death of her husband. She narrates the story of his dying, and she narrates the story of making and fulfilling a promise, which leads to new strength in her life. Yvonne loses her husband and receives a valuable gift in his passing.

In telling us about losing her husband, Yvonne first gives us some history that informs us about what she thought her life would be like. As the last sentence in the first paragraph states, her dream was not to come true.

In the second paragraph, Yvonne starts her narration nine months into her marriage telling about the event that would turn everything upside down. Yvonne's comment, "We didn't know it at the time, but this was the first day of the end," lets us know that what she relates about her marriage to Mark will be the events that led to losing him. From the chemotherapy, through her obligations in caring for him and the effects of those obligations on her, Yvonne takes us to the day they learn that despite surgery, her husband's cancer had reappeared. When Mark and Yvonne make a promise to each other, the other story about discovery begins, even as the story about loss continues. Later Yvonne writes, "When Mark died, he took a part of me with him, but I am one of the few who can say I saw where that part went." Narrating Mark's final days, she is also narrating the source of her new strength. Loss and discovery intertwine.

As I said earlier, what you are discovering about your subject by telling your story guides you in where to start and where to stop and how much time to spend on any one event in the story. In Yvonne's first draft of the essay you just read, she wrote about the diagnosis and then about losing Mark. It was only after peer response that she realized her story had to include the events of caring for Mark and the event of his death. No matter how painful those events were to recall and to evoke, that was where the deepest part of the story lay — in his actual giving of the gift she received from him. She could only fully realize the gift by fully realizing on paper what that time in her life felt like, looked like, smelled like, sounded like, tasted like. Mark's seizures, her shallow sleep beside him, the hand with which he strikes her shoulder, the movement in his body as his spirit leaves are a narration inside the narration. Without the details in this narration, the other narration, the one about a promise and its fulfillment could not be fully realized.

Yvonne did not sit down and plan that one story would unfold from another story. But by staying with the details that her early responders insisted on hearing, she found her discovery, the story within her story. The five-year-old who strings events together is telling only events. The essayist who shapes where to start and where to end is revealing life-changing understandings gathered from inside the events, understandings that are re-experienced by the writer and readers alike.

After you read your first versions of a story to a person or a writing group, you will be able to adjust your narration if the sequence or importance of events is not quite tuned up. You will be able to do this when responders report the feelings they get from hearing your work.

EXAMPLE: NARRATION ESSAY

Let's look at Robert Roden's story about almost losing his life, a story that leads him to an appreciation of how nature can be a guardian angel helping one to find life again and again. Notice as you read this story, which events are emphasized and which are briefly told as the author writes his way to discovery.

ANGEL IN THE WOODS

Through my teenage years, I enjoyed a freedom that most kids only dreamed about. I could pretty much do what I wanted, as long as I went to school and kept my grades up. I used to hang out with a small group of friends that were living in similar situations. Every spring, when the snow was melted and the days grew warmer, we would all get together, Paul and Sue, Bill, Freddy, Peter and I, to plan a camping trip to the White Mountains in New Hampshire. We would pull out a map, choose a spot where we could hike in and we would go up for a long weekend. We pooled together what little money we had. The first thing we would do was fill the gas tank in Freddy's car. That would be enough to get us there and back again. What was left, we spent on food. We would take our camping equipment, the clothes we were wearing, our toothbrushes, shorts and coats and off we'd go.

It is always beautiful in the White Mountains, but in the spring it is even more beautiful. The nights are cool, in the forties, and the days are warm, usually in the high sixties, sometimes as high as the eighties. The trees are covered with bright green buds, like little rose buds just before they burst open, and the sky is a brilliant color blue. This time of year also brings high water levels, with the snows still melting away in the higher elevations. The rivers are bursting with torrents of ice cold, crystal clear water. On the hot days, we would always find our way to one of these wild rivers, and if we were lucky, we would find a cascade or natural slide area. On one occasion, we found a cascade about eighty yards long and just steep enough to get a good speed going. Nature had done its work well. The rushing water had carved a trough down most of the cascade. The walls were worn smooth, and it was a perfect size for sitting in. At the bottom, the water shot out of the trough like a fire hose, landing right in a big pool of water.

Paul was the first one down. Whoosh, off he went, picking up speed all the way down. We had to run down the rocks to see him shoot out the end and land in the pool, his arms and legs flailing in the air. From the top of the cascade, we could not see the bottom. One by one, we took our turns. We spent the rest of the day there, sliding down and climbing out to warm up in the sun.

Near the end of the day, I decided to go down one last time. While everyone else was lying around on the rocks, I slid down. Out the end I popped through the air and landed in the pool. This time, instead of climbing out, I swam around exploring. I swam in behind the rushing waterfall and back out the other side. That is when I realized I wasn't making any progress. I was actually being drawn backwards by a strong current. It was like an invisible force pulling at me. I tried to swim harder, but I was still being pulled back. I could feel my heart pounding harder. Despite all the water around me, my mouth felt dry as dust. I called out for some help, but there was no one close enough to hear. How could they? I could barely hear myself over the sound of the crashing water. The thought of drowning was very real to me at that moment. I swam as hard as I could, kicking and stroking frantically, but I was just standing still. I felt myself getting very tired and frightened, when out of the woods stepped a young man. He walked over to the edge of the pool, bent down onto one knee, and asked me if I needed help to get out. I squeaked out a desperate yes, and he reached out, grabbed my hand and pulled me out. I thanked him sincerely, and just as suddenly as he had appeared, he disappeared back into the woods. I sat there for a while looking at the woods where the man had come from thinking how lucky I was to be alive.

While I was walking back up along the river to rejoin my friends, I couldn't help but think someone, or something, was looking out for me. Was that my guardian angel that stepped out of the woods to help me?

It was good to see my friends again. They looked like a family of seals sunning themselves on the rocks. Although only minutes had passed, it seemed like hours since I last saw them. I had decided during the walk back not to tell them what had happened down below. I knew that it had happened, the fear was real enough, but the appearance of that man out of nowhere seemed almost a dream.

There have been other times in my life when I have felt my guardian angel was watching over me, but those memories are not as strong as that time in the woods. In my life, I've grown to love the woods even more, the solitude, the wildlife, the calming sound of a rushing stream and the memory of that man reaching out and saving me.

The Discovery in "Angel in the Woods"

In this story, some events are described in detail and some events are told only in the author's transitions from paragraph to paragraph. We know before the end of the first paragraph that escaping to the White Mountains was a yearly spring ritual for the author and his friends. In the second paragraph, we find out about the author's love of the mountain woods and the rivers, and then we learn about a particular trip to a particular cascade. In the third paragraph, we go down the slide with Paul and run with the others to see him land at the bottom of the slide in a pool of clear snowmelt. In the fourth paragraph, the author skips to the end of the day when he decides to slide one more time and, once in the pool, to explore behind the waterfall. Here time slows down. We feel the water pushing him back. We tire as he does in the urgency of being unable to swim forward. We hear the crashing water muffle his cries for help. Our mouths remember the taste of fear as he describes it: dust in the midst of so much water. We welcome the man stepping from the woods, wonder at the seeming slowness of his rescue as the author tells us the man didn't reach in right away but asked if the young swimmer needed help. The author does not repeat the conversation in which he thanked his rescuer; perhaps this would take the reader away from the magical, ethereal qualities the author was experiencing. It would certainly take the focus away from the author's desperate "yes."

In paragraph five, the author makes the transition back to his friends, thinking while he walks about this man being his guardian angel, sent by some protector to save him. In paragraph six, he sees his friends again. They are as undisturbed, as unaware of his drama as seals sunning themselves on a far off coast. We learn now, after the fact, that our author had already decided not to tell his friends what had happened. The event was like a dream he wanted to savor. This is a man who loves solitude, he will tell us in paragraph seven. We will believe him, partly because of this small detail of self-revelation. And so a story about almost drowning and being rescued becomes also a story about love of solitude. This narration is more than just a retelling of a sequence of events. It is about how being rescued from under a waterfall in the White Mountains has become a story that heals the author time and time again.

LOCATING YOUR NARRATION MATERIAL

Answer the "write" question for narration by clustering your thoughts about "What times do I remember when I lost or found something, someone, or some opportunity," or "What times do I remember while _____ (for example, again, getting divorced, becoming a parent, adjusting to an illness, fighting a war, visiting another country) that I lost or found something, someone or some opportunity?" Put the words "lost and found" or just the word "lost" or just the word "found," in the center of a piece of paper. Draw a circle around what you wrote there. Let yourself associate times that go with the words and write them down on the page, circling them and connecting the circle to the center circle with a line. If you think of more details to go with the memories, make little clusters around the circles that shoot off from the middle words. Don't censor your memories. Just get them down. Circle them. Connect the circles with lines.

After you cluster, chose one of the images and memories and freewrite about it for ten minutes. Try to recount the events that led up to the loss or the find in the order that they happened. Put your freewrite away for now.

Doing these two exercises, you will have put yourself on the trail of material from your life experience. Later it can be organized using narration to lead you to new insight. You might have thought of a time you lost money your parents had given you or when you were with a dying relative, friend or pet. You might have thought of a time you lost a job or a part in a play. You might have remembered finding a precious object, a new friend or an unexpected chance to travel.

You might also want to do the This Is a Poem exercise or the analogy exercise from the description essay chapter. They can also be helpful in developing material for a narration essay, especially since, as you have seen, many of the events in the sequence must be aptly described. But in addition to the exercises I already showed you, there is another poetry exercise that can help you collect information about the event you are writing about.

This exercise is modeled after Gary Snyder's poem, "Things to Do Around a Lookout." He writes:

Wrap up in a blanket in cold weather and just read
Practice writing Chinese characters with a brush
Paint pictures of the mountains
Put out salt for deer
Bake coffee cake and biscuits in the iron oven
Hours off hunting twisty firewood, picking it all back up and
    chopping
Rice out for the ptarmigan and the conies
Mark well sunrise and sunset—drink lapsang soochong
Rolling smokes
The Flower book and the Bird book and the Star book
Old *Reader's Digests* left behind
Bullshitting on the radio with a distant pinnacle, like you, hid in
    clouds
Drawing little sexy sketches of bare girls
Reading maps, checking on the weather, airing out musty Forest
    Service sleeping bags and blankets
Oil the saws, sharpen axes
Learn the names of all the peaks you see and which is highest
Learn by heart the drainages between
Go find a shallow pool of snowmelt on a good day, bathe in the
    lukewarm water
Take off in foggy weather and go climbing all alone
The Rock book—strata, dip and strike
Get ready for the snow, get ready
To go down

Think about what you have decided to write about and title a piece "Things That Happened When I Lost/Found _____." Just make a long list of things that happened. You might enjoy using lots of the "ing" forms of verbs as Gary Snyder does in some lines, but if you do, later in your essay, remember to fix these phrases to avoid incomplete sentences. For instance, phrases in a list like "tying knots in a rope" and "walking along the railroad tracks" might have to become "I was tired of tying knots in a rope so I walked along the railroad tracks." But for the exercise stage, just write phrases as they occur to you.

You might try this exercise again entitling it, "Things That I Didn't Do When I Lost/Found _____." In this way, you might come up with good details that make you see how different that time was from other times.

WRITING YOUR ESSAY

After you have done your exercises, review the sample essays. Remember that the narration essay is organized by a chronological sequence of events, but note how these essays begin. "The Promise" begins with a description of what the perfect married life was supposed to be, albeit a picture gleaned from television. By the end of this first paragraph, though, we are told our author was not to experience this kind of marriage. In "Angel in the Woods," the author begins with a description of how his teenage years were filled with freedom and camping trips to the White Mountains. His second paragraph tells more about the mountains and finally focuses our attention on one particular trip.

Langston Hughes, a famous writer from the Midwest who became part of the Harlem Renaissance in the thirties, started "Salvation," a narrative chapter in his autobiography, *The Big Sea* (1940), with these three sentences: "I was saved from sin when I was going on thirteen. But not really saved. It happened like this." Hughes goes on in his first paragraph to give a synopsis of a big revival that had been going on at his aunt's church for weeks. He tells how excitement was building for a special meeting for children. And he ends his paragraph with the sentence that focuses the story he will tell: "That night, I was escorted to the front row and placed on the mourner's bench with all other young sinners, who had not yet been brought to Jesus." We are about to learn the events of that night and the outcome in terms of what he lost and what he gained as he sat and waited for the moment of his salvation.

Now try your hand at a draft of your narration essay. You might want to start with a sentence like, "This is a story about the time I . . ." or "Usually things went like _____ for me, but this time something else happened." Write as best you can from what seems to be the beginning of the story to what seems to be the end. Even when your essay is not fully developed, you can feel when you are onto something. Trust that feeling.

DEVELOPING THE DRAFT

We are going to watch as Elizabeth moves from description essay writing to narration essay writing. Note how she carries the lessons of description into her narration. Note where she starts her story, how she introduces it, what events she includes, and where she ends her story. Does she arrive at an insight in this draft?

UNTITLED

Every few months I load up my little brown Honda with a suitcase full of clothes and books that I have half read and head toward Vancouver to the Sylvia Hotel in search of rest and relaxation. Once I arrive in the West End, the trendy neighborhood where the Sylvia has stood for years, I'm always eager to reacquaint myself with her tree-lined streets where friendly neighbors stroll or sit leisurely sipping espresso at the outside cafes. I look forward to these familiar scenes and to the discoveries, perhaps a new bookstore, foreign film or friend, that might cross my path.

The last time I was in Vancouver, I had an adventure of a lifetime. Just a day before I left Seattle, a friend, who never calls unless she has big news to share, called me at work quite out of breath. A good friend of her husband's would be in Vancouver and would I be interested in showing him the sights? Before I had a chance to ask a question or even dare object, she was spelling his name off with a phone number to match. *Cleavon Little*, at the Le Meridian Park, number 433-6767.

"Cleavon Little," I rolled the letters off my tongue as if to search for some taste of familiarity. My long-term memory kicked in with lively scenes of two old men sitting on a bench in Central Park, laughing and bickering about life. Cleavon had had the lead in a play my mother had taken me to years ago at the grand old Forest Theater in Philadelphia. His performance was very moving, and I remembered how I had cried all the way to the car after the final curtain.

Cleavon Little wanted to go sightseeing with me! I could hardly believe my luck. On my drive to Vancouver, I rehearsed out loud little facts I knew about French wine and modern art so I might have some interesting conversation to share with this worldly person. Back in high school, I had relied on this exercise to loosen my tongue and build my confidence before placing a call to the boy in homeroom I had the latest crush on. As I rambled on, I could hear the high nervous pitch in my voice. I prayed that with repetition, I would sound graceful, my words flowing with ease in his presence.

We met the next day in the lobby of his hotel. As he stepped off the elevator with his brown fedora hat and his beard filled with grey flecks just as he had described over the phone, he looked much younger than I remembered. We exchanged a firm friendly handshake. At breakfast earlier, I had overheard a new bride talking excitedly about walking on air as she made her way down the aisle of the church. As we headed out the door into the newness of the day, I knew just how she felt!

Cleavon seemed content to let me take the lead as I directed us towards the waterfront ferry station. We boarded a tiny blue tug that didn't seem large enough to fit all eleven people that were waiting in line for passage. With room to spare, we chugged fearlessly through the choppy ice blue water over the wakes of power boats hurrying by.

Through the light fog that had settled on the bay, we could see the brightly painted set of Granville Island. Housed among the buildings were art galleries, rare book stores, cafes and pricey boutiques with jewelry I can only dream of wearing.

We started our tour at the Granville Island Brewery. I didn't waste a second sampling every ale and lager they offered us. Giggling, we compared notes on our favorites and the lightheadedness we were both experiencing.

As we strolled along the cobblestoned streets from gallery to gallery with Indian carvings made of aqua jade and earrings created from recycled bottle caps, our conversation evolved like the interesting pieces of art we had witnessed. I asked Cleavon questions, more than he could field at once, about his life and work. Why had he become an actor? What did he think about when he was performing? Was he ever afraid? Smiling, he answered each one in great detail. He seemed to be enjoying the attention as he shared that actors never really leave the stage.

I suggested we lunch at Bridges Restaurant, famous for their steamed clams. We took our places in the crowded room of faceless voices at a table with white linen. The sky seemed particularly grey framed against the glittering lights of the city's skyline. For a few minutes, we stopped talking to watch the rain as it fell against the window exploding into abstract patterns upon impact. It was a perfect day for sitting and observing anything and everything.

We ordered two glasses of chardonnay, a plate of hummus and pita and a bucket of clams steamed in garlic and sank back into our conversation about life. As if learning our lines, we quizzed one another back and forth about our families, our happiest moments and our regrets.

Somewhere between the brewery and the restaurant, the intimidation that had consumed my body with fear of not living up to this role was left behind like an antiquated prop. I don't think I ever mentioned a silly fact about French wine or modern art. I had successfully survived my first dress rehearsal.

Again, before you redraft your essay, think about what you admire and what annoys you in this draft. Follow me through the response method.

THE THREE-STEP RESPONSE
Step One: Velcro Words

From Elizabeth's draft, the following images stick with me: "Cleavon Little," "rehearsed out loud little facts I knew about French wine and modern art," "high nervous pitch," "tiny blue tug," "wakes of power boats hurrying by," "Indian carvings made of aqua jade and earrings created from recycled bottle caps," "rain as it fell against the window," "somewhere between the brewery and the restaurant."

Step Two: Feelings

In tracking my feeling response both to the piece as a whole and to the writing sentence by sentence, I would say:

On the whole, I feel excitement about meeting someone famous, the awkwardness of feeling too mundane in the face of that fame and celebrity, and the satisfaction of getting to the person-to-person contact that helps each of us grow.

Now sentence by sentence: Every sentence in the first paragraph makes me feel like I am being kept from getting started on a particular course. First I load up a Honda full of clothes and half-read books. Then I am set up to think that once we arrive in Vancouver, there will be espresso sipping and people watching. What happened to reading? Finally, despite all the half-read books in the car, there is hope of a new bookstore or seeing a film.

In the second paragraph, the phrase "adventure of a lifetime" puts me in a competitive mood. I want to say, "Oh, yeah, really? Prove this to me." Having this feeling, I am not at ease in the essay. But the phone call from the friend and the remembering Cleavon Little absorbs my interest. Then the phrase "my long-term memory kicked in" makes me feel separate from the essay again. I feel my attention being drawn from the memory to the speaker aware of herself remembering.

I enjoy the paragraph about the speaker in her car rehearsing conversation as a way to deal with her excitement. But when she first lays eyes on Cleavon, I feel confused. She describes his beard as grey-flecked, but she says he looks younger than she remembered him. After the handshake, when the speaker goes back in time to describe a bride she overheard earlier in the day, I feel interrupted. She finally gets to meet Cleavon and she is thinking of a morning conversation she overheard? And then I really feel let down—the intrusion of the bride memory was only in the service of getting to the cliché "walking on air!"

Despite the fact that I feel some of the speaker's nervousness and excitement about spending the day showing a famous actor around Vancouver, the paragraphs that describe boarding the tug, walking among galleries, bookstores, cafes and boutiques leave me feeling flat. These actions don't seem different from what any two tourists might have done. My interest is back again when the speaker mentions Indian carvings made of jade and earrings of recycled bottle caps, but I am disappointed with the phrase "our conversation evolved like the interesting pieces of art we had witnessed."

I feel amused by the questions the speaker asks Cleavon and by her observation that he feels comfortable with attention. I don't mind knowing they are off to Bridges Restaurant, but "faceless voices" places me unwillingly in the *Twilight Zone* or some existentialist novel. A "particularly grey" sky doesn't help bring me back, but the two stopping their talk to watch rain on the window does. The sentence, "It was a perfect day for observing anything and everything" makes me feel like a child given a quarter to go get lost. "Hey," I want to say, "why are you closing the door on the interesting part? What else did you observe?"

I'm back in the story with the chardonnay, hummus, pita and clams, but I feel confused by the idea of the speaker and Cleavon learning their lines and quizzing each other as they are sharing stories about themselves. I want to shout, "Don't leave me feeling teased. Where's the quiz? Where's the script?"

I like the phrase "somewhere between the brewery and the restaurant" because it comes directly from the event and I feel comfortable looking back now to earlier in the day. But the idea of fear getting left behind like an antiquated prop puts me off. I feel like the speaker is trying too hard to use Cleavon's theater experience to describe her own experience when hers is different! Lastly, I mistrust the phrase, "survived my dress rehearsal." This is a real event with a real person. This isn't going to happen again for another audience, is it?

Step Three: Curiosity

In the third step of my response, I want to indicate where I am interested to know more:

I want to know more about Cleavon's performance at the Forest Theater and what moved Elizabeth. I want to see Cleavon more often and see what Elizabeth saw and heard that made her feel so light-footed. I want to know what they talked about as they wandered around Granville Island. I want to know why the jewelry was so important to Elizabeth that she singles it out. I want to know Cleavon's answers to Elizabeth's questions of him. Does Elizabeth see any gestures that remind her of the character she had seen him play? I want to know the happiest moments and regrets and family stories they shared. I want to know what Elizabeth is pleased about as her lunch draws to a close. It seems deeper than that she merely never mentioned facts about French wine and modern art. And finally, how did they say goodbye? Right now the essay seems to stop in the middle of the event.

Get the response you need to your first draft. Then, before you begin a second draft, read Elizabeth's developed draft.

THE SECOND DRAFT

THE LINES I LEFT BEHIND

Every few months I load up my little brown Honda with a suitcase full of clothes and books that I have half read and head toward Vancouver to the Sylvia Hotel in search of rest and relaxation. Once I arrive in the West End, the trendy neighborhood where the Sylvia has stood covered with ivy for years, I'm always eager to reacquaint myself with the tree-lined streets where neighbors stroll or sit leisurely sipping espresso at the outside cafes. I look forward to these familiar scenes and to the discoveries, perhaps a new bookstore, foreign film or friend, that might cross my path.

My last trip to Vancouver was two months ago and just the day before I left Seattle, a friend, who never calls unless she has big news to share, called me at work quite out of breath. A good friend of her husband's would be in Vancouver and would I be interested in showing him the sights? Before I had a chance to ask a question or even dare object, she was spelling his name off with a phone number to match. *Cleavon Little*, at the Le Meridian Park, number 433-6767.

Cleavon Little, I rolled the letters off my tongue as if to search for some taste of familiarity. Lively scenes came into view of two men, senior in their years, sitting on a bench in Central Park, laughing and bickering about retirement and how they cheated each other at chess. Mother had taken me years ago to see Cleavon Little in performance at the grand old Forest Theater in Philadelphia. His spry and quick-witted character reminded me of a funny little man I used to pass on my way to class in the morning. Charlie, or Chubs, as he preferred to be called because of his rosy full cheeks, used to hang out in front of the campus coffee shop and always had a joke to share or a quick tune on his harmonica. Irish jigs were his favorite. I would usually stop for a chorus or two with the other regulars. Like Cleavon, his smile was bright and engaging and made you feel as if you were the only person he was playing to in the audience.

Chubs died suddenly my senior year of college, three months before I saw Cleavon's play. After the final curtain fell, I cried the entire six blocks back to the parking garage. Though Cleavon didn't die in the play, the revelations he shared over the course of the play about his life and his fear of dying were very real to me.

After Loree's news I found myself in quite a stir, which for me is a combination of jubilation and raw panic. What on earth would I say to Cleavon? "Oh, by the way I really enjoyed your play?" I guessed that would be a successful place to start, but what else? I remembered during the first act of that long-ago play he told his friend how much he loved information, any kind of information.

On my drive to Vancouver, I rehearsed out loud little facts I knew about French wine and modern art so I might have some interesting information to share with this worldly person I was about to meet. Back in high school I had relied on this exercise to loosen my tongue and build my confidence before placing a call to the boy in homeroom I had the latest crush on. As I rambled on, I could hear the high nervous pitch in my voice. Silently, I prayed that with repetition, I would sound graceful, my words flowing with ease in his presence when we met the next day in the lobby of his hotel.

It was Easter Sunday and pouring rain. I had called my mother hours earlier to wish her a happy holiday, and she in return had reminded me to be myself, breathe deeply and get Cleavon's autograph on a napkin.

Having arrived early, I settled myself adjacent to the elevators in one of those large overstuffed chairs that seem to swallow you whole. My heart was pounding as I wrestled with the velvet cushion hoping to look somewhat poised. Cleavon entered the lobby at exactly 2:00 P.M. There underneath a beige fedora hat and framed on either side by his thin black beard was the familiar smile. He showed little hesitation in picking me out of the crowd. When he had inquired as to how he might recognize me, I assured him I would be "the friendly looking one."

We exchanged greetings and laughed. It was all I could do not to run around the room telling everyone who would listen I was with Cleavon Little, *the* Cleavon Little, as in actor of stage and screen.

Loree had told Cleavon that I knew the city like the back of my hand. I would have to take the lead so I suggested that we head for the waterfront ferry station.

On the tiny blue ferry, I paid our fare and sat down next to Cleavon who had started taking pictures of the boats moored in the marina. As we chugged fearlessly across the bay, he told me how much he loved sailboats because they always appeared to be steering their own course with the help of the wind's conviction.

The image of sailboats in the wind stayed with me as Cleavon told me he was once told by an instructor that he would never be an actor. "In spite of this encouragement, I applied for a fellowship to acting school in New York and was chosen with thirty-five other recipients out of one thousand. Elizabeth, you must always do what you think you cannot."

I thought then about how much I wanted to go to Europe and how I seemed to be losing confidence about going alone. I wondered if somehow it showed that I needed encouragement in my life.

I had been planning an itinerary waiting for the "right time" to leave. Over the last year, I had made three departure dates and had cancelled the first two. It was always some variable like a friend convincing me that I couldn't be picking a worse time to be in the south of France. I thought back to when my father tried to teach me over and over how to sail his fifteen-foot ketch one summer. After countless failed attempts to master the timing of the sails to the wind's commands, I found myself one day with a blustering sail and the wind coaxing me along. Cleavon's words of confidence left a lingering taste. This time there would be no cancellation.

As we walked up the gangplank, Granville Island was barely visible in the fog. I could feel the friendly energy, though, the buzz of fellow explorers wandering that keeps me coming back time after time. Housed in the many buildings are art galleries, rare bookstores and cafes that beg you with their comfortable surroundings to spend hours over coffee eavesdropping on nearby conversations. Where to start?

Today I chose the Granville Island Brewery, home of tasty micro-beer, for our beginning.

"Micro-beer?" Cleavon asked curiously. "This is certainly new information!" We tasted a schooner each of lager, some thick brown stout, and some pale ale as I explained the Northwest was famous for homemade beers. "What do you think?" I asked, wiping the foam from my lip.

"It's strong stuff!" he exclaimed. "Kinda reminds me of the bootleg my Daddy used to make." He had just finished telling me about his older brothers and how he tried desperately to keep up with their frisky behavior. I imagined him pleading to be included as they crouched secretly under the front porch passing the bottle of forbidden juice.

As we strolled along the cobblestoned streets from gallery to gallery filled with Indian carvings made of aqua jade and earrings created from recycled bottlecaps, our conversation evolved like the interesting pieces of art we had witnessed. There were inside stories about Hollywood as he referred to his friends Dustin and Richard. I tried not to be obvious with my questioning, but I really wanted to know how difficult it was to live a public life. "Elizabeth," he sighed, "for every bit of glamour there is the consequence of lost privacy. Think about your own life; aren't there trade-offs?"

The wisdom and perspective in his voice seemed very much to match that of Frank's, the seventy-year-old retiree I saw that Sunday on stage. Cleavon, named after his grandfather who was a Baptist minister known countywide for his spirited sermons, was just sharing information, the kind that mattered in life, not the details of fine dining or expensive champagne.

When we reached Bridges Restaurant, a table was waiting with a perfect view of the bay framed against the glittering lights of the city's skyline. My attention drifted off into the conversations that filled the room as Cleavon pored over the wine list. We ordered two glasses of chardonnay and entertained ourselves over a plate of hummus and pita and a bucket of clams steamed in garlic and wine. Was it the fearlessness of rain falling hard against the window and exploding into abstract patterns that prompted Cleavon to ask me about my fears? "I am afraid of failing to live my life," I shared, not quite believing I was being so very candid in my response. "I know exactly how you feel, my dear, but the best we can do is take risks. It is like learning your lines, Elizabeth. We all have them; the challenge is figuring out which ones really work for us."

I thought about the information I was given today by Cleavon, the information that was a gift with no price tag or pastel-colored tissue paper concealing its contents. It stood on its own, the lines I would have to learn.

Notice that this draft is titled. Elizabeth has learned why she is writing about the time she was given an opportunity to show a famous actor around a favorite city of hers. She gets to rediscover and affirm that when she lost her nervousness, she gained a new personal courage and a new friend. It is interesting to note that in "The Lines I Left Behind," a second story is woven into the chronological order of the Vancouver trip events — there is the phone call, the remembering who Cleavon Little is, the drive to Vancouver, the phone call from the hotel to her mother just before she goes to meet Cleavon and, of course, the day of sightseeing with him. The other story is of the memory of Cleavon Little in a play in Philadelphia and how he is connected in the author's mind to her real life experience of an old man who hung out in front of a college area coffee shop. Cleavon's performance as a character something like that man meant a lot to

Elizabeth since the old man had died just a short while before she saw the play. Now she associates Cleavon with the play's character's wisdom and with her own deep feelings. By the end of her day with him, his own wisdom and personality have affected her deeply. The placement of one story inside another is one of the things that happens when a writer trusts chronology and images. The events of our lives contain wisdom. We write to find out what is wise in what we have lived.

KEEP DRAFTING

If you'd like, use the response method on Elizabeth's developed draft. Then begin writing your own second draft. Get response to this version of your work. Keep on developing your narration essay and getting response as many times as you want.

As you write and get response, you will discover why you are telling the story you have chosen. You will get in touch with what you learned from the event you are narrating. It is not that you must state directly what you learned. Rather, what you learned becomes the real story and the details you chose and the events you describe are the ones that serve that story.

CHAPTER FOUR

The How-To Essay

Writing About What You Know How to Do or to Make

... there is the mnemonic potential of language — the capacity to use this tool to help one remember information, ranging from lists of possessions to rules of a game, from directions for finding one's way to procedures for operating a new machine.

— *Howard Gardner*, Frames of Mind: The Theory of Multiple Intelligences

In our culture, we are very familiar with the how-to style of writing. It is not hard to find how-to books and articles on subjects as wide-ranging as making a marriage work, becoming a super learner or performer, wiring a house, lowering cholesterol, and preparing for alien abduction. All of us read about how to accomplish procedures and/or make products.

In getting an education, pursuing hobbies, raising families, and doing jobs, we have learned how things are made or work. Some of us know firsthand how government works or how airplanes are built or how nonfat frozen yogurt is made. Some of us are knowledgeable about how to juggle two jobs while raising a family; others know something about how to resolve conflict successfully or how to play badminton. But why would we write about how to do these things in a personal essay?

There is a difference between a how-to article and a how-to personal essay: When you write a personal essay using the how-to form, you are writing about how something is done or how something is made because *you want others to appreciate the process you are writing about.* You want them to understand not the process alone, but how the process of making or doing a particular thing has affected your life. You want them to learn that doing or making it may affect their lives.

Any instructional writing, personal or otherwise, involves paying attention to:

- the steps in the process you are describing
- the order in which the steps must be performed
- the special terms you need to understand for success
- the tools required to do the process
- the variations allowed in approaches
- the signs that show a desired outcome has been achieved

This system of organization is similar to that of a narration essay because it contains sequence much like narration contains chronology. It contains description because you must evoke both stages in the process and objects — the five senses are involved. In addition, it can contain little stories, called anecdotes, as a way of describing any of the steps.

In addition to these six characteristics, any how-to personal essay must make clear what you are really telling your readers while you are also telling them how a particular thing is made or done.

Some of the most thought-provoking how-to essays explain step by step how to do something that we actually wish we didn't really know how to do: how to fall in love with someone who isn't right for us, how to lose our hard-earned savings, how to destroy the environment, how to lose a wife or husband, how to have practically no friends. We can write to help someone we care about avoid doing what we have done. Sometimes we write about how to make something because we think others will want to make it for themselves someday. Sometimes we write a how-to for someone who had meaning in our lives to say thank you to them and to show them they were influential. No matter why we are writing or to whom we are addressing our thoughts, we also write to understand our own experience more deeply.

I am going to concentrate on one form of the personal how-to in this chapter — the epistolary, or letter form. Many popular non-fiction books are currently using this form in which authors share life experience with their children. Two of these are Kent Nerburn's *Letter to My Son* and Marion Wright Edleman's *The Measure of Our Success, A Letter to My Children and Yours.*

By thinking of both something you know how to do or make and someone you believe needs this information, you will be in a good position to write a how-to personal essay.

Again, if you have an area of experience you are writing about, ask yourself the "write" questions: "What do I know how to do or make concerning _____ (for example, once again, divorce, parenting, adjusting to an illness, fighting in a war or visiting another country)? Who do I most want to tell this to?" Answers to the first question might range from how to file for divorce and how to work out joint custody to how to make divorce harder on yourself and everyone you love. When you think about to whom you might want to tell the information, you can narrow the possible topics. Perhaps the topic that is most appealing is the one about joint custody, for instance, addressed to your children so their new life is easier for them. Or perhaps this topic is addressed to your ex-husband to make the point about how important it is that children's lives continue as easily as possible.

After you figure out whom you want to address, you might find yourself rearranging the topic a little. Maybe you see that you want to write to your ex-husband about the need for joint custody and you realize the most effective way to do this might be to write about how to wreck a joint custody situation and wreck the kids' emotional lives, too.

If there is no particular topic you are thinking about for your writing, you can ask, "What do I know how to do or make? Who do I most want to tell this to?"

Whether you have a particular interest area or not, create two clusters. In the first one, put "how is made or done" in the middle of the page and circle and connect whatever words come to mind. You might find yourself thinking about how to make your grandmother's rhubarb pie, how to cheer up a toddler, how to mess up a house, how to earn points with the boss, how to find a new friend, how to care for a sick friend. You will be surprised at what you can explain to someone else. Next, cluster around the phrase, "To whom do I want to tell something?" Pretty soon you will think of some surprising people, or even inanimate objects, you might want to write a how-to personal essay for—a former teacher, a dead relative, a close friend, the annoying business associate at the next desk, your favorite stuffed animal from childhood, your mother, father, spouse, lover or children.

After asking the "write" questions and answering them with the help of clustering, you will find a topic and an audience you are interested in. Once you have a topic, do image-gathering exercises using the Things to Do and This Is a Poem strategies. I will introduce a new exercise for gathering how-to material for your own how-to letter essay, but first let's look at two sample essays and see how they work.

EXAMPLE: HOW-TO ESSAY

In the following example, Suzanne Pitré writes her stepdaughter to share a requested recipe, but in telling her stepdaughter how to make a certain soup, the author also tells her how to create something even more important to families and friends. Notice how Suzanne interests her readers in what she is going to say, how she describes the steps in her soup recipe and how she explains the other process as well. Are there short narrations in this how-to? Which images appeal to which of the senses?

LETTER TO MY STEPDAUGHTER

Dear Amanda,

Your Dad told me you called today while I was at work. He said you were planning a special dinner party and wanted to know if I would send you my recipe for Good Vibes Potato Leek Soup. You know, of course, I am delighted you asked.

Because I have strong feelings about the importance of cooking and feeding people, about what it means spiritually, before I give you my recipe, please indulge me.

Do you recall when you left home for Ann Arbor to start college? You had been assigned to a suite in the dorm which had a kitchen so just before you left we went to the grocery store to stock up on some food and other supplies for your new home.

I recall my mixed feelings as we were cruising the aisles pushing the half-full cart in front of us. I was happy for you in your excitement at being able to go to Ann Arbor. But I missed you already, your late night cookie-making binges, your friends in and out of the house and especially the ingenuous way you walk into a room full of people knowing everyone there will like you.

You picked up several cans of tuna fish and put them in the basket. I glanced distractedly into the basket and mumbled something about your not wanting those, picked up two of the cans, replaced them on the shelf and selected two other cans. You asked what was wrong and I said, "They're bent." You, in your natural curiosity, asked why I didn't want bent cans. My very distracted answer was, "Because they give you bad vibes."

We laughed over that: it became a good family joke and favorite non sequitur. We even extended the concept to encompass the opposite, good vibes, and attached that handle to favorite dishes, like my Potato Leek Soup. But as ludicrous a response as that seemed, there was a basis for it.

I believe that the art of cooking is in not strictly following recipes. Recipes are important, certainly, but to be a really good cook, you have to have some feeling for food, for flavors and textures, for the colors and aromas. Foodstuffs are living or formerly living things. Preparing food to eat sets up vibrations akin to breathing—vibrations that form a bridge between the once living food and the person who consumes it. As the preparer or cook, you can attune yourself to your senses and respond or you can ignore the vibrations and slavishly follow the recipe. If the latter, what you have will certainly be edible and probably be tasty, but it won't be special. It won't say to the people who sit at your table, "I'm glad you are here. I want to share with you a part of me."

I say this because I feel that cooking is a personal statement of caring (or not caring) and it involves putting something of yourself into (or withholding yourself altogether from) what you do.

My recipe for Potato Leek Soup is very simple, but the better your sensitivity, the better the soup will be.

To feed four people, you'll need eight man-fist-sized white potatoes, five leeks as big around as a quarter, a bunch of green onions, a small yellow onion, three French carrots (the short, stubby kind), a quarter pound of butter, a pint of heavy cream, salt and pepper to taste, hearty red wine (a Burgundy or a Beaujolais is nice) and some sour cream.

Peel and quarter the potatoes; scrape the carrots and cut them in thirds; slice off the roots and split the leeks lengthwise (this way you will be able to wash out all of the sand lodged in the layers) and slice them; peel and quarter the onion and clean and slice the green onions, reserving the tops.

This next is important. You should cook the vegetables in a sealed cooker which requires little water or liquid. This is because after the vegetables are cooked, you do not drain off any of the liquid. The less liquid you have, the more intense the flavor of the vegetables will be. I use a pressure cooker and find it infallible.

Just put the vegetables in the pressure cooker with the rack and one cup of water, bring up to pressure, reduce the heat to one-third and cook at fifteen pounds pressure for five minutes.

While the vegetables are cooking, you should warm the soup plates and chop the green onions for five minutes.

Remove the pot from the heat, cool immediately under cold, running water and remove the lid and the rack. Leave the liquid in the pot. Add the butter and half the heavy cream. With a portable electric mixer, beat the vegetables until they are reduced to a puree. I like to beat the mixture until the orange flecks of carrots are a little less than half the size of raisins and the puree is the consistency of Cream of Wheat. This, of course, is a personal choice. If you prefer your soup thinner, add more cream. If you haven't already, taste the soup and add whatever salt and pepper you like. White pepper is more pleasing visually, but this soup is so hearty and provincial, I don't find black specks of pepper objectionable.

Depending on how long it has taken you to reduce the cooked vegetables to a puree and how much heavy cream you have added, you may want to put the pot back on the stove for a minute or so to be sure the soup is nice and hot.

To serve the soup, splash a little red wine (a little goes a long way; you won't need more than a tablespoon) into each warmed soup dish, and carefully ladle in the soup. The wine will not mix with the soup and will form a lovely burgundy halo around the golden eggnog colored soup. Place a dollop of sour cream in the center of the soup and sprinkle the sliced green onion tops on and around the sour cream (again, a little goes a long way). Now you are ready to present your masterpiece to your guests.

Sour black bread and a simple green salad go very well with the soup. If you want more, I suggest a cold meat of either boiled ham or rare roast beef or, if you can get it in Columbus, smoked salmon.

You may be surprised that I didn't start with a chicken stock, which is the way most recipes for potato soup in all its variations start. The reason is that when I created this recipe, what I wanted was the taste of fall, which to me is root vegetables. I didn't want chicken soup with potatoes and leeks in it. This is an example of what I mean when I talk about "vibes."

When you make the soup, pay attention to your instincts. If you feel like altering the recipe somehow, do it. See what happens. That way, this soup, or some variation, will ultimately become yours. You will learn how to avoid "bad vibes," or worse, "no vibes," and share with your guests food that nurtures the soul as well as the body, food that has been enriched with your caring, because we are all enriched by sharing something of ourselves with others.

Love,

Suzanne

The Discovery in "Letter to My Stepdaughter"

Suzanne has taken the opportunity of being asked for a recipe to tell her stepdaughter how to make not only potato leek soup but the good vibes of caring and attention. She tells her stepdaughter the recipe because she has been asked to do that, but she tells her the method for creating good vibes because she loves her. In literature, there is a long tradition of writing a letter to an audience of one person when actually a wider audience will read the work.

This letter starts with a short paragraph telling why Suzanne is writing the recipe. The next short paragraph tells about the creation of good vibes. Then the longer paragraph following is a narration of a past event and the family history it created, so anyone reading the letter will understand the derivation of the phrase "good vibes." That established, the writer goes back to the soup—step by step in the order necessary, we see what is needed, what must be done, and how to know when the mission is accomplished. Then after the soup is made, we get information on why the speaker's variation of the soup does not start with chicken stock. This is the start of the how-to about creating good vibes. We heard previously that it is important to create them; now we learn what to do to create them. Lastly, with the phrase "food that has been enriched with your caring" we feel the entwining of both how-tos. Suzanne has enriched her own sharing of a recipe with the care she takes to nurture her stepdaughter.

Go back into the essay. Name the steps to make the soup:

1. Get the ingredients.
2. Prepare the vegetables for cooking.
3. Cook the vegetables.
4. Warm the soup plates.
5. Handle the pot of cooked vegetables in a particular way.
6. Make the vegetables into soup by adding ingredients and making a puree.
7. Prepare each bowl of soup for serving.

Notice the special terms included in each step and how they are defined. For example, French carrots are named and described as "the short, stubby kind" and the size of the white potatoes needed is described by analogy as "man-fist-sized." In how-to, special materials or tools needed to accomplish a particular step are named. One example in this essay is the pressure cooker.

Also in how-to, the reader is told about variations in what steps can be taken or what tools or materials can be used. In Suzanne's essay we hear, for instance, about differences in the consistency of the puree, using black pepper versus white, and water versus chicken soup as liquid. In how-to, readers are told when they will know their task has been accomplished. The soup is ready once the burgundy halo, dollop of sour cream, and sprinkle of onion tops garnish each bowlful. Where does the writer tell the reader why she should be interested in accomplishing the task described? Well, we know Amanda has actually requested the recipe, but why should she bear with Suzanne's whole essay in addition? Because cooking is a personal statement of caring and in telling Amanda how to prepare the soup, she is also demonstrating the caring.

Go through the essay and look at the other how-to Suzanne has written simultaneously to the soup recipe, the how to create good vibes essay. See if you can separate the process into steps and name them. When would you know you have created good vibes? Why should you want to create good vibes?

Notice that to organize parts of the how-to essay, various forms of rhetoric are used inside the main organizational plan. Description provides precise images and details. Short narrations (anecdotes) help demonstrate and set scenes about why one should think about the process being discussed (there is a story in Suzanne's essay about shopping for groceries with her stepdaughter). Comparison and contrast (we will discuss these more in chapter five) come into play as a way of telling the reader how to know if she is doing something correctly—a standard is given to which results can be compared.

EXAMPLE: HOW-TO ESSAY

In the next how-to letter, Mary Meza wrote down the heartfelt thoughts many fail to communicate to those they love who depend on them. As you read, say in your own words what Mary is teaching her son to do. What are the steps? This essay has much in common with the previous essay. You might want to list the steps in each essay and then describe both the outer and inner processes the essays deal with in a few sentences. Pay attention also to the images the author uses. Which ones are doing the most work in terms of the inner process being described? This author uses more short narrations than the other author. Think about why there are more anecdotes in this how-to letter than in the previous one and how they help explain the process.

LETTER TO MY SON

Dear Brian,

I've thought about writing a letter like this to you since you were two years old. It was around that time I began to fear that I might die sometime during your childhood. I guess I feel that way because my mother died when I was still young, and it's taken me so long to adjust. There were so many questions she could have answered for me. I don't think she would have mapped out a step-by-step plan of action that would propel me effortlessly into adulthood nor do I think she might have had a magic formula that could evoke instant womanhood and perpetual happiness. But she'd been there before me. She could tell me what worked for her and what didn't. At least I would have had a foundation — a place from which to start. So I won't presume to tell you how to live your life, but I will tell you what I've discovered, what you might need to watch for, and what I believe helps to lead a human being on a road to personal peace.

Think of a river. Picture the crystal clear waters flowing gently past you, moving fast here, a little slower there, slapping the bank at the bend. Abruptly the current changes and things speed up. Watch out! Rough waters ahead — gray, murky, rough and raging. But then it slows down, becoming gentle, until, again, it flows past calm and slow. That's life. It can be wonderful when things are going your way, when you're feeling on top and in control with exciting new adventures just around the corner. But, just to keep us on our toes, it can turn us upside down. You feel blocked at every turn, friendless, alone and adrift. But the point is it keeps right on flowing. And what seems very important at the moment may pass or sink, or it may take root and bloom into something beautiful. You never know, but if you hold onto this image during the bad times, it might help you remember that, "This, too, shall pass."

There have been times when I've lost sight of the river, when I've gotten out of step with the rhythms of life. I guess the worst time for me was when your grandfather had a stroke and we had to put him in a nursing home. I felt so much pain for him and for myself that I didn't want to see the river. I wanted to see nothing, feel nothing, believe in nothing. With time, though, circumstances changed, as they always do. Your grandfather died, and slowly I recovered the ability to see the river. And I realized it was okay to turn my back for awhile because that is what I'd needed to make my way through the experience. And the wonderful thing is, Brian, the river was still there! And it kept right on flowing.

Your grandfather always said, "The only thing you can count on in life is change." And I agree, but I'd like to amend that a bit. (Amend means change — see how that works?) I think you can always count on yourself, too, if you take the time to learn about yourself and love yourself. You can look at your life in two ways: the what of Brian and the who of Brian. Don't ever make the mistake of thinking that you are the what. There was a man I knew who lost his job at the age of fifty who then spent the next several years of his life in deep depression. He had become his job and had defined himself in terms of what he did rather than who he was. Your success as a person doesn't come from how much money you make or how prestigious your job is. Your success as a person will come from knowing who you are, knowing your weaknesses and strengths, loving yourself and from that love reaching out to touch others with love.

"Know yourself." "Love yourself." I've heard these directives all my life from various sources and so will you. If you know yourself, you'll love yourself; if you love yourself, you'll know yourself; and if you have both knowledge and love, you'll have life licked! I'm still working on it. What I have found so far to be of the greatest help to me is becoming totally involved in helping someone else. When a friend needs to talk and I listen — trying to understand, trying to help, trying to "walk a mile in his shoes" — I sometimes astound myself with what I say, not even knowing I thought this way or that way until my focus was on someone other than myself. Or now, as a weight counselor, helping people battle their personal demons, I have had to come to terms with or at least give a passing nod to some of my own. In helping other people, you'll learn more about who you are, what you think, and what new directions you might want to consider than you ever would sitting off by yourself, thinking only about yourself. And whatever you learn, Brian, it will always make for an exciting discovery!

But don't be impatient in this search for yourself because it's really just growth. You may think there's not much to the who of you, but somewhere in your thirties, you'll find that there's a wealth of personhood inside you, and I'm told the forties are even better!

As you grow, your experiences will work on you; the people you touch will touch you in return; and the more you grow the more you will learn about yourself. As you learn who you are, love who you are. Say to yourself, "I like myself unconditionally!" Say it every day and pretty soon you will and then loving yourself will be easy.

Loving you has always been easy for me.

Your Mom

The Discovery in "Letter to My Son"

Children long to hear their parents' experience. Directing her thoughts to her son, Mary tells how she missed out on learning about experience from her mother. She tells her son what he will get from paying attention to her experience—not a lecture on how to live his life, but information about what his mother has discovered, what she believes anyone might need to watch for, and what she thinks helps lead a human being to personal peace. The modest tone combined with the focus on big issues lures the reader.

Mary's steps toward personal peace require:

1. viewing life as a river
2. forgiving yourself when you seem to step out of it
3. counting on change
4. knowing the difference between who you are and what you are doing
5. loving yourself and remembering you are loved.

Mary writes about how she has learned these steps and about the optimism with which she looks forward to her older adult years.

Though she has taken on what we would usually consider a big topic with many intangibles, Mary weaves the steps toward self-growth and affirmation together with examples and detail that give information a reader can absorb through the senses. Her comparisons refresh our experience of living. As we read the process toward self-growth that Mary outlines for her son, we experience an interesting process — love from Mary pouring out so her son can learn to allow love into himself, and, in turn, pour it out to others. There is a story within a story within a story here, a flowing that hasn't stopped for Mary despite the early death of her own mother.

EXERCISES FOR DEVELOPING YOUR MATERIAL

Although you may have felt familiar with description and narration as writing styles, other styles may seem unfamiliar. They require organizational patterns that you may not be using in your writing. You have, however, used these organizational patterns in your life. To help you realize the experience you already have with these patterns, I will share exercises in this and the next chapters that help you reconnect with your experience of the patterns.

The If-I-Can-Do-It-You-Can-Understand-How-to-Do-It-Too Interview

Find someone to interview about something he or she knows how to do, someone who is also willing to interview you. For example, someone you know may know how to develop film or use public transportation efficiently or prepare soil for vegetable gardening. Bring a pen and pad and ask your interviewee to tell you why the task to be described is an important one. Jot down the reason. Ask why it might be important for others to know how to do the task. Jot this down. Next, ask your interviewee to describe the steps, one by one, performed in doing the task under discussion. Take notes. If the steps are not making sense to you, ask questions until you have all the terms and procedures straight and you understand what is done, in what order, and how to do each part of the process.

Referring to your notes, tell the process back to your interviewee. Did you get it right? If not, you probably need a further description or a different order to the steps given you. Let your interviewee help until you are both satisfied that you could perform the task using the directions.

Now that you have experienced *receiving* how-to information, switch roles. Have your interviewee become your interviewer. With pad and pen for taking notes, the new interviewer will ask you to designate something you know how to do and listen to you tell why someone else might want to know how to do it. Perhaps you will discuss how to stop smoking or how to unclog a toilet or create a savings plan that works. Whatever your subject, your interviewer asks you to tell the steps needed to accomplish the task, one by one, in the right order. Your interviewer must be sure to ask questions to clarify any special terms, tools, materials, variations, or precautions another needs to know about. After the interview is completed, your interviewer must describe your process back to you. Would it be done the way you instructed? If not, you know what you need to do — correct a step, add steps, or give more information.

Anytime you have given someone directions to get somewhere or shared a recipe, you have experienced communicating in the how-to style. Anytime you have tried to assemble something from manufacturers' directions or used a product according to instructions, you have experienced receiving information in the how-to style. You know how important clarity, precision, correct order and inclusion of all pertinent information is for the receiver! Whenever you are using the how-to form, whether it is to make sure family members know how to do Thanksgiving the way your grandparents did it or to tell your best friend how to overcome the grief of an unwanted divorce, that same kind of thoroughness creates essays that are rich, full, and well-received.

LOCATING YOUR HOW-TO MATERIAL

Now that you have practiced noticing the steps in a process, look back at your clusters and any image-gathering exercises you did on the topic discovered through your cluster. With these in front of you, create a freewrite. Let yourself write sentences continuously for five to twenty minutes. When the time is up, shake out your hands and leave the freewrite for a little while.

WRITING YOUR ESSAY

When you feel ready, make a draft of your how-to essay. Look at your freewrite. You can add to it by writing a short account (narration) of a time you remember sharing with the person you are writing. Or you might want to focus on a future time for which you want to prepare this person. After grounding your addressee in a situation, state what process you want to explain. Move along by describing the steps that need to be done to complete the process. Take care to get the order right and not to leave any important steps out. Pay attention to your use of description and terms in the steps. Are the images true to the situation and senses? Do any of the terms need explanation? How will the addressee know when the task is accomplished?

If you get stuck describing any of the steps in the process, stop and do a cluster or a This Is a Poem or a Things to Do exercise especially for that step. You will generate images that will get you unstuck.

Before you take off on your how-to personal essay, consider a sentence from Latin American writer Eduardo Galeano in his book *Days and Nights of Love and War* (Monthly Review Press, 1983): "I believe in my vocation; I believe in my instrument." If the idea of telling a story to start yourself off doesn't appeal to you, use Galeano's words as a prompt. The next sentence will be your own.

DEVELOPING THE DRAFT

Now that you have written a first draft, let's look at Elizabeth's first draft of a how-to letter essay. You will notice that this draft is missing the strong personal subtext of the sample essays. It doesn't seem to have a universal premise like the sample essays do. As you read, instead of being put off by this, look for your responses. What would you tell the writer in the three-step process? When you read my discussion of her draft, you will see how responses help the writer arrive at deeper meaning.

HOW TO SAMPLE SEATTLE
IF ONLY FOR A DAY

Dear Ruth Ann,

It was wonderful to receive your letter and learn that you and Jan will be venturing to the Northwest for his annual bar convention. Last year Mexico City, this year Seattle. You certainly know how to get around! I know how much you have wanted to visit Seattle since I moved here three years ago. The early letters I sent you were filled with what I'd uncovered as I explored my new home. There were the midnight ferryboat rides across the sound, the "to go" cups of espresso that seemed to be a permanent fixture in people's hands and the rain that fell and fell but never dampened a spirit of adventure or dissuaded me from stepping out. The curiosity in your correspondences prompted me on. I told you how at Seattle's Pike Place Public Market fishmongers pitch salmon through the air like baseballs and yell "incoming" like umpires yell "play ball."

I must respond to your request that I sketch out an itinerary that includes "everything" even though your travel schedule permits you only one full day for sightseeing. That is quite a task. I believe, my friend, that it is what you will see during your time here that will be more memorable than how much you see. I want for you to leave Seattle having tasted a sampling of the diversity of its people, sights and sounds. I know they will be rich and lasting and will provide you with the very flavor that attracted me. You can always come back and enjoy a full meal. For now, let's concentrate on a combination plate of appetizers I have tried to design.

As you requested, this will be a walking tour with a few jaunts on public transportation. Please bring good sturdy shoes with traction as the terrain of the city tends to be a bit hilly in spots. The weather even in August can be unpredictable so I would suggest a lightweight slicker just in case and a backpack for storage that will leave your hands free to roam.

Please leave your guidebooks at home. If you have any questions beyond the information that I enclosed for you (see downtown map I included numbered) just ask a friendly someone on the street for directions or suggestions. I think it is important that wherever you travel you get a feel for the people, and what better way to start than to engage them in conversation? Believe it or not, I made two very good friends on my first visit to Seattle. Seattlites love to show off their city, so fear not!

What better way to orient yourself than a bird's-eye view of the city from the Space Needle? If it is a clear morning take the number twenty-four bus from the front of your hotel to the Seattle Center. Just follow the path 'til you're at the base of the tower and take the elevator, a two-minute ride, to the top. The view is spectacular. To the west, you will find the snowcapped Olympic Mountains gracefully preceded by a sea of blue known as Puget Sound. To the north is the ship canal. Let your eyes follow it eastward through Portage Bay into Lake Washington. Due south is downtown Seattle. The streets look more confusing than they are. Just remember the avenues run north/south and the streets run east/west.

"Help!" Elizabeth wrote on a note to me accompanying this draft. She didn't know why she felt trapped and unable to continue.

Let's go through the three-step response method and see why Elizabeth got stuck and couldn't write from beginning to end.

THE THREE-STEP RESPONSE
Step One: Velcro Words

Here are the images that stick with me: "Midnight ferryboat rides across the sound," " 'to go' cups of espresso" like "fixtures," "rain that fell and fell," fishmongers who throw fish "like baseballs," bringing "sturdy shoes and a lightweight slicker," talking to "a friendly someone," "Space Needle," "snowcapped Olympic mountains," "ship canal," "Portage Bay," "Lake Washington."

Step Two: Feelings

I feel the pleasure of having a friend visit, the happiness of feeling comfortable in a new place and eagerness about helping someone have a good tour.

My feelings about the language as I go through this draft are: I feel settled in with the opening overviews. I know who is coming to Seattle, why she is coming and why Elizabeth is writing a trip guide. Well, sort of why—for some reason Elizabeth isn't going to tour with her friend and show her around, and I feel left out not knowing the reason. I feel comfortable hearing the images Elizabeth reports she wrote to Ruth Ann about Seattle.

Phrases like "my friend" sound nervous to me. The city "tends to be a bit hilly in spots" sounds like someone trying to appear English. I feel a loss of confidence that I am in the presence of a speaker whose diction I trust. "Hands free to roam" brings me uncomfortably back to a seventh-grade joke about boys with Russian arms and Roman hands. Phrases like "I am," "I believe," "I want," "I would suggest," and "Please leave," that are sprinkled through the three inside paragraphs put me off. They draw attention to the author as leader, something like a teacher standing at the front of the field trip bus. If Elizabeth worded her sentences without phrases like this, attention would be on the tour, what she wants to communicate to Ruth Ann, not on how she feels about communicating it. She must trust that her enthusiasm and exactness will come through in the very images and instructions she writes for Ruth Ann.

I like hearing that Elizabeth made two very good friends on her first visit to Seattle. It leaves me with confidence about Ruth Ann's afternoon.

I feel forced into considering the question, "What better way to orient yourself than a bird's eye view of the city from the Space Needle?" First of all, as a stranger to the city, I wouldn't know the answer. Secondly, I'd rather stay on the ground and meet those Seattlites who love to show off their city. I feel so much enthusiasm for them, it is a disappointment to be told to go all the way to the top of the Space Needle where I can't touch, see, hear, taste and smell what Elizabeth mentions being so fond of.

Herein lies the source of Elizabeth's getting stuck—she has diverted her attention as well as the visitor's away from the sounds, textures, smells, tastes and sights that are in the daily experience here. Popping up to get an overview of the lay of the land does not help one get a feel for the people and their activities.

There is another overall feeling I get reading the draft and that is one of discomfort at being an unwilling eavesdropper. Why am I reading this letter? Do I care that Ruth Ann and her husband Jan have gotten to travel a lot recently? Do I care that Elizabeth is ecstatic over her friend's short stay? And why does Elizabeth tell Ruth Ann things she already knows like how long Elizabeth's been in Seattle? For my benefit as reader? Is this what I need to know? I feel like a tagalong and I'd rather leave Ruth Ann and Elizabeth to their tête-à-tête and find something else to do.

The letter form does come with this problem—how can you address your thoughts to one person and make the resulting essay good reading for a wider audience? My answer is that once you write your way all the way to the discovery, the insight, the subtext, the real reason you are writing this essay, you will be able to cull away all that is off-putting to a general audience. Once your piece discovers what it is about, the personal images you do use will place any reader in your moment.

Step Three: Curiosity

Here is where I am interested to know more: I want to know why Elizabeth isn't in the tour. I want to know more about why exactly Ruth Ann might want to have her hands free. I want to know more about all the espresso, the fishmongering, and the rain and hills as someone on the ground might experience them. I want to know how to get around the city—which buses, which streets. I want to know what the climax of the tour will be.

Now, get the response you need to your first draft, but before you rewrite, take a look at Elizabeth's developed draft. Notice how even the salutation "Dear Ruth Ann" is no longer necessary. The occasion of addressing her friend is so neatly woven into her essay that the title alone takes care of placing the reader.

THE SECOND DRAFT

TO RUTH ANN WHO WILL VISIT FOR A DAY

The early letters I sent you were filled with what I'd uncovered as I explored my new home. There were the midnight ferryboat rides across the sound, the "to go" cups of espresso that seemed to be a permanent fixture in people's hands and the rain that fell and fell but never dampened a spirit of adventure or dissuaded me from stepping out. The curiosity in your correspondences prompted me on. I told you how at Seattle's Pike Place Public Market fishmongers pitch salmon through the air like baseballs and yell, "incoming" like umpires yell, "play ball."

And now I can look forward to seeing you and sharing my city, if only for a day. When you will be here, another close friend of mine is being married on a boat on Lake Union. I will see you at the beginning and end of the day, and I will offer you a plan for exploring Seattle on your own in between. I believe that it is what you will see during your time here that will be more memorable than how much you see. Please come back to enjoy a full meal. For now, though, I'll concentrate on a combination plate of appetizers.

Most of the day I am describing will be a walking tour with jaunts on public transportation. Bring good sturdy shoes with traction as the terrain of the city is hilly. You might want a backpack for slicker storage, since the weather even in August can be unpredictable.

If you have any questions beyond the information that I am enclosing for you (see downtown map with numbers) just ask a friendly someone on the street when you get here for directions or suggestions. That way, you'll get a feel for Seattle people. Believe it or not, I made two very good friends on my first visit to Seattle.

In the morning, I'll meet you at your hotel, and we can walk to my neighborhood and start your day with a steaming cup of espresso and a brioche at Cafe Septieme, a cozy little coffeehouse in the heart of Belltown. Belltown is stuffed with funky clothing shops, art spaces (a Northwest term for art galleries) and classic brick apartment buildings. I spend hours at Septieme writing letters, reading or just watching the cast of characters that make their way in and out the French doors. The air is usually thick with the sweet smell of butter pastries, conversations about foreign films or the latest play two young writers are struggling over as they chain smoke in a state of dissension.

After breakfast, I'll have to return home to get ready for the wedding, but I'll point you in the direction of Myrtle Edwards Park for an invigorating walk. Usually, I lose myself after a long day at work by listening to the soothing sounds of Elliott Bay lapping against the rocky shoreline. Sometimes I walk with my eyes closed breathing the fresh salt air and letting the calls of the seagulls direct my way. The winding path guides you along the water for a mile and a half with a stunning view of the Olympic Mountains to the west. If it were evening, you could see how the Olympic Mountains' cutout paper shapes contrast against the pink sky.

At one end of the park, the largest grain elevator on the West Coast loads tankers with wheat and barley destined for the Far East and Central America. Look out at the Sound and enormous barges are inching across it, their decks piled with orange cargo containers destined for the docks. Seattle is a major port for the international import/export market.

Your journey will continue with a ride on the waterfront trolley car. Within minutes, you'll arrive at the base of the hillclimb, the backstairs to Seattle's famous Pike Place Public Market. A bill-board of green and blue swimming salmon will welcome you and, believe me, these fish are a familiar signature in and around Seattle. This is salmon country, home of king, chinook and coho to name a few. Maybe you will see the Metro bus painted with bright blue and pink salmon inviting all to "swim aboard."

The Pike Place Market is what many Seattlites consider to be the heart and soul of the city. It was almost lost to the wrecking ball some years back but was saved by a group of tenacious citizens who recognized its worth as an integral part of the community. As you make your way through the main arcade where the day stall vendors sell their wares, you'll notice hundreds of floor tiles en-graved with the names of generous people who contributed money to save the market.

At first, your eyes, ears and nose will compete for your attention! I call it the market buzz. The gentle harmony of musicians' dulcimers will dance through your ears only to be interrupted by echoes of the hand-slapping gospel pulsing across the street. As you move towards the beat, your eyes will be drawn to the colorful tie-dyed clothing hanging from the rafters and then to the endless row of tables with samples of homemade honey on popsicle sticks, wooden puzzles or fire-glazed pottery. As the aromas of freshly baked cinnamon rolls and dark roast coffee tease you on in search of their origin, your eye may catch a curious yellow star-shaped fruit that one of the Asian grocers is slicing and offering to the people as they pass.

Treat yourself to lunch up on the balcony of the Copacabana overlooking Pike Place. From there you will have a great view to observe the diversity of people that work, live, or just play at the market. They are young and old, and they come from such lands as India, Mexico, and our own East Coast. They wear pinstriped suits, Birkenstocks and vintage clothing. Some only wear black and die their hair purple. They buy flowers, produce, wine, pastel-colored wind socks, incense and lattés to go. Some come to the market to entertain and others come to be entertained. Sit back and enjoy the crowd as they weave a colorful tapestry before your eyes.

You can keep track of the time on the large clock that hangs adjacent to the huge red Public Market sign. After a couple of hours at the market, I can imagine you will look forward to a little rest, and I can't think of a better spot than on a ferry named Spokane. To reach the terminal take a #18 bus heading south on First Avenue. Tell the bus driver to let you off at Yestler, and the terminal is one block west. Once you get inside the terminal, you will see the ticket taker located in a glass booth. She will ask your destination. Tell her you want to go to Winslow. When you get there, you can visit shops and bookstores that are only a short walk from the ferry dock. Best of all, the Winslow ferries have top decks that stretch the length of the boat where, if it is sunny, you will find commuters soaking up the sun's warm rays and the fresh air. If it's a cool day, you can sit under one of the orange glass awnings that extends from either end of the ferry where rectangular heaters hang to keep the chill off.

From the open deck, you'll see the cars load into the vast belly beneath you as the deckhands wave them on, pointing left and right. This is a good time for striking up a conversation with other passengers who often exchange forecasts about how many cars waiting in the loading area might still squeeze onto the ferry before it leaves the dock.

All the day you are here, when I hear the distant horn of the ferry, which sounds once as it departs and twice before it docks, I will be thinking of you. I'll wonder about your thoughts as you travel back to Seattle across the bay, showy Mount Rainier in the background. I'll remember my first ride and how I felt welcomed by the city's skyline, all lit up against a dark evening sky.

When you arrive back at the Seattle ferry terminal, I think it will be about time for you to head to your hotel to get ready for dinner. Go into the bus tunnel at Second and University near the ferry terminal. You can catch the shuttle heading up to the West-lake Station. Traveling the bus tunnel will give you a chance to see some of the city's newest public art. Each station is decorated with colorful murals and other playful works. The Westlake Station, where you will get out, has a wall with tiny blinking neon lights seeming to represent the pace of commuters at rush hour.

I have made dinner reservations for you and Jan at the Space Needle. When he is done working, you can meet him there by taking The Monorail at the Westlake station. It will whisk you to the Space Needle and then you will board an elevator to the restaurant. The restaurant revolves slowly and you can view both the Cascade and the Olympic mountain ranges as you eat. From the viewing decks, you can see Seattle's lakes and Puget Sound very well.

I can't think of a place more perfect for you to share the stories of your day with Jan than overlooking the city where you can point out the market or the ferries crossing in the distance. I will join you there after the reception and take you for dessert to Cafe Sophie. I have written you about their creamy rich cheesecake loaded with plump strawberries. You won't be able to make up your mind between that and the double chocolate espresso torte. I promise.

Until dessert time, from the wedding boat on Lake Union, I will look up to you, as I have done often in my life. When my friend Lisa slips the gold band onto Jeff's finger and promises to stand with him in times of joy and of doubt, I will think of you and Jan and the ten years of marriage you will be celebrating in December. I wish I could give Lisa the wisdom you have gained for when she needs help navigating the early storms in a new marriage.

Strength and character, you always said, help in the toughest times. When I first moved to Seattle and knew so few people, I remembered those words amidst the others you whispered in my ear as we hugged goodbye. Strength and character—they are what I find in my new city.

I was pleased with this version and its richer emotional subtext. We can experience the occasion upon which Elizabeth is speaking to her friend on two levels—that of Elizabeth as guide and that of Elizabeth as one who has been guided. How nicely our real lives include images and occasions that lead us to discovery. Is it a coincidence that just when her happily married friend is coming to town, Elizabeth is attending the wedding of another friend? This is the synchronicity writers count on. Remembering words of Ruth Ann's wisdom that she wishes to share with her newly marrying friend, Elizabeth is led into stating what is meaningful to her.

Did you notice how phrases from the first draft that tell more about Elizabeth's writing anxiety than about seeing Seattle in a day have disappeared? She no longer patronizes Ruth Ann by inserting "my friend" in the middle of a sentence and by putting on a kind of British diction when she describes the city. "Tends to be a bit hilly in spots" becomes "the terrain of the city is hilly." When Elizabeth trusts the exact images of what she has seen and done in Seattle, she gets to her real subject, which isn't about food or about Seattle being a playground; it is about the values of strength and character she hopes for in herself, her friends, and her city. For Elizabeth, this strength includes diversity, good taste, friendliness and safe transport, which means dependability.

Elizabeth has made good use of an occasion for writing. In telling her friend how to visit Seattle (and enjoy its food), Elizabeth has drawn a portrait of what her city and friendships mean to her. She has gotten to evoke for herself just how far she has come making herself comfortable in her own life.

KEEP DRAFTING

Once again, if you feel like it, go through the response method for Elizabeth's developed draft. Then get back to your draft and the responses you received. Let yourself write more from beginning to end. Can a reader both *follow your steps* and *feel why* you are really addressing them about how something is made or done? Gather new responses to your continuing drafts and develop your work until you feel satisfied.

CHAPTER FIVE

The Comparison and Contrast Essay

Writing About How Things Are Different From How You Expected Them to Be

World is the pattern of meaningful relations in which a person exists and in the design of which he or she participates.
— *Rollo May*, The Courage to Create

We use comparison and contrast to make choices — between jobs, consumer goods, vacations, etc. We examine similarities and differences. We compare an unknown to something with which we are already familiar. We can also use comparison and contrast to learn about ourselves. For instance, a person might learn more about his or her attachment to a hot rod by comparing it to having a celebrity in the neighborhood. Another person might learn more about why he or she likes swimming in a pool better than swimming in the ocean by discussing the differences between the pool and the ocean in accessibility, temperature, and depth. Yet another person might compare and contrast both kinds of swimming and find characteristics that make each a favorite way to swim.

We also use comparison and contrast to write personal essays that lead to self-discovery. I developed a "write" question for using this essay style from a statement made by a friend who had recently returned to the U.S. after living in Morocco. He felt the magic of living in Morocco was discounted in America where our need to pay the bills forces us headlong into *making* a living rather than *living*. He said sorrowfully, "It's not the way it's supposed to be." I rushed off to teach a class with the phrase still in my head and used it successfully with my students to develop comparison/contrast essays from their personal experience.

I urged my students to use the phrase to compare and contrast the way they were living to how they or others close to them would wish them to live. I wanted them to explore ways in which their lives were both like and unlike what they or someone else might wish.

We think we know what other people want or expect from us and, covertly, we contrast what we are doing with those expectations. Often, we feel we are doing less than what we are "supposed" to be doing. But what if we stopped for a moment and examined our lives according to the comparison and contrast style of essay writing?

Ask yourself, "In my life, what is not the way it's supposed to be?" See how the question opens up new areas for writing and thinking. Let things come to mind that contrast with how you or someone else thought "it" would be. Are you a school teacher instead of a doctor? Single instead of married? Living on a farm instead of in a city? Adopting children instead of having them? Living far away from family instead of close by? Baking your own bread instead of buying it?

You might start thinking of how you selected a career or a boyfriend and defied your parents' expectations, or how you worked a job because the money was good and you could buy what you were supposed to want but discovered you wanted something quite different. You might compare what you picture as the right of all children with the actualities of what has happened to children you know or to yourself as a child. Things somewhere in your life "are not the way they are supposed to be."

If you have a writing subject in mind, insert it into the question. To use our examples once again, "What about divorcing, parenting, adjusting to an illness, fighting a war, or visiting a new country, is not the way it's supposed to be?" Your parenting style might contrast with how you hoped you'd parent. Your life with diabetes is different from before you had it. Actual battle experiences differ from movie battles. We are all different from the norm, from an idealized version of life, from our old selves, and from those who came before us. Here is an opportunity to examine the differences and see what you have gained or what is missing for you.

Let's turn to two sample essays and see how they are organized and how their authors accomplish self-discovery. Note how descriptive, narrative and instructive elements that we covered in earlier chapters are used in these essays.

EXAMPLE: COMPARISON AND CONTRAST ESSAY

Here is an essay by Syeda Rizwana F. Kazmi. She left her home in Pakistan and was new to Seattle when she thought about the city's rain and how it differed from the rain of her childhood. As you read her essay, notice that by contrasting the rain in Seattle with the rain in Pakistan, Syeda creates a way to contrast her youth with her adulthood, the American culture she finds herself in with the Pakistani culture she grew up in, and her life when she lived close to her family with her life far away from them. As you read, make note of any comparison or contrast, no matter how small, to see how the mind gets into the comparison and contrast groove and grows an essay.

THE RAIN IS NOT THE WAY IT'S SUPPOSED TO BE

The present moments never prevail over our lives. They keep chasing us in their own bewilderment. The old broken carriage of life is pulled by the cruel and blind animal of time. Our moments follow the carriage of life in the form of clouds, showering tears, telling stories of the time when they were present.

Before I came from Pakistan, I had the rainy season, the only weather I wanted to stay in forever. I remember myself in a strange sort of ecstasy: I am out on my swing, singing and swinging, sometimes wildly and sometimes very smoothly. Marble floors which used to be red brick floors are fresher than before the rain. All sorts of colorful chips are brighter and their colors are deeper than they were before being washed by the rain, which is pouring down, humming and tapping the floor rhythmically. I smell the soil everywhere, even in my room. I run upstairs. At the top of the roof, soil is getting its seasonal shower. It is getting fragrant. I am barefoot, dancing, jumping and running madly. The flat rooftop has a four-foot-high concrete fence all around it. It has a little geometrical and floral pattern in it. I peep through these patterned holes and watch people moving in the street.

It's thundering horribly. Rain is pouring heavily. I am soaked in the water. I am trying to stuff the mouth of a drainage pipe to make a swimming pool at the roof top. I am looking for old garments, towels, curtains or sheets which I can use without any fear of my mother. She is calling me down. She is in the kitchen frying pakoras (vegetables dipped in a spicy gram flour paste and deep fried). She is worried about me. Whenever it rains, I am mad. Afterwards, I always get sick, but the next day I am out in the rain again wilder than the day before. She knows my passionate love for rain. She does not keep me from doing my crazy things.

The cold breeze is blowing west to east. The old oak at my grandmother's house is singing its own old sad song in the memory of those who left it to stand there forsaken forever. Its pale and dead leaves can no longer resist the wind. They are separating from the tree unwillingly. Some of them are getting away from me. I can't bring them back to their original place. I'm running with my arms stretched in the air as if I am trying to catch them. Suddenly, I feel a pang of pain in my right foot. It's bleeding at my big toe. It's cut somehow. I'm crying and the old oak is singing the lyrics of abandonment.

The rain stops. I can smell different kinds of savory, sweet and deep fried foods in the air. I know that my grandmother is downstairs talking to my mother. She has brought sweet colorful rice (zerda). My mom is getting ready to make pooras (sweet thin pancakes), one of the dishes of a rainy day. My brothers are out, playing with my cousins and uncles. Soon they will come home colder and paler than I am. I should go downstairs and wash and wipe the marble floor before someone slips and breaks bones. My sisters are playing hide-and-seek inside the rooms. I want to take a warm shower and to wear warm clothes.

"Hi, Rizwana, I am coming; get my tea ready," my uncle is yelling at the corner of the street as he is approaching my home. He is my dad's only and elder brother. He's brought three or four dozen pink lotus. They are floating in a big round ceramic pan in my house. He'll sit by me in the kitchen. Everybody will gather there and we'll drink tea, eat pakoras, pooras and zerda. We will have hot discussions about cricket, hockey and politics. The day will end with a fight between my uncle and me or with television.

I have spent innumerable days like this, but things are no more the same since I have left my home. The rain is not the rain I experienced in Pakistan. It's not the rain which smells like a spring full of fresh water spurting from the heart of the earth, spreading an immense fragrance of soil in the air. Here in Seattle rain showers the concrete and asphalt roads. It floods the grassy lawns which are already watered by the sprinkler systems and soaks through the wooden houses which get moist, damp and cold. There is no aroma of food to give a feeling of celebration. The rain pours down with no thundering. The winds knock down the trees. I sit in my tightly closed room near the window. My eyes are fixed on the views outside. I analyze the trickles down the window glass, tears on my cheeks. My madness is dying within me. My old true companion is leaving me.

The cold weather is freezing my limbs and chilling my soul. Am I growing old? Would I be able to go back to my past's delightful days? Why is time constantly forcing me to move from place to place? I'm scared.

Outside of my bedroom window heavy branches are falling down from the tall trees. They don't recognize me. I am a stranger to them like I am to the inhabitants of this city. I want to catch them and tell them who I am. I want to celebrate the rainy season, but there is nothing to celebrate. People can not play and dance wildly with me in this rain. For them, it is a miserable day.

Since the rain does not smell as before, I feel its water is full of acid and chemicals, artificial like the smile on a salesman's face. How can I welcome it wholeheartedly? How can I get crazy when there is no swing hanging in my backyard? There is no rooftop where I can pool the rain water, where I can jump and play. I am forlorn in grey, ice-cold weather, and the rain is weeping on my fate. The rain is supposed to bring new things to life. The rain is supposed to be a divine blessing. The rain is supposed to resuscitate the earth. The rain is supposed to spread joy among the living beings. The rain in Seattle is not the way it is supposed to be.

The Discovery in "The Rain Is Not the Way It Is Supposed to Be"

This essay opens with comparisons: life is like a broken carriage pulled by the animal time; our present is already a group of clouds telling sad stories just behind us. Certainly this is not what most of us think when we think about how "it is supposed to be," yet on reflection, we know that our lives may be much less under our control than we would like to think. These short contrasts set a mood and a tone. We know this will not be a happy story.

The second paragraph opens with the phrase, "Before I came from Pakistan, I had the rainy season, the only weather I wanted to stay in forever." Before and after. After we close a door, we often see most clearly what we left behind. Rizwana sees her mother, her grandmother, her uncle, brothers and sisters. She sees the red marble, the old oak tree, the pink lotus flowers, the colorful zerda. She smells the pakoras, the pooras, and the pungent soil of her home where she knew the comings and goings of her family, and they knew and delighted in her.

Since she has come to Seattle the rain is not the same for her. To Rizwana this rain smells not of earth, but of chemicals. It sounds different, and it looks different. There is asphalt, spongy overwatered grass lawns, sprinkler systems, blown-down boughs of trees, icy cold air, forced solitude inside, and no savory aromas from familiar cooking. Contemplating the differing landscapes, Rizwana ultimately names what she mourns the most — the passing of her own wild girl-spirit, the part of her that danced ecstatically in the rain. With this perception we are back to the beginning — the carriage that is life drawn by the blind animal time pulling us always just a little beyond where we had wanted to linger.

The comparison and contrast essay could not be accomplished without the sensory detail of description and the short stories of narration (think of Rizwana's stories about her mother and her uncle). The description of the rain in Pakistan also becomes a how-to spend a happy rainy day at home in Pakistan. As you write in the various styles, your dexterity in mixing them increases. This dexterity then allows you to tackle the complexity of some of the more elaborate essay styles to come.

EXAMPLE: COMPARISON AND CONTRAST ESSAY

Kate Wright's essay compares her life as a young adult to her toddler brother's life. As you read, notice how at first Kate's observations seem to carry only an entertaining irony: We appreciate what we had when we were younger only after we grow up. That old adage, "Youth is wasted on the young," comes to mind. But notice, too, how Kate's observations lead beyond the irony to a very Thoreau-like or Wordsworthian longing.

I WISH . . .

There are times when I get home that all I can do is relax, for fear my mind or body might explode. It is during those times that I end up watching — or if I'm really energetic — playing with my little brother. His life seems so carefree compared to mine: he spends his day exploring new corners of the house, eating and sleeping. If he should break something while playing he is naughty — but the responsibility falls onto the shoulders of whoever was watching him. His food is prepared for him, his laundry done for him, and whereas my mother makes sure I am up in the morning, she is careful not to make noise outside his door. He gets twelve hours of sleep; I'm lucky if I get eight. Most of all, there are no little jobs he is responsible for, such as dishes, cleaning or phoning someone. All that he does is pleasure. He may not always be pleased, such as when his lunch is not gotten quickly enough to satisfy an empty stomach or when something he wants to examine is out of reach, but his trials and tribulations don't grip him or restrain him as responsibility does me.

So, while my barely toddling strawberry-blond brother is enjoying his discoveries in life, I am slaving over some assignment I must get done. My brother has no tests, unless they are remembering that he's not allowed to play with our books, and I pass from class to class being forced to learn too quickly what could have been interesting. I learn; he discovers. I have due dates; he can remember lessons at leisure. Moreover, while I'm responsible for organizing the entire junior class for rummage sale muscle power, he is growling at his stuffed bear and saying hello to his seal. It is easier to build a block tower with not-yet coordinated hands than it is to manipulate people into doing boring jobs well.

I envy him because he has not yet been molded by society into its sense of right and wrong and its prejudices. He does not have any code he must live by, no manners he must have. I watch him impolitely push his way into someone's lap who is reading, or sit absorbed by a seat cushion making all sorts of excited shrieks and giggles, oblivious to what is around him. He does not notice when my mother and I exchange funny looks and laugh at what he does; he just does. I miss that freedom — I no longer sing loudly in public because I know my voice is awful. I will occasionally break free and dance a few untrained steps, but the reactions I get — surprise, uncomfortable laughter, teasing — are enough to limit the number of times I let myself go.

But even more than self-consciousness bothers me, the loss of interest and alertness makes me despair. When I look at how my brother can be so fascinated by a puddle of water, a belt, a string or any other equally trivial item, I realize that somehow I have lost that innocent amazement at life. I no longer see things I used to. Now I rush from class to class, and the quivering leaves moist with rain elude me. My mind spins trying to keep track of everything I need to do, so I miss the bushy-tailed gray squirrel that streaked across my path.

It is sad to think I can get so caught up in the world of society: I would enjoy living in the world my brother does for a bit. I only wish he could realize what he has while he has it, because too soon he will be in my place. Maybe he will be glad he is no longer a dependent and vulnerable child, but for me, there are times I am so exhausted I would gladly trade my independence for the joy of discovery.

The Discovery in "I Wish" . . .

Kate calls her essay "I Wish . . ." and the ellipsis after "Wish" shows that her subject is elusive. Through exploring her wishes, which she may think are unattainable, she finds out how much she treasures certain ways of being when she compares her life to the life of her toddler brother. Kate sees in his doings that life is supposed to be about discovery, not self-consciousness, deadlines, and pressure to perform. Life is supposed to be about engaging in the world, not withdrawing from it, about noticing the gray squirrel across her path and singing at the top of her lungs. Kate evokes the difficulty in putting away carefree enjoyment. By keeping her eye on her brother and the feelings she has watching his particular actions, Kate lets us know a great deal about what we are missing if we allow ourselves to be entirely caught up "in the world of society."

I believe these contrasts between herself and her little brother served Kate well. She contemplated her life as it had been and her life as it was in the present, strip-mined of so many qualities she valued. The act of writing this comparison and contrast contemplation may have helped her restore some of those qualities to her life.

EXERCISES FOR DEVELOPING YOUR MATERIAL

There are two helpful listing exercises you can do to get your mind working along comparison and contrast lines.

Telling It How It Never Was to Find Out How It Is

One of the exercises is the metaphorical thinking exercise I already introduced in the description chapter. When you try it, you will realize how things that are different are also alike. A doorknob is something like a knee in size and in shape. The straps on the top of some sandals are like highway overpasses.

You can use constructions like this to help you learn to write comparison and contrast essays. For instance, if you said, "Writing is like mining for gold," you could explain the writing process in terms of gold mining—what equipment is needed, how to pan in the river of information, how to recognize a nugget and what to do with it. This mining may not be anything like the way I hoped writing would be with well-shaped essays, stories and poems appearing rapidly on my computer screen, unstoppable as pedestrians crossing New York's streets.

If you said, "My old boyfriend was like a McDonald's," you might find yourself writing about how unsatisfying the relationship was — the same old menu, the pre-spread ketchup-mustard combo on the rolls meant to please without taking a stand, the flashy packaging over the skimpy meal. This relationship may be nothing like the one you'd hoped to have, the one like the Louvre filled with unlimited beauty and treasures.

To do this "like" thinking as a warm-up exercise, make a list of things going on in your life and compare these things to something you have never thought of before. For example, arguing is like rowing with one oar or my mother is like a library. Next take one of these likes from your list and see if you can extend the analogy you are making as in the gold panning and writing example or the relationship and McDonald's example. Go on at greater length talking about one subject in terms of another. Some of what you say may seem silly, but keep going. Metaphor can help you be brilliant!

Before and After

Here is another listing exercise that greases the comparison/contrast mind. It comes from my interest in before and after pictures, from the ones people have of their houses before and after "the remodel" to the ones in magazines about women's cosmetic makeovers and diet plans. We are all being remodeled, made over, thinned or fattened as time goes by.

To do this exercise, make a list of sentences that begin with "before" and continue with "after" such as:

> Before I turned sixteen, I put up with my curly hair;
> after that I straightened it every month.

Before my divorce, I lived in a huge old house on a tree-lined street in the artsy part of town; after I remarried I lived in a smaller old house in a working-class part of town.

Before I was remarried, I never ate pecans on my cereal; after I remarried I learned to look forward to a whole pile of pecan halves on the Rice Chex in my bowl.

Before I had children, I didn't know myself; after I had children, I learned more and more about who I am.

Write before and afters on subjects important and unimportant, physical and spiritual, silly, mundane and esoteric. Have fun seeking out lots of ways in which you have experienced change. Reread your list. Notice that the changes (contrasts) work against a background of sameness (comparisons). Before and after my divorce, I lived in houses; where and what kind changed. I am myself before and after having children; the difference is I know myself better after having children. I ate cereal before and after my remarriage, but what I put on the cereal changed. You don't have to worry about whether you are comparing and contrasting or about whether they are balanced in your writing. Your mind will do this kind of thinking naturally.

LOCATING YOUR COMPARISON AND CONTRAST MATERIAL

Write the phrase, "It's not the way it's supposed to be" in the center of a blank page. If you are working without a particular topic, let yourself think of circumstances in your life, big and small, that differ from how you'd like them to be or differ from how someone close to you would like them to be. Your cluster can include topics like your job, marriage, home, hobby, vacation or social behavior. If you are working with a topic in mind, such as visiting another country, your cluster might include things like how learning the local expressions hindered rather than helped you or how taking the buses turned out to be more fun than using your international driver's license.

When you have decided what you want to work on, cluster what you or others wish things tasted, smelled, sounded, felt and looked like in this area of your life. Then begin a freewrite. You might start it out with a "like" construction or a "before and after" sentence. For instance, "Before I was a part of the group called senior citizens, I thought growing older meant growing wiser." Or, "When I took my family to the Grand Canyon, I felt like the clown who doesn't see the gun-toting villain coming up behind him." Or, "Before I went to Paris as an exchange teacher, I thought I would spend all my free time there in cafes writing in my journal, but within a few weeks I was farming."

Go on for about ten minutes. Whichever your focus is—how your life is different than you thought it would be or how it is different than someone else wishes it were—keep writing the particulars.

WRITING YOUR ESSAY

Next, write a draft of a comparison and contrast essay. You can begin with an image or anecdote that sets you and your readers in the situation you are writing about. Remember how Kate lets herself relax when she comes home from school and plays with her little brother. Remember how Rizwana thinks of life and memory and remembers herself as a little girl in the rain before she tells us where she now sits.

You might want to start something like novelist Amy Tan does in an essay called "Watching China," which appeared in *Glamour Magazine*, September, 1989:

> I am an ignorant observer of the situation in China, un-versed in politics, a citizen of the United States, where "inalienable rights" have been a fact of life from the day I was born.
>
> But over the the past months, I have been watching the televised coverage of events in Beijing. . . .

She tells who she is in relation to her subject and what she has taken for granted in her life. Then the word "but" acts as a hinge opening the door for contrasting American and Chinese events. In your writing, you can begin with who you are and what you are doing. Then with a "but" you can enter the domain of how things were supposed to be. Or you can begin with a description of how things were supposed to be and with a "but" throw yourself into a description of how they actually are.

Once you start, write your draft from beginning to end. Then put the draft away for a little while as you consider my response to Elizabeth's draft.

DEVELOPING THE DRAFT

Elizabeth's draft of her comparison and contrast essay developed from her interest in a "before and after." She wrote, "Before I was grown up I couldn't wait to be grown up; after I grew up I couldn't understand what all my hurry was about." She also clustered and freewrote on the topic of how she wanted to hurry and grow up but her mother said she wasn't supposed to be in such a rush. Then she wrote:

UNTITLED

To this day I can't remember what all the hurry was about, hurry, that is, to grow up. "After all, you only live your childhood once." It was one of my mother's standard lines she'd recite to me as I kept after her to let me play with the older girls in the neighborhood. They were at least five years ahead of me and filled with stories about how their bodies were changing, their breasts growing round and firm. My mother grew weary answering my questions, which I asked methodically, over and over. When could I anticipate these changes not to mention when could I pierce my ears and stay up past 11:00 P.M.? My inquiries were always met with a polite, "In time, dear." Sometimes, I would cry when mother told me not to wish my life away. I thought she really didn't understand. As I came to discover years later, she knew best that childhood was a time one never had privilege to again. To her, childhood was a time not to be concerned with anything other than what was in the immediate moment, like wondering what might be for dinner. Still, I wanted a promise that special things were going to happen for me. All of it, boys, breasts and happiness.

Yes, I wanted to be older; in fact, I was downright infatuated with being an adult. This intrigue went far beyond playing dress up and house. I studied the adult world. It seemed filled with the glow of routine and stability. I saw this especially in my parents. My father used to rise at the same time every morning, kiss my mother on the cheek and make his way for the train station to board the high-speed line for the city. He always looked so important and sure of himself dressed in his dark suit with his raincoat draped over his arm and his briefcase in hand. At night when he returned, he would again kiss my mother on the cheek. I always melted when they kissed with a warm hopefulness that I too someday would bestow such loving affection on someone else's cheek.

Mother and Dad worked as a team around the house, she taking care of the meals and daily upkeep and my father doing projects which seemed to vary depending on what household improvement Mother felt they needed, such as new wallpaper for the kitchen. They were like a recipe when it came to making decisions about the children. You couldn't have one ingredient or input without the others. I never saw them fight or even raise their voices to one another. They held hands when they walked down the street and referred to each other as "doll."

Twice a year my parents would give dinner parties for six couples, usually old friends from town. They would arrive in their fancy cars, and the women looked poised and elegant in their silk dresses, their diamonds glittering like stars from gold chains around their necks. I used to love the smell of their sweet French perfumes which lingered in the dining room long after the women had gone home.

Once the dishes were cleared and the brandy was being poured, I'd hide in the kitchen with only the counter light casting a shadow against the wall. I'd fix a plate of the leftovers, often vegetable pâté and caviar and swallow them down along with the jovial sounds from the next room. Overhearing their stories, I would lose myself somewhere between the white sandy beaches of the Caribbean and the bright lights of the Broadway theater marquees. It all sounded so exciting and exotic, much more so than the two weeks I spent with the mosquitos in the woods at summer camp.

As they spoke, I heard a certain strength and evenness in their voices. Their words sounded full, robust with knowledge and experience. I really believed that once I was an adult I would be capable of projecting, like an image upon the screen, the very same self-assuredness.

I wanted nothing more than to grow up and assume my position alongside those I had long admired. I am not certain at what juncture in my life I was officially welcomed to adulthood. Was it when I graduated from college and my mother wrapped her arms around me as we prepared food for my graduation party and whispered in my ear, "Welcome to the real world, Sweetie"? Or could it have been after my twenty-fifth birthday, when Dad announced I was now a quarter of a century old, and suddenly I could feel thirty breathing down my neck?

Well, here I am almost thirty, and the adult world is not the fanciest foil-wrapped package under the Christmas tree filled with promise. The glitter has long faded as the reality of my responsibility to earn a living to pay bills and keep a roof over my head leaves me little time to enjoy my life. There were moments I never worried about tomorrow; now it feels like that is all I do. Is this what caused my father to be so exhausted at the end of his day that after he'd kissed my mother hello, he sought the solace of his chair, falling asleep until dinner?

Long gone is the concern and eagerness over when my body would sprout from a little girl's into a woman's. Now, each year as I count another candle on my birthday cake, I look deeper into the mirror and see the roots of age. Tiny lines, as if etched in stone, now define the skin underneath my eyes. As I run my fingers down the sides of my hips, I can feel the distance they must travel apart from one another.

Back in high school when I'd get bored in class, I'd scribble my favorite children's names on my note pad just to try them out. They were beautiful names like Tess, Elizabeth, and Daniel. By the time I was thirty, I had planned, I'd have my third child. Instead, I am a godmother who dotes on two beautiful godchildren, ages three and six, who make me laugh and bring tears to my eyes as they explore their world.

As far as being single, it is a bit like drowning. Especially when I find myself among a crowd of couples. Just their mere presence can suffocate me with painful reminders of what I don't have in my life, like security and companionship, despite my arms that flail madly about trying to pull them into reach.

THE THREE-STEP RESPONSE
Step One: Velcro Words

I find memorable the fact that Elizabeth's friends were five years older than she. I remember the questions Elizabeth asks her mother about staying up late and piercing her ears. I remember Elizabeth's desire for boys and breasts. I remember the image of the father kissing his wife on the cheek and leaving for the train in his dark suit with a raincoat draped over his arm and his briefcase in hand. I remember the team of Mother and Dad working on Mother's priorities for the house, their hand-holding and calling each other "doll." I remember the dinner parties, the jewels, dresses, perfume, caviar, pâté and conversation about the Caribbean and Broadway. I remember the graduation from college and the checking now for face wrinkles. I remember the image of life not being a fancy foil-wrapped package under the Christmas tree.

Step Two: Feelings

I feel the author's sense of impatience with the lack of glamour in childhood, the weariness of her mother in answering the same questions over and over again. I feel the author's enchantment with adults, and her disappointment, even despair, in her own adulthood.

Tracking my response to the words and sentences in this draft, I begin with a sense of anticipation knowing the author will contrast this hurrying with why it isn't worth hurrying. The specific questions asked of her mother, the feelings of being misunderstood in her desires, and impatience with her mother's view of childhood refresh my memory of being a daughter.

I am drawn in, too, by her study of the adult world and her description of her father's routine and aura of stability. I am, however, wary of the wording, "I always melted when they kissed with a warm hopefulness that I too someday would bestow such loving affection on someone else's cheek." "Warm hopefulness" does not capture the experience of her wishing. "Loving affection" makes me tired. I already experienced the kiss on the cheek, and hearing it labeled keeps me from moving forward.

From this point, I can report being carried along very nicely for many paragraphs. I feel well placed while I watch the mother and father's domestic partnership. I like the details I am given: what household improvement Mother felt they needed, the comparison of their decision-making style to ingredients in a recipe, the unraised voices, the hand-holding, the pet name "doll." I liked the dinner party replete with fancy cars, silk dresses, diamond jewelry, French perfumes, brandy, dirty dishes, and leftover caviar. I like the author's comparison of the glamour she conjures in the words "sandy beaches of the Caribbean" to the yearly mosquito-ridden two weeks of summer camp. These are images I can see, taste, smell, touch and hear. They are also consistent with a young girl's viewpoint. And they are mindful of the comparison and contrast format.

But when Elizabeth wonders when she was welcomed to adulthood I hesitate. The idea that someone waits for an invitation is unusual to me. Her mother's phrasing, "Welcome to the real world, Sweetie," makes me wonder what world her mother had her in up until then.

Being told she is a quarter of a century old seemed like an occasion upon which one would reflect upon adulthood, so I relaxed again. I am interested in the turn the essay takes with, "Well, here I am almost thirty...." I like the new view of seeing what her father did (fall exhausted into a chair) after he kissed her mother hello. I like the contrast of how now instead of worrying about when she'll look like a woman, Elizabeth worries about lines and weight gain. Same fixation on the body, different way of looking at it. I like hearing the contrast between dreaming of the kids she would have by thirty and herself at thirty with godchildren instead of biological children. I go easily with the speaker to her feelings about being single. But the short amount of time spent on missing having a partner, the one who she always dreamed would be there, leaves me unsatisfied.

Step Three: Curiosity

Now, where I am interested to know more. When Elizabeth talks about having moments when she never worried about tomorrow in contrast to now, I am interested to know what she worries about now and what about adult life tires her out. After she talks about what her father did in his fatigue at day's end, I wonder what Elizabeth does in her fatigue. When Elizabeth remembers her high school self scribbling the names of the children she'd like to have by thirty, I am interested to know more of what she imagined she'd be and have by thirty. At the end, I am interested to know much more about what security and companionship are in Elizabeth's life. I wonder if she can say where she finds security and whether that security carries some sadness for her because it is from sources other than she had expected and counted on. I am interested to know whether the kind of security she finds now is more real than what she dreamt of as a young girl.

After you get the response you need to your draft, read Elizabeth's developed draft:

THE SECOND DRAFT

ONE WITH AN OLIVE AND ONE WITH A TWIST OF LEMON

"After all, you only live your childhood once," my mother used to say. It was one of her standard lines she'd recite to me as I kept after her to let me play with the older girls in the neighborhood.

They were at least five years ahead of me and filled with stories about how their bodies were changing, their breasts growing round and firm. My mother grew weary answering my questions. When could I anticipate these changes? When could I pierce my ears and stay up past 11:00 P.M.? My inquiries were always met with a polite, "In time, dear." Sometimes, I would cry when Mother told me not to wish my life away. I thought she really didn't understand. To her, childhood was a time not to be concerned with anything other than what was in the immediate moment, like what was for dinner. Still, I wanted promise that special things were going to happen for me. All of it, boys, breasts and happiness.

My father used to rise the same time every morning, kiss my mother on the cheek and make his way to the train station and board the high-speed line for the city. He always looked so important and sure of himself dressed in his dark suit with his raincoat draped over his arm and his briefcase in hand. At night when he returned, he would again kiss my mother on the cheek.

Mother and Dad always worked as a team around the house, she taking care of the meals and daily upkeep and my father's projects varying depending on what household improvement Mother felt was needed, such as new wallpaper for the kitchen. They were like cooks using a shared recipe when it came to making decisions about the children. Each of their inputs was an ingredient. I never saw them fight or even raise their voices to one another. They held hands when they walked down the street and referred to each other as "doll."

Twice a year my parents would give dinner parties for six couples, usually old friends from town. The friends would arrive in their fancy cars, and the women looked elegant in their silk dresses, their diamonds glittering like stars from gold chains around their necks. I used to love the smell of the sweet French perfumes which lingered in the dining room long after they had gone home.

Once the dishes were cleared and the brandy was being poured, I'd hide in the kitchen with only the counter light casting a shadow against the wall. I'd fix a plate of their leftovers, usually vegetable pâté and caviar, and swallow them down along with the jovial sounds from the next room. Overhearing the stories, I would lose myself somewhere between the white sandy beaches of the Caribbean and the bright lights of the Broadway theater marquees.

I wanted nothing more than to grow up and assume my position alongside those I had long admired.

In high school, I used to scribble my favorite children's names on my note pad when I would get bored listening to the teacher. Tess, Elizabeth, Oliver and Daniel. Assigning them made motherhood feel that much closer. Just like my Aunt Debbie, I planned to have my third child by the time I was thirty.

I am not certain at what juncture in my life I felt officially welcomed to adulthood. Was it when I graduated from college and my mother wrapped her arms around me as we prepared food for my graduation party? Or could it have been after my twenty-fifth birthday, when Dad announced I was now a quarter of a century old?

Well, here I am almost thirty and the adult world is not the fanciest foil-wrapped package under the Christmas tree. The glitter has long faded under the reality of earning a living to pay bills and keep a roof over my head. There were moments I never worried about tomorrow. Now, every evening before I leave work, the brown leather briefcase my father brought home from Poland sits by my desk overflowing with articles I need to review for the next day's meetings.

It is 8:30 or 9:00 by the time I arrive home. I remember now that after my father kissed my mother hello in the evening, he fell asleep in his chair till dinner. I sit on the floor, my shoulders resting heavy against the wall, as I open my mail. Dinner consists of celery sticks and hummus that I haven't bothered to spoon out of its plastic container into a dish. The only glamour to my meal is the cotton napkin I've draped over my lap to serve as a table. I stare blankly at the opposite wall listening to phone messages from friends who ask, "Where have you been?" and "Are you alright?" There isn't time for coffee at the Honey Bear Cafe or long walks in the park. This must be what my mother meant when she sometimes said, "There is never enough time to do it all."

Long gone is my concern and eagerness over when my body would sprout from a little girl's into a woman's. Now, each year as I count another candle on my birthday cake, I look deeper into the mirror and see the roots of age — tiny lines in the skin underneath my eyes. As I run my fingers down the sides of my hips, I feel the distance they must travel apart from one another.

I think about the lovers I've held. No commitment ever seems to last longer than two or three months. I share the ingredients of my life and wonder why I have not yet found compatible ingredients in another to make a marriage.

These are increasingly vulnerable times for me as I share my fears with my mother about the previously unimagined landscape of my life. When she came to visit recently for a long weekend, I took her to my favorite restaurant in Vancouver, Delila's, nestled under the tree-lined streets of the West End, an elegant place. As we each sipped from our frosted martini glasses, hers with an olive and mine with a lemon twist, she added more ice cubes to my drink to keep it from being too strong in just the same way she tries to dilute my worries. With just one clear swallow left, I looked down at my drink and saw I would have to look further for comfort now. I am blazing my own trail through adulthood. I need new reference points, new trail markers, though the ones I followed this far were lovely and long my favorites.

The most distinguishing aspect of this developed draft is the nice way the end loops back to to the beginning. The daughter is with her mother again at the end. But now the daughter is thinking something that contrasts very deeply with how she usually thinks about her mother. Her new thoughts contrast to the remembered dialogue with which she opens her essay. By the end of the essay, the contrast of how Elizabeth's adulthood was supposed to be with how it actually is brings her some resolution. She acknowledges and accepts that she is different from her mother and that she is different from how her mother expects her to be. The essay's title expresses this in images. As readers, we experience not only these differences, but the adult Elizabeth as well.

Notice the balance in this comparison and contrast essay. For just over half of it, Elizabeth remembers what she thought adulthood would be like from watching her parents and their friends. Then the contrast is ushered in with the words, "I am not certain at what juncture in my life I was officially welcomed to adulthood." No matter when, now at "almost thirty," Elizabeth's world is not the one she expected. The images she includes next are well chosen for evoking a tired, working, unglamorous, single woman. Wisely, Elizabeth makes a statement about her vulnerability that brings her mother back into the picture: "These are vulnerable times for me as I share my fears with my mother about the previously unimagined landscape of my life." Then Elizabeth ends with a short narration of a recent dinner with her mother. Her eye on her mother's gesture, she comes to a new, though slightly painful, truth. As readers we are left to contrast this new Elizabeth with the Elizabeth who used to "swallow whole" the images of her parents to define her world.

KEEP DRAFTING

Run through the response method with Elizabeth's developed draft, if you wish. Then continue developing your draft and getting the response you need. As you write, you'll find that the structure of the comparison and contrast form combines naturally with the details and images of the life you are describing. Use sensory detail, tell anecdotes, make analogies. As you write you will be thinking concretely about the details of your expected and actual lives. You will tell stories about yourself and the people in those lives. You will be drawn to make analogies to enliven your writing. Though you will be thinking only about putting down the words, you will be carried along by the words to new understanding. This is how insight comes — obliquely. The images and details and situations you write down keep hinting at meaning until the meaning can't be missed.

CHAPTER SIX

The Division and Classification Essay

Writing to Sort Things Out in an Original Way

And where did I find, other than in living day to day, the sense of the complex that made such sense to me?

— *Marvin Bell,* Writers on Writing, *edited by Robert Pack and Jay Parnini*

How many times have you heard a comedian or a speaker proclaim, "There are three kinds of people" and then go on to give each type a name and draw examples of each? In the course of our lives, we recognize, often subconsciously, types of people and their behavior, as well as types of places, situations, things and events. When we organize them according to unique categories, we impart our special point of view. Then we can inform and often entertain others and ourselves.

In a division and classification essay it is important to divide your subject according to a trait each group has in common. It is important to have at least three groups because otherwise you are in the realm of comparison and contrast. Your skills with description, narration, how-to and comparison and contrast will help you as you write to evoke and explain the categories and their differences and to move your essay along.

In a column that appeared in the *New York Times* in 1968 and is reprinted in *The Riverside Reader* published by Houghton Mifflin, author Russell Baker takes on the voice of a professor to explain the three major categories of inanimate objects: "those that don't work, those that break down and those that get lost." The categories are introduced in the order that they vex humankind. I still laugh to the point of tears when I read this essay because I get in touch with my usually unconscious, though unavoidable, frustration with the objects in my life.

Be original when you ask your yourself, "What *types* of people, situations, places, things or events do I experience in my life?" Types of waiters and waitresses who serve me, types of responses machines have to me, types of phone calls I get, types of Sundays, and types of neighbors I have had are on my list. You should try for categories that you haven't encountered before or new ways of looking at categories that are common. Types of supermarket shoppers can be made more original by narrowing the subject, perhaps to types of cart pushers or ways people accept food samples at demonstration tables.

If you have a topic you already want to explore, insert that topic into the "write" question. For instance, using the examples from before, if you are writing about parenting you might say, "What situations in parenting do I know enough about to evoke by using categories? If you are writing about visiting a new country you can do the same thing: "What situations to do with visiting this new country do I know enough about to evoke by using categories?" In the case of parenting, you might think of kinds of children's misbehaviors, school conferences, requests children make of parents, or requests parents make of children. About visiting a new country, the categories might turn out to be types of responses you get when you tell people you have done that, medical problems to prepare for, sadness you experienced away from home, locals you met there, tourists you met or tours.

But before you work on gathering the answers to your "write" question, turn your attention to the sample essays and discussions that follow.

EXAMPLE: DIVISION AND CLASSIFICATION ESSAY

In the following essay, written by Robert Lowery, we look through his eyes at the kinds of phone calls he receives from his mother. As you read the essay, notice Lowery's introduction to his material and then the way he designates each kind of phone call, either by name or by topic discussed. Notice the details he uses to fully describe each call. Notice especially the order in which he describes the types of phone calls he gets from his mother.

E.T., PHONE YOUR MOM

Phone calls from my mother are all attempts to reach out for love and caring, but are camouflaged with heaping tablespoons of guilt thrown in my general direction. My mother fits all of the stereo-types of a Jewish mother even though she is Southern Baptist. She is overprotective, likes to worry, and shows love by smothering me with correction and concern. Raised by an overprotective aunt after her mother became disabled, she knows no other way to raise her child. She is a person more suited for life on a gentle and proper southern plantation prior to the unpleasantness of the Civil War. I have the misfortune of being her sole target of attention and weekly calls which fall into four different types.

The first type of call is to verify that I am well and eating right according to her standards at the moment. The first sentence or two inquire about my last known illness. I hear, "Do you still have your cold?" immediately after answering the phone's ring. It has been two years since I was sick, but to my mother, time has no relevance in matters of my health. Even after replying, "No, I'm fine and just got home from running the Boston Marathon," I know that I'm going to have to listen to the standard "chicken soup" home remedies for my long-gone cold. Rule number one: I never voluntarily mention any illness to my mother; I let her dig for the information.

The "chicken soup" is really no attempt to bring relief to the cold, but a clever way to change the subject to my diet. "You're not still eating those awful frozen dinners that I saw in your freezer are you?" she next queries. Never mind that these were my emer-gency stock for when I get home late from work and have to leave in fifteen minutes in order to get in my 25-mile bike ride before dark. She has determined that I exist on TV dinners except when I'm not eating fast food greaseburgers and french fries. I have been found permanently guilty, even after proof of my innocence. Rule number two: I never have frozen dinners in the freezer when Mom comes to visit. Home-cooked leftovers are OK.

The second type of maternal phone call is the reverse of the first in that it is an urgent summons for sympathy when she is sick. I get comfortable because this is always a long call. I take notes on the medication that she is taking as there will be a test later. I will be expected to remember which of her current pill collection is upsetting her stomach and which makes her dizzy. I plan on hearing all the details of where it hurts and how it is worse than last time. She is much worse than Aunt Nell who had this same thing last year. Rule number three: I strive to become an amateur pharmacist.

Oops, I was not listening carefully; she has changed the subject again! "Speaking of Aunt Nell, you know what a lowlife your cousin Will has turned out to be, living with that woman and all," I hear her as she begins the down-home news and comment. This is a limb-by-limb discussion of the family tree. I continue taking notes. Life requires that I know who bought a new car, who has money problems and which of my relatives has just done something incredibly stupid . . . again. Now is the time to insert the latest dirt on my ex-wife and the ex-kids. I have to be careful here because these winds can blow in both directions. Sometimes I'm the good guy, sometimes the bad. Rule number four: I can't win, no rules help here.

Next is the "Let's Make a Deal" call. We now depart from matters of health to material goods. My mom tries to imitate Monty Hall and find out what I want for my birthday, Christmas or Groundhog Day. I must choose door number one, two, or three. "I don't know," or "I can't think of anything," is the wrong answer. Rule number five: I keep a current list of wishes stashed away in my wallet. This allows Mom to hit the stores with minimal delay and worry.

I sometimes try to turn this game around and discover a good gift for my mom's birthday, etc. This never works. The "You don't need to get me anything," whine serves as her standard answer. Rule number six: I remember her birthday with flowers or perfume. I do jewelry every fifth year to keep her in suspense.

The final type of call puts fear in the hearts of all of us who live in different cities than our parents. This is the when-can-I-come-visit-you phone call. My mother often buries the question deep in idle chitchat which purposely serves to let my mind wander. She then fires this fast ball across the phone line catching me unaware. A coming-to-visit call differs from all the previous calls because this one is a true threat to my mental health. Remember the guilt thing I mentioned earlier? This is the infamous offer which I can't refuse. Rule number seven: Forget about excuses; I've already used them all. I make a leap of faith and pick a date.

This visit could be fatal unless I observe some cautions. I go through my closet and take any clothes which might be out of style to a rented storage garage. I remove all clothing belonging to anyone of the opposite sex. This saves me months of cross examination. I do my laundry; there cannot be a single piece of dirty laundry in the house when she arrives. I wear something and throw it away if necessary. Next, I clean out the refrigerator. I get rid of any frozen meals and all previously opened jars or packages of food. I take them to the rented storage garage with the clothes. I restock my food supply with an all new stock in unopened containers and buy lots of fresh vegetables. I make the refrigerator look like a display at QFC. Next comes the worst: I clean the bathroom with the "white tornado" or something appropriately industrial strength. I'm dead meat if she even smells any germs.

As in all other matters of life, the best defense is a good offense. Rule number eight: I call my mother often, catch her off guard and ask lots of intrusive questions. She loves it and speaks highly of me to all her friends.

The Discovery in "E.T., Phone Your Mom"

Robert introduces his essay by placing his mother in a category and describing the characteristics for membership there. She is the stereotypical Jewish mother even if she is a Southern Baptist — smothering him with worry and inducing guilt. And for her adult son Robert, it all comes down at this late date to phone calls which he tells us he divides into four types. First, second, next and final. These are the words that move Robert from type to type through his essay. Inside the types are details that make the calls as unforgettable to us as they are to him.

In type number one, we see Robert heading off disaster by making up two rules. We also see him as a physically fit bicyclist and a man with his own past. While the topic of the first kind of call from his mother is his health, that of the second kind is *her* health. This contrast helps Robert move from category one to category two. Now Robert must strive to belong to a category himself, that of amateur pharmacist. But that is not all — he must know the trials and tribulations of relatives his mother informs him about and be one of them with his own accounts of trials and tribulations. His accounts may evoke sympathy or disapproval from his mother. He cannot know which, hence the rule that he cannot win. Beneath the humor of his essay, there is sadness and resignation.

Robert moves to the third kind of call by announcing its name, "Let's Make a Deal." He compares this kind of phone call to a television game show to explain the way it works. Robert generates two more rules for his survival and moves to the final, and most feared, kind of call from his mother. It is the most feared because the rule is he must say yes to her proposed visit. In the frenzied finale of the essay, Robert cleans his bathroom, does his laundry, goes through his food and clothing and moves to storage anything that will be unacceptable to his mother. Then he shops for those fresh vegetables hinted at in call number one and makes a nice loop back to his opening. The calls are arranged in order of the magnitude of disruption to Robert's life. He builds to the big one that will lead to an actual visit from Mom, which is much harder to handle than the phone calls.

Since he can't reach outside the phone call categories to end his essay, how will Robert get to an ending that reaches some sort of closure and satisfies? He uses a truism, "The best defense is a good offense," in the final paragraph of his essay. Rule number eight leads him to call his mother. And what kind of phone call is that? Just one more of the four kinds of phone calls with Mom, we have to think. Does making calls to his mother actually stall dreaded phone call type number four coming his way? Our author is playing a game he never asked to play, one he seemingly can't quit, whose own vicious circle is perpetrated by his mother no matter what he does. With the tone of the anecdotes and details, Robert evokes the frustration of his situation. He discovers or relives the degree to which this circle of behavior rules his life, the depths to which he participates in what it takes to be his mother's son.

EXAMPLE: DIVISION AND CLASSIFICATION ESSAY

Michelle Ramsey classifies three responses to an "ex." As you read, notice the names for the kinds of responses, the details that describe them, and the order in which the author introduces them. Notice, too, the essay's introduction and conclusion and how they state why the author is classifying these responses.

THE EX

My "ex"; I have always disliked that phrase. Technically, it is just a prefix meaning "former" or "not." I never pictured myself having an "ex," but once I had one I began to realize how appropriate the term really seemed. Ex-boyfriend, ex-husband, ex-wife, they all sound the same. They sound like one is taking a big, fat, black magic marker and placing a huge X over the part of one's life that the "ex" once occupied.

At the time I acquired an "ex," I didn't consider that I would occasionally still have to deal with this person. Two long years later, I have determined that there are different ways to categorize the manner in which one deals with an "ex."

I'll begin with the manner that is usually used soon after a break-up: the "I Despise You" response. While in this stage, an individual will generally cringe at the very sound of the "ex's" name. Any conversation or chance encounter with the "ex" will be accompanied by yelling, screaming, mouthing obscenities or making obscene gestures. This stage may be therapeutic in getting the anger out, but it is not personally recommended by the writer for use over any long period of time. Allowing hate to consume one's every thought will eventually result in making one unhappy and miserable. The despising or hate will overshadow memories of the "good times" that one and one's "ex" may have shared in the past. These memories of the "good times" may be missed in the future. Good memories of one's "ex" can be very useful as well as necessary when there is a child involved. Personally, I enjoy having those "good" memories to look back on later in life.

Since the "I Despise You" response can also be a cause of great embarrassment for both parties if these chance encounters occur in public places, it gradually goes underground anyway, changing into the "Revenge" response. Here the individual will spend endless hours plotting or thinking up ways to get even. These plots will include such things as throwing bricks through windshields, slashing tires, and sending packages of brightly wrapped animal feces to home addresses. In reality, this stage is a head game to be played out scenario after scenario in one's mind. This stage should not be acted out. One needs only to pick up the nightly edition of any newspaper in any metropolitan city in this country to read of love triangles or fatal attractions erupting into violence and often causing death to those involved. The movie *She Devil* is a prime example of the "Revenge" response going to the extreme. The character played by Roseanne Barr devotes her entire life to plotting and carrying out the perfect revenge.

Most of us want to get on with our lives, so our responses shift again to "The Silent Treatment." While practicing this response, one will pass one's "ex" without an acknowledgement or glance in that direction. When a persistent "ex" is telephoning during this time, the individual will conveniently be "not at home right now," "out of the office," or suddenly "dead." This stage is denial and avoidance at its best. By ignoring the source of the annoyance or discomfort, one believes the problem will go away. Blocking that someone out of your life may help begin the healing, but it can also backfire. If one attempts to use "The Silent Treatment" to cover up any unresolved feelings of wanting or desire for the "ex," these feelings may resurface again, either directly in interaction with the "ex" or as extra baggage carried into any future relationships with others.

The next kind of response is generally used when one must deal with an "ex" in some capacity. The "ex" may be the parent of your child, a coworker or the relative of a friend. These close ties may require the "Cordial" response. This is a time of trying to be civil. One attempts to sit through a dinner with the "ex" or carry on a conversation without any of the previous responses coming into the picture. The event will generally be uncomfortable and strained, but to those who are unaware of the situation, it may actually seem normal. To those who know the situation it will seem "under control." This response is frequently required of parents to be sensitive to the needs and spirits of their children.

The "Death Thoughts" response is often related to an "ex" missing a child's birthday, moving in around the corner with a new significant other, or purchasing himself or herself new expensive toys while the child support remains unpaid. This stage is again a complete head game. The thoughts will be of the "ex's" death and may frequently involve plastic explosives. When one has these thoughts, the reality of the belief that the "ex" may actually be dead, will often shock or frighten one back to reality. One will then begin wondering, "Would I cry?", "Would I attend the funeral?" This response can be surprising when it sometimes resurfaces again and again even though the situation seems resolved.

The last response is the one that makes most people laugh in disbelief. Perhaps it is the one that tries to make it full circle back to something of the beginning of the relationship. It is the "Mutual Break-Up" or the "We're Still Friends" response as seen in the popular movie, "Three Men and a Baby." Like the characters in this movie, individuals will meet willingly for lunch or a walk in the park; they may even continue to share the same home. These couples will hug at the end of an encounter and often share the details of their current relationships with one another. Since they are no longer a couple, they may then advise or assist each other with problems in these new relationships. Unbelievable as this response may seem, the advice may go, as in the movie, to the extent that one even suggests a new partner or spouse for the "ex."

With any luck, these stages will not become permanent responses to one's "ex." More often than not, one may experience all or a variety of the mentioned responses at different stages following a break-up. Be assured, however, that like most things in life, discomforts over one's "ex" can heal with time. In the meantime, if one finds oneself dreaming about dynamite and hit-men, fear not; it happens to the best of us.

The Discovery in "The 'Ex"

My "ex"; Michelle begins, a semi-colon there to make us pause as if she'd written a whole sentence. In fact, the phrase *my "ex"* lumbers weighty as a doctoral dissertation. How wise of the writer to let the phrase speak for itself.

Just as there are categories of "ex" people in one's life, so the author tells us in her second paragraph, there are also categories of responses one has to an "ex." Whereas we are all familiar with the kinds of "ex" people one has in life, we may be more intrigued by the author's original thinking about our responses to them. These responses share the common trait that they contradict the idea of finality, of marking the "ex" off like a day gone by. The author orders the types of responses she discusses chronologically, as in narration. The order in which you are most likely to have the responses is tied to how much time has passed since the break-up. This order also goes from the hottest response closest to the break-up to the cooler responses as time passes. The author moves between types of responses by showing how or why one response can become another. If a child is involved, however, there are other criteria for the kinds of responses and they are presented to us from cooler to hotter, cool if others are around, hot if the "ex" disappoints the child.

Finally, a sixth response is included and leads to the author's conclusion. Although the author cannot credit herself with having this sixth response, it has been presented in at least one popular movie. Saving this made-for-the-movies, almost-impossible-to-execute response for last ensures the reader will contrast it with the very real and strong feelings the author has already reported. Though entertained by the author's catharsis, the reader also sees how much maturity it has taken to name, understand and live through the experience of having an "ex."

A WORD ON LOGICAL SUBDIVISIONS

When you write division and classification essays, you must be sure you have made subdivisions that are logical and comprehensive. Remember that they must total at least three because having only two divisions creates comparison and contrast rather than division and classification. Logical division requires that there be a single governing principle to the divisions — phone calls from my mother, responses I have to my "ex," kinds of English teachers, kinds of fathers — and that the divisions seem comprehensive.

An example of non-comprehensive subdivisions is dividing stores into types, such as department stores, convenience stores and boutiques. This leaves out many types of stores — shoe stores, for example, country general stores, electronic and appliances stores, furniture stores and warehouse shopping stores, among others. There is no way you could cover all the types of stores when they are divided this way without writing a telephone book. When categories are this large, you must think of a new principle upon which to base your subdivisions. It must be a principle that allows you to deal with a certain chunk of the broader classification. It must provide a framework for you to use in looking at your subject. If you worded your category, "the three kinds of stores I shop in" the subdivisions department stores, convenience stores and boutiques would seem odd but comprehensive.

Dividing kinds of stores into groups such as stores tourists like, stores community members like, and secondhand stores disrupts having a consistent principle of organization — the last kind of store could belong to either or both of the other categories. A division such as stores I like, stores my husband likes, and stores my children like is consistent and complete for purposes of organization. So are divisions such as stores in my city that tourists like, that residents like and that residents of neighboring communities like. So are divisions such as stores I use daily, monthly and once a year.

EXERCISE FOR DEVELOPING YOUR MATERIAL

Here is an exercise for thinking along division and classification lines.

A New Whirled Order

Brainstorm a page-long list of things, people, places, events and situations you don't usually think of in categories but that you feel you could: freeway drivers, bosses, billboard ads, radio programs, food in your pantry, people ordering coffee, people walking their dogs, mothers, fathers, daughters, sons, workers, people courting, phone machine message leaving styles. After you have brainstormed a page of possible areas to categorize, choose a few of the ideas and create subdivisions for them. Food in my pantry may divide into groups like the following if I view it through the eyes of my teenage son: pop-it-into-your-mouth-whenever-you-are-hungry food, consider-if-you-can-pop-it-into-your-mouth-even-though-it-would-taste-better-cooked food, overlook-it-altogether-because-it-takes-more-than-ten-minutes-to-prepare food.

A fun way to do this exercise and expand your ideas is to sit down with a group of friends or your family and have everyone write down, on separate pieces of paper, kinds of things, people, situations and events: parental lectures, punishments, downtowners, ways to spend quality time, collectors, music buffs. Have everyone fold up each of their pieces of paper and drop them into a bowl or a hat. All will select the same number of pieces from the hat as they put into it. Then they will all think of original ways to subdivide the classifications they selected. Listening to everyone's categories and ideas about subdividing them will loosen up your thinking and bolster your willingness to search your life for original divisions and subdivisions.

The principle you use to subdivide your subject should communicate an original outlook, a new way of viewing the presented classification. Ultimately this form provides a way of viewing your own behavior as well as that of others.

LOCATING YOUR DIVISION AND CLASSIFICATION MATERIAL

Ask yourself the "write" question for this essay style: "What things, people, places, situations, and events do I know enough about to explain by subdividing into categories?" You can put the words "things, people, places and events I can divide" in the center of a page to start a cluster. You might want to do a separate cluster for each of the four words. After you cluster from these words, you will find you have a topic that interests you. Put that topic in the middle of a blank page and do a cluster around it. Shoot off all the subtypes you can think of from the central word, circle them, and then off those circles, cluster traits and examples of each type. Allow yourself to be silly and farfetched. You never know where one image will lead. You never know when a silly idea will uncover a brilliant one.

What do your subdivisions have in common? Are they about what bothers you, amuses you, makes you angry, is most important to know? Have you been able to subdivide your selected category into at least three divisions? On what basis have you made the subdivisions? The answers to these three questions will help you start a freewrite.

WRITING YOUR ESSAY

Freewrite for ten minutes on the topic that interests you from the clusters. When you are ready, write a first draft of your division and classification essay. You might want to start with a short anecdote in which you re-experience why this discussion is important in your life. For instance, if I were to relate the scene in which I last grumbled at my family that I was going to give up writing, buy a suit and look for a management job downtown, it would lead, for me, into writing about my own types of writing behavior—ignoring writing, accusing my family of taking up all my time, having outbursts, locking myself up with my computer. The lesson here for me would be that as unlike writing as some of these behaviors look, they are, for me, part of a cycle of writing.

Or as you begin, you might remember how Robert starts his essay about his mother's phone calls with a paragraph about what category of person his mother fits into and what the distinguishing characteristics of such a person are. Then he proceeds to describe the phone calls. Michelle starts with a paragraph about the category "ex" before narrowing her discussion to responses to an "ex." In "The Plot Against People," Russell Baker plunges right in with a general principle: "The goal of all inanimate objects is to resist man and ultimately to defeat him, and the three major classifications are based on the method each object uses to achieve its purpose." Whether you back up to give category history or announce your principle directly, write from beginning to end.

Not only will the divisions you make take over and direct your hand, you have already practiced with several essay styles that will naturally come to aid you in your writing. Description with precise images helps you make subdivisions. Narration offers little stories inside the divisions to further evoke them or to let your readers know how you came up with the idea of exploring your subject. Comparison and contrast helps make transitions from one subdivision to the next and distinguish how one division is different than another. How-to can even make its way into a division and classification essay if you instruct your readers on how to classify something they might not have thought of classifying!

Stay with the sensory images in your subject, and you will find that you naturally use all these styles to make connections, evoke the categories and travel toward discovery.

DEVELOPING THE DRAFT

Once again we'll look at and respond to Elizabeth's draft. She got the idea for this draft from her list of classifications to divide. When she decided on ferryboat riders, she drew a cluster on this topic to bring more images and details to her mind before she started her draft.

This draft doesn't read as a completed essay. In it, Elizabeth is searching around in the vicinity of her real writing. It is almost as if she stopped where she did hoping for the encouragement my three-step response would give her to continue in her original thinking towards the end. Note your responses to the kinds of divisions she makes in the category ferryboat rider, how she introduces her topic, how she orders and moves from one division to another, and how she exits her draft. Pay attention to which descriptions delight you and which confuse or bother you. Read in order to pinpoint the opportunities Elizabeth has for good revision. Compare your responses to the ones I share with Elizabeth.

UNTITLED

In the Northwest, sometimes the shortest distance to travel between two points is across the steel blue water known as Puget Sound. The Washington State Ferry or "the boat" as some frequent users refer to it, gives new meaning to the words "public transportation" for an East Coast transplant. These large white flat-bottomed vessels are as much a part of the scenery as the sound and jagged, snow-peaked Olympic Mountains beyond.

From the side of the dock, the ferry is shaped like a milk carton lying on its side, its sharp edges rounded off with a tunnel running through its center where cars are parked eight lanes across and four lanes up top. It dwarfs even the largest semi-diesels that are loaded on board. The ferry's design is symmetrical, the front distinguishable from the back only by noticing which way the ferry is travelling. A control tower, bedecked with radar antenna and an American flag, sits at each end overlooking two narrow balconies, that extend like the brim of a baseball cap over the car deck. Centered between the towers sits a white square pedestal with two tall black smokestacks reaching towards the sky. As nighttime sets in, the brightness of the ferry's red and green safety lights glisten like jewels against the darkness.

During the day, the ferries hustle from each side of the waterway, passing in the middle of the sound like two gondola cars. As one pulls from the dock the engine's thunderous roar plays concert to the whirlpool of green, capped with white foam that swirls in a frenzy between the loading ramp and the thick rubber bumper that encircles the base of the ferry. A long-winded horn resonates from the bridge announcing its departure. It is this deep familiar sound I hear nightly as I am falling off into sleep that calls out reminding me of the uniqueness of life in the Northwest.

Hundreds of people ride the ferry each day to reach destinations of business or vacation pleasure. Every hour, shiny American and Japanese cars line up end to end below the terminal like obedient students. Passengers congregate on a cement walkway reading newspapers or just standing watching others who are watching them. They are waiting for a shrill ring signalling loading has begun. As the metal gate slides out of view, a blur of color pushes forward, briefcases and shopping bags seeming to jockey for a position down the loading ramp. Not until the confusion of people begins to disperse onboard can one really see the types of passengers that ride the ferry. Based on personal observation I have divided them into three categories.

First and by far the largest group of passengers is comprised of the commuter, territorial in nature, who boards the ferry with a sense of urgency hoping to secure a favorite spot along the window or under the sun deck. Usually dressed in business clothing, commuters carry at least one, though I have witnessed up to four, personal items such as briefcases, backpacks, radios or lunch boxes that are placed around their seat to mark their space. Within minutes after seating, they begin to look very involved working on laptop computers pulled out of their briefcases or sitting in a sea of paper they spread over the table of a booth. Sometimes you can't even see their faces because their noses are buried so deep in the folds of the *Wall Street Journal*. Truckers may be hidden under their caps while stretched out on the seats, coffee thermoses wedged under their heads as pillows.

Not all commuters focus on solo pursuits. Some sit with friends, usually neighbors, sipping soda and sharing popcorn from the snack bar. They converse, loudly at times, about their jobs and families. I have always imagined that for those commuters who travel every day, twice a day, after a time, the passenger cabin begins to feel very much like their own living rooms.

Next are the tourists, dressed in leisure wear and sporting smiles that are acknowledged by the commuters they encounter. They travel in groups and enter the cabin from a staircase below, cameras hanging round their necks, arms encumbered with guidebooks or coolers of lunch. Appearing more concerned with a head count of their children who wander off or with stopping to explore the pamphlet racks that offer colorful brochures of what they should see while in the Northwest, the tourists are left to take whatever seats remain.

On the deck, they can be overheard making comments about the size of the city's skyline or asking questions about how much it really rains in Seattle. As the ferry pulls away, one of my favorite moments of the ride, they are busy snapping pictures of Mount Rainier or chasing their squealing children who are running about the deck.

During the last three years, I have burrowed in a corner like the commuter to study notes for a meeting with business clients on the peninsula. As a tourist, I have missed half the lush scenery of the ride trying to capture the perfect shot of the Space Needle. It is the activity of the third passenger that I prefer to engage in, that of the transformer.

Unlike the commuter or tourist who relies on the ferry to reach a specific destination from which to move on, I look forward to times the boat can provide me safe passage in the quest that always takes me closer to my thoughts.

I carry nothing with me except a simple pouch fastened round my waist. Avoiding the mild chaos of boarding, I wait to descend the loading ramp until I hear a quick snort from the ferry's horn that signals three minutes to departure. Crossing onto the deck I feel the familiar resonance of the engine's vibration under my feet. Where I travel to next depends on my mood and the weather, though I usually spend most of my time on the top deck.

THE THREE-STEP RESPONSE
Step One: Velcro Words

This draft is loaded with images, both visual and auditory. It has a number of images drawn by metaphor. The ones that follow are the ones that stick with me: "steel blue water," "East Coast transplant," "large white flat-bottomed vessels," "milk carton on its side," "dwarfs even the largest semi-diesels," narrow balconies extended "like the brim of a baseball cap," "sound I hear nightly," "briefcases and shopping bags seem to jockey for position," cars line up "like obedient students," "largest group is the commuter who is territorial in nature," "carry . . . up to four personal items," truckers with thermoses "wedged under their heads as pillows," cabin like the commuters' "living rooms," tourists in "leisure wear," "cameras hanging round their necks," "coolers of lunch" and "guidebooks" encumbering them, "snapping pictures," "chasing their squealing children," asking "how much it really rains in Seattle," "commenting about the size of the city's skyline," "burrowed in a corner," "quick snort," "transformer," "closer to my thoughts."

Step Two: Feelings

From the draft as a whole, I feel the familiarity Elizabeth has with the ferry having studied its appearance, its setting, its sounds in the night. I feel the variations of liveliness on board the ferry—busy or sleeping commuters, active tourists, pensive transformers. I feel, too, the urgency of Elizabeth's ongoing wish for a journey and the calm she feels knowing "the boat" is always there for her.

My feeling responses to the words and sentences go like this: I feel sure of what I am reading about from the first paragraph, and I like knowing where my feet are, so to speak, in this essay. Then, although I feel enlivened by much of the detailed description of the boat in the second two paragraphs, I feel dizzy, too, from so much darting of my eyes—from inside to out, up to down, across to near. I settle down with the last sentence of the third paragraph with the words "as I am falling off to sleep." Perhaps resting just sounds nice to me after all that looking, but I am also drawn to the boat as a personal, comforting image. But I do feel rushed with that image because I don't know yet all the boat means to Elizabeth.

Well, no sooner am I off to sleep than I am in the midst of hundreds of people who ride the ferry each day. I feel jarred. But once into that paragraph, I am interested to know what classifications Elizabeth has come up with. I want to read on.

I enjoy seeing the commuters and their things and their behaviors as much as I enjoy seeing the tourists, their things, concerns, actions and their interactions with the commuters. I feel smoothly led by Elizabeth from these two categories to her third category because she says she has belonged to each of the two categories she described as much as she'd been an observer. I feel safe with this kind of attitude. I don't feel like I may be attacked for having been one or the other or both myself.

Once Elizabeth introduces the word and category "transformer" my interest is peaked. When she says the transformer goes on a quest bringing herself closer to her own thoughts, my interest continues. But when she leaps to what she wears, when she boards, and where she sits on board, I feel a "so what" coming on. I don't want to be distracted from what the quest is about, and how the quest is made.

Step Three: Curiosity

This discontent I am feeling leads to a discussion of where I am interested to know more. Why is the ferry important to a transformer? Who else on the ferry belongs to this group? How does carrying a little pouch lead to transformation? What is an example of such a transformation? I want to know what a transformation is so I, too, can fall asleep content listening to the ferry's horn and wake up eager to take transformational trips.

Get the response you need to your first draft according to the three-step process. Having collected the response, take some time away from both the response and your draft while you look at Elizabeth's developed draft.

THE SECOND DRAFT

CROSSING STEEL BLUE WATER

In the Northwest, sometimes the shortest way to travel between two points is across the steel blue water of Puget Sound. The Washington State Ferry or "the boat" as some frequent users refer to it, gives new meaning to the words public transportation for an East Coast transplant like myself.

When I stand on the waterfront, I see these large flat-bottomed vessels crossing by each other like gondola cars on a ski lift. They are as much a part of the scenery here as the sound itself and the jagged snow-peaked Olympic Mountains beyond.

When I go to the ferry dock and watch the boats slowly head toward the tie-up for disembarking and embarking passengers, I look up high at the two control towers on top, each with radar antenna and an American flag. Two narrow balconies sit below them like the brims of baseball caps over car decks. The boats appear like giant horizontal milk cartons, the ends of the cartons open and rounded off.

Inside are four car levels, each with eight lanes across. Even the largest diesel semis appear dwarfed inside this cavern. Every hour, shiny American and Japanese cars line up end to end below the passenger terminal like obedient students. Passengers congregate on the cement walkway. They read newspapers or just stand watching others who are watching them. When the metal gate that separates them from the gangplank slides out of view, they push forward in a blur of color, briefcases and shopping bags crowding down the ramp. On the ground, orange-vested men and women direct the waiting cars, trucks and buses onto the vehicle decks.

By the time a long-winded horn resonates from the boat's bridge announcing the boat's departure, its passengers are sorted.

First and by far the largest group of passengers is comprised of the commuters who, territorial in nature, have boarded the ferry with a sense of urgency hoping to secure a favorite spot along the windows or under the sun deck. Usually dressed in business or work clothing, commuters carry at least one, though I have witnessed up to four, personal items such as briefcases, backpacks, radios and lunch boxes. Within minutes of finding their seats, some of them begin to look very involved working on laptop computers pulled out of their briefcases or sitting in a sea of paper they spread over a booth table. Sometimes you can't even see their faces, their noses are buried so deep in the folds of the *Wall Street Journal*. The commuting construction workers and truckers may be hidden under their caps while stretched out on the seats, coffee thermoses wedged under their heads as pillows.

Not all commuters focus on solo pursuits. Some sit with friends, usually neighbors, sipping soda and sharing popcorn from the snack bar. They converse, loudly at times, about their jobs and families. I have always imagined that for those commuters who travel every day, twice a day, after a time the passenger cabin begins to feel very much like their own living rooms.

Next are the tourists, dressed in leisure wear and sporting smiles that are acknowledged by the commuters they encounter. They travel in groups and enter the cabin from a staircase below, cameras hanging around their necks, arms encumbered with guidebooks or coolers of lunch. Appearing more concerned with a head count of their children who wander off or with stopping to explore the pamphlet racks that offer colorful brochures of what they should see while in the Northwest, the tourists are left to take whatever seats remain.

On the deck, they can be overheard making comments about the size of the city's skyline or asking questions about how much it really rains in Seattle. As the ferry pulls away, one of my favorite moments of the ride, they are busy snapping pictures of Mt. Rainier or chasing their squealing children who are running about the deck, only a metal mesh guardrail between them and the water.

During the last three years, I have burrowed in a corner like the commuter to study notes for a meeting with business clients on the Olympic Peninsula. As a tourist, I have missed half the lush scenery of the ride trying to capture the perfect shot of the Space Needle as the boat pulls away from the city. It is the activity of the third kind of passenger that I have learned and most prefer to engage in. Outwardly, they are not going anywhere except across the water and back. But inwardly, they are provided safe passage in a quest to come ever closer to themselves and their thoughts.

I call this group transformers. They travel alone and carry little with them although occasionally you'll see one with a personal journal in hand. Like the commuters, transformers have favorite places to sit—the upper deck under the sunroof or against the front of the bridge. Unlike the commuters and tourists who study newspapers and maps, transformers keep their eyes on the water in front of them or on the sunset and birds in the distance. They listen to the cries of gulls and feel the crisp salt air.

Unlike the commuters and tourists who operate on a schedule and are headed toward a specific destination, the transformers use the boat anytime. When the boat docks across the sound, they stay on board for the return crossing and congregate on the front deck to watch the passengers and vehicles unload, the clang of the metal off ramp under the tires almost a mantra.

At the boat's return, transformers leave the ferry fifteen minutes or so behind the other passengers and amble down the ramp filled with the sensation that they have been gone for hours, not just the sixty minutes of a crossing and return. That is when their transformation is complete and the solitude of the crossing has brightened their inner landscapes.

As I see the ferry gliding across the sound or hear its distant horn as I drift off to sleep at night, I think about the transformers on board and the last time I was among them. I imagine myself deep in thought walking on deck, breathing the fresh air that rejuvenates. I know the boat is there. I know I can ride whenever I need to make the passages that help me.

In this version, Elizabeth's beginning is much more integrated. She is the "I" on the waterfront looking at the boat. She is the "I" who goes to the ferry dock and watches the boat head toward tie-up. Once she starts to tell us about the inside of the boat and the groups of people on it, we imagine we have boarded the boat with her.

By looking closely at the Washington State Ferry and the people on board, Elizabeth has recognized that although she has, and may well again be, a commuter and a tourist, she has also developed what might be a lifelong habit of using the ferry to make a different kind of crossing—an inner crossing, a tranquil meditation that puts her back in touch with herself. Recounting her experience via the division and classification style, she rests content knowing opportunities for such passages into herself are always available.

Notice that Elizabeth's division and classification essay is couched inside a narration structure—boarding, riding and unboarding the ferry. When as a writer you are paying close attention to your experience, the experience itself seems to arrive with the proper blend of essay styles needed to evoke it. By now you realize I will never advise you to sit down and say to yourself, "I will use this style and this style and this one to build my essay." It is far more productive to trust the design part of your mind by sticking to the truths your senses tell. You start with a main strategy via the "write" question. Then remember what you saw, heard, tasted, touched and smelled and the images seek out the mini-strategies you need for writing a strong essay.

KEEP DRAFTING

Review the responses you got to your first draft. Sit down and write a developed draft. Get responses to it, then rewrite and get new responses and rewrite as many times as you feel you need to. Between drafts, look at how you introduced your category and how you moved in the writing from one division to the next. For instance: Did you use comparison or contrast to move along? Did you describe a location to move along? Did you find some other trait of the category to use in making good transitions? Can you articulate in one sentence what dividing this category into groups has helped you see?

CHAPTER SEVEN

The Cause and Effect Essay

Writing About Decisions and Events That Have Changed Your Life

If we are able to make the best sense of our lives — if we persist in trying to do so and truly commit ourselves to this task — perhaps we can even affect the course of history and change the flow of events. Who knows?

—*Malcolm Boyd*, Edges, Boundaries, and Connections

You are familiar with reading the cause and effect style in newspapers and books. For instance, you may have read articles that report on FAA investigations of plane crashes. To answer the question, "What made a plane crash?" the FAA investigates material, equipment, weather, and human errors. A thorough investigation may show which sequence of events and problems caused the crash.

You may have read books in which historians and social scientists study the causes of Nazism and the rise of Hitler, the rise and fall of communism or the reasons behind economic failures. Medical researchers write articles exploring causes of diseases. They want to know why there is a sudden upswing in the number of tuberculosis or meningitis cases reported.

When something happens to you, you may ask, "Why?" This is a natural way to think. However, in our culture, we are so used to using hindsight to find causes in the hopes of applying knowledge to future situations, we forget the wisdom in looking further down the chain to see the effects of decisions and actions. Sometimes there is no "why" to what a situation is doing in your life. It is just there. It is important to discover "what" has happened in you as a result of living with or through that situation.

"What decisions or actions have I or someone else made or taken that have affected my life and what are those effects?" You may find yourself remembering your parents' decision to move or have another child or send you to camp. You might remember your decision to return to school after a decade out of high school. You might think of your decision not to seek a promotion at work or to seek one. You might think of a best friend moving away. You might think of a time you were a victim of a burglary or scam.

The question can be adapted to your particular area of writing interest by inserting your topic: What decisions or actions have I or someone else made or taken concerning (to use our usual examples once again) my parenting, divorcing, illness, fighting or visiting and what are the effects of those decisions on my life? Perhaps you moved to a retirement community or were forced to become a single parent or left Morocco before you wanted to or suddenly deserted the army.

Using the cause and effect style is valuable in personal essays written for self-discovery. Most of us believe that because of such and such happening, we are stuck and cannot change our behavior, our circumstances, our mood. When writers apply cause and effect thinking to personal essays, however, changes certainly can occur. And we don't have to limit our thinking to the one most pivotal time in our lives. In 1909, Mark Twain wrote in an essay called "The Turning Point in My Life," which appeared in *Harper's Bazaar*, "I know we have a fashion of saying 'such and such an event was the turning-point in my life,' but we shouldn't say it. We should merely grant that its place as *last* link in the chain makes it the most *conspicuous* link. . . ."

To write good cause and effect essays that lead to discovery and new ways of seeing, think in specifics. Once again, approach your subject obliquely. Writing often works best when it is about subjects you feel less invested in. You might have an easier time, for instance, writing about the consequences of not going to a dance on your night off as a camp counselor than about how meeting your husband changed your life. Writing about meeting him because you didn't go to the dance can offer you more details than you realize. But sometimes you have to meet a subject head-on because until you write about it, you may not be able to write about anything else.

In the following sample essays, you will experience with the writers the effects of mourning a recently deceased relative and the effects of making a simple decision to get up early despite the cold. As you read them, watch for the incident(s) that are the causes and ones that are the results or effects. Notice how other essay writing styles are used inside the cause and effect structure — especially description, narration, comparison and contrast. If you find other styles, note those, too.

EXAMPLE: CAUSE AND EFFECT ESSAY

Michael Kuntz wrote under the duress of having just lost his step-father. His essay progresses over a few days time, almost in journal form. As you read, notice the detail about the immediate effects on the author of his stepfather's death. Then notice how this discussion leads to a eulogy, which contains a discussion of his stepfather's influence on him. Notice, too, how Michael reveals the impact of his stepfather's illness. Notice how even the effect of the weather is important to Michael in this time of mourning.

A LIFE IN THE FAMILY

Riding downtown on the #7 this snowy November morning, there is plenty of time to think. Stuck in traffic, there is little else to do. It is in these moments, with no escape, and no real activity to distract me, that the pain surfaces. Few things in life alter our world so completely, and finally, as the death of a parent. For me, the days immediately following the passing of my stepfather, Lee, are a time of confusion, when feelings come with alternating ease and difficulty. My ability to suppress pain is being put to the test, and I am particularly aware of my efforts to do so. In the process, I am rediscovering that the very emotions I try to stuff down rise up with a sharp insistency when I least expect them.

The feelings have risen this morning on this bus and, by comparison, something like being late for work seems too trivial to warrant a sustained thought. Life seems a little cruel at times. For several days, I have struggled with the notion of writing about the effects Lee's death have had on my world, but the pain seems too fresh, and the idea of facing it head-on overwhelms me. A bus connection later, I arrive at the office and another day's distraction.

◆ ◆ ◆

Fate has a way of putting us where we need to be, whether we like it or not, and two days later, I am snowbound on Capitol Hill without even the diversion of the crowded bus to keep me from my thoughts. And my thoughts inevitably return to Lee.

The stepparent is much maligned in fact and fable. In reality, they are sometimes an improvement over the real thing. Such was the case in my life. I know that when my mother made the decision to divorce my father and later to marry Lee Patrick Kelly, she was seeking a better life for both of us. That was certainly what we found.

I was a curious adolescent: overweight, shy, and socially withdrawn—yet gregarious within the safety of the family structure. It must have taken no small amount of courage for Lee to assume the responsibility of joining our family in my sixteenth year. We hit it off immediately. With his devilish humor and rousing sense of fun, he was vastly different from the remote father figure I had been accustomed to.

Some of my earliest memories of Lee are of the times I made him laugh. Specifically how or why, I have forgotten. His laughter was contagious. It would begin as a spasmodic hissing through clenched teeth and gradually escalate into a boisterous, uncontrollable chuckle which, as he would attempt to catch his breath, would be punctuated with sharp, ear-splitting bursts. His laughter always made me laugh and vice versa. On and on we would go, tears streaming down our faces, until my mother would have had quite enough of us, which only made us laugh all the harder.

Lee also had a stubborn streak and could hold his ground in the face of the most rational of arguments. Many a heated discussion would end with the opponent (often me) giving up out of sheer frustration. Sometimes the hint of a gleam in those Irish eyes might make you suspect that he was being contrary for the pure enjoyment of it!

For almost forty years of his life, Lee was an auto mechanic who hated cars but felt a strong sense of responsibility toward the care of them. Time and again he would try in vain to instill the same sense in me. He succeeded as far as teaching me to change a tire (I still remember to loosen and tighten the nuts in a specific pattern and to place them safely into the hub-cap as I go about the dreaded procedure) and to check the oil periodically (when I remember). But I always depended on, and trusted in, his advice on any car problem of a larger nature. The work ethic was firmly a part of his makeup, but his work was something done of necessity and not choice. He confessed to a childhood fantasy of being an orchestra conductor. The 1930s, however, were hard times, and such a fantasy must never have seemed even remotely within the realm of possibility.

My recent memories of Lee tend to center around what he endured in his three-year-long battle with cancer. Beginning with the laryngoscopy, which forever robbed us of the sound of his laughter, and through his second surgery, exactly one year to the date later, in which his esophagus was removed, he must have suffered an enormous amount of emotional and physical pain. And yet, throughout it all, he retained his feisty good humor and his stubbornness.

The frail, hurting man in the hospital bed those last few days seemed a far cry from the robust Irishman of 18 years ago. What a strange, foreign thing the human body seems when it finally wears out. Standing by him, I could sense that the spark, the essence, the soul of the man was still very much there, yet somehow unable to fully realize itself in that now inadequate frame. How glad I was for him when at last the spark was free and how sad for myself that I could no longer be in its presence.

What, other than death, is so undeniably a part of life and yet so easily denied? We are all dying as surely as we live — yet we live our lives as though our tomorrows were in endless supply. We plan for all the things we want to do "someday," until we are ultimately faced with the fact that "someday" has come and gone, and there are no more tomorrows.

♦ ♦ ♦

Two days after the first snowfall, the Seattle skies are clear and blue. I walk to Volunteer Park in yet another attempt to lose myself in my environment. The landscape sparkles before me like all the Christmas cards of my childhood — the ones which left a glittering trace of stardust in the envelope, and on my fingers when I handled them. The air feels sharp and icy against the tear which rolls down my cheek.

Surrounded by the serenity of this early winter scene, I see it in a simpler way. My task seems clear. My "someday" is now. I needed to write about Lee, and I have. He was, and he is gone; I loved him and I will miss him very much.

Ultimately, I believe, we are judged in life by what we teach and learn — the gifts we exchange both consciously and unconsciously. Lee Patrick Kelly taught me how to change a tire and check the oil in my car. He also taught me about the positive and negative aspects of obstinacy and a great deal about courage. Walking home in the snow, I realize that perhaps, even in death, he is still teaching me a little bit more about being alive.

The Meaning in "A Life in the Family"

I finish reading this essay with a lump in my throat. The snowy November Michael's essay is set against will be forever entwined with the sadness of loss and the sweetness of gathering new insight and refreshed love. The essay winds its way through the slow traffic of grief with patience and with persistence. Loss causes pain, memory, and confusion. Snow halts business as usual, and Michael is off from work and able to submerge himself in his grieving. He remains aware of his surroundings and his activities. They provide a small narrative inside his cause and effect essay that helps him keep it moving as he realizes the effects of his loss. When the skies clear, two days after the storm which allowed Michael to stay with his grieving, he realizes he has accomplished something—writing about Lee, who he was and how he was loved. Michael names the effects his stepfather had on his life starting with the concrete details of tire changes and oil checks then moving on to lessons about obstinacy. Next, Michael moves to the greatest of life's lessons—how to let go and hold on at the same time. Michael shares with us the most long-lasting effect of his loss, that of consciously taking Lee Patrick Kelly, who is gone now on the outside, into his own being. This final effect revealed, Michael walks home in the snow, knowing he has learned "a little bit more about being alive."

A close reading of this essay for the purposes of seeing essay styles also reveals the use of comparison and contrast and division and classification. The opening two paragraphs announce the *contrasts* in Michael's life right now—the more he tries to repress emotions to continue his life, the more they rise up insistent when he is not expecting them. When the feelings do arise, they make other feelings or fears trivial in comparison. There are three kinds of memories Michael employs to explore the effect of this death on him. These are memories from childhood, from Lee's recent illness, and from what Lee has taught him with death, the final departure.

EXAMPLE: CAUSE AND EFFECT ESSAY

Sometimes the decisions we make that are instrumental to our well-being are very small ones. Tri Nguyen, the son of refugees from

Vietnam, writes about how a small decision affected him. As you read, notice the effects on Tri's well-being and character development that stem from his small decision.

SIMPLE PLEASURES

"Cock-a-doodle-do." The remote cry of the roosters awakens me from a peaceful sleep. Lazily, I open my eyes and see the window in my room. It is still dark outside. I remember promising myself the night before to wake up early the next morning to see the sunrise; but now in the early morning the promise seems to be insignificant compared to this warm bed. Reluctantly, I stir myself out of bed, saying to myself, "A promise is a promise," although I yearn to return to the warm bed's embrace. As my bare feet touch the ground, I am stunned into full awareness by the cold floor. The coldness fades as my body warms up leaving me with a clear mind and impatient spirit for a walk outside, to feel the cool fresh air and see the rising of the sun. These actions may seem ridiculous to most of my cousins on the farm, but to me, this is what I cherish most about living on the farm.

I was born in and spent most of my life in a fairly big city. Every day, I am rudely awakened by the cold sound of metal bells from my alarm clock. Opening my eyes and looking out the window, I can only see houses and towering buildings bunched together to block out the light of a new dawning sun. By the afternoon, the noise of the factories' machines running at full speed can be deafening just as the smoke from the smoke pipes of hundreds of cars and factories can pollute the air we breathe, choking out our breath and the sunlight from the city.

But not here, not at this five or six acres of farmland. My aunt has had this farm for as long as I can remember, and although my mother has told me, "You have been here before many times," our earlier visits were when I was too young to truly appreciate the tranquillity of the place. I stand on the front porch with the condition of the big city racing through my mind. I come back to this reality with a cool breeze and the call of the rooster, "Cock-a-doodle-do." I turn my head in the direction of the sound and walk toward it.

Still in bare feet, I slowly step from the front porch, and my feet touch the soft earth. The sun has not risen over the mountain yet, but there is enough light from the sun now to see the dew on the grasses glisten from the sunlight. I can see dimly the silhouette of the chicken barnyard and the sack of grain near the barnyard door. I scoop a handful of grain with my left hand as I enter the barnyard. Throwing some grain on the floor for those chickens that can see and want to eat, I walk slowly to the nearest nest. And without much noise, I pick up a small chick with my right hand and walk out. Returning to the front of the house, I quietly sit down cross-legged on the wet grasses. As I bring the hand with the grain to the one with the chick, I think of the simplicity of the world and how the sun just now has risen over the mountain peak to warm the earth and my face. This is a new day.

The Discovery in "Simple Pleasures"

Tri's decision to keep his promise about rising with the rooster's cock-a-doodle-do results in a small ritual in the quiet of dawn: "I bring the hand with the grain to the one with the chick. . . ." And the small ritual results in the large journey back to simplicity, to being, to self-renewal.

Tri employs some comparison and contrast between the city and the farm, between the attitude of his cousins and himself, and between how he feels in the city and the country. He, of course, narrates his morning at the farm and uses simple, precise descriptions. But once again, the style that propels the discovery in this essay is cause and effect: he has asked himself about a decision he made and what resulted from that decision.

EXERCISE FOR DEVELOPING YOUR MATERIAL

Try the following exercise to help you find and develop material for writing your own cause and effect essay.

One Thing Leads to Another

Two or more friends or family members can help you get warmed up with cause and effect thinking. Each of you must write down, individually, three bogus "policies" or "facts." Put each on its own piece of paper. Here are three examples: four out of every five dogs are barking more loudly this year than last year. All restaurant workers in the state of Washington now wear green clothes both at work and outside of work. The normal wintertime temperature in Seattle is eighty-two degrees with low humidity.

When everyone has finished, each person passes the papers to someone else in the group. Everyone writes something that could result from each "fact" or "policy" received. For instance: Now that dogs bark more loudly, there are fewer house break-ins in the neighborhoods, but there are worse tensions between neighbors because no one is sleeping very well. Since restaurant workers wear green clothes all the time, workers in other fields have adopted particular colors for their clothes and now at parties no one ever asks the question, "What do you do?" Seattle has become a vacation paradise and people there are turning their homes into bed and breakfast places. In addition to community gardens called pea patches, there are now community swimming pools called plunge patches.

When everyone is finished writing down effects for each "policy" or "fact," pass the lists once again. This time look at the "facts" and "policies" as well as the effects written on the pages. Think of some reasons (causes) for these "facts" and "policies." In my examples, maybe dog food companies began injecting dog food with a certain hormone to increase shelf life, and it affected the dogs' barks. Maybe there was a severe hepatitis outbreak in Washington State, and having restaurant workers wear green made it possible to manage the epidemic. Maybe global warming gave Seattle a tropical climate. When you are all finished, take some time to read what you have written.

If you can't arrange to do this exercise with a few people, skim some newspapers or magazine ads. Write down some of the claims manufacturers make for their products, putting each claim on a separate piece of paper. Chose a few of the claims and write your own ideas of what the results of such a "truth" might be. Stray as far from the product and the manufacturer as you can. Next write reasons for the validity of the claims.

For instance, I open a magazine and see an ad for a CD. "This recording will replace what you used to expect from music," the ad proclaims. Writing the effects of such a claim I state: I now expect to hear vacuum cleaner noise when I put my stereo on. I expect not to have to eat anymore once I play the CD I bought. I expect to meet the recording artist in a virtual reality software package that comes along with the CD. Then, when I get around to writing the causes for this claim, I think: The producers wanted to transform the sound of background music. The producers wanted to make a lot of money.

The producers wanted to pass off what they had recorded already without spending more money on a better recording.

Inventing results before thinking about causes and inventing causes without thinking about results loosens up our thinking so we can absorb the fact that although one thing leads to another, we can be surprised at what that is. In our society, we rely on cause and effect for analysis in order to control, in order to preserve the idea that we are in charge and can conquer and shape our environment and lives. Maybe in writing from personal experience using cause and effect, we can cultivate a different kind of understanding about events in our lives. Perhaps we can cultivate a desire to learn from them and see where these events have left us with more perception, more whole than we were before.

LOCATING YOUR CAUSE AND EFFECT MATERIAL

You can explore some of what has happened in your life by viewing circumstances as having been touched off by a decision. When you ask the "write" question, "What decision have I or someone else made that affected my life?" you can begin a cluster with the word "decision" in the middle of the blank page. Cluster around the word "decision," all of them you can think of that either 1) you made, 2) were made for you, or 3) others made for themselves that affected you. Cluster images and phrases around each of the decisions that come to you. Next ask yourself, "What action have I or someone else taken that has affected my life?" Start a cluster with the word "action" in the middle of the page.

Between these two questions, much will come to mind. Did you decide to marry someone or not to? Did you spend your money seemingly foolishly and enjoy something wonderful contrary to what others predicted? Did you go through this doorway instead of that one? Did you surrender something hard to let go and grow as a consequence? Did you refuse to surrender in the face of everything and receive something important? When you feel interested in a particular memory, start a freewrite. Do a This Is a Poem exercise if you need help coming up with more details about the decision or action you are writing about and its effects on you.

If you are exploring a particular topic, insert it into the question like this before you do your clusters: What decision concerning _____ did I or someone else make that has affected me? What action concerning this topic have I or someone else taken and how has that affected me?

WRITING YOUR ESSAY

Now that you have gathered the details through these exercises, choose an action or decision that interests you and begin writing a draft that shows and explores its effects on you. Look back at the sample essays. Notice how both of them start where the author is speaking from: a #7 bus, a farm at dawn. Perhaps you can start your draft by describing yourself physically in a location. Another way to start is to offer the dialogue in which the decision was told. Did you talk to yourself? Were you talking with someone else? Were you overhearing someone else's dialogue?

Writer Michael Dorris begins a cause and effect section of "Fetal Alcohol Syndrome, A Parent's Perspective," written for the Centers for Disease Control and now collected in his 1994 book, *Paper Trail* by getting right to the point: "When you're a parent of an FAS or FAE child, your goals change with the passing years." He will examine the effects of adopting a fetal alcohol syndrome child on his own sense of self and value as a parent.

Whatever you use to start writing, images of where you are, bits of dialogue from the time you are remembering, or statements of the cause itself, try to write from beginning to end. You can trust your dexterity in using sensory detail, events organized through time, contrasts, comparisons, how-tos, and even divisions and classifications. If those styles can help you, they will occur to you as you are writing. They always arrive if they are needed.

DEVELOPING THE DRAFT

Put your draft away for a while, and read Elizabeth's essay. She had been in an unsatisfactory love relationship during the time we were working on writing together. She knew she needed to examine a decision she had recently made. In order to tell her ex-lover why she was saying no, she had to look at and describe the causes, the reasons, for her no. To do this effectively she went to the spot most likely to bring up images of meeting her lover and beginning her romance, the park where they had met and often ran. Notice how Elizabeth uses the place she is writing to shape metaphors that explain her feelings and situation.

ALONG THE PATH

Today you are on my mind as I set out to walk along the path where I have seen you jogging many evenings after work, your hand always rising to give me a quick wave as you pass from the opposite direction. Today I passed the wooden bench at the entrance to the park where you asked me out for the first time. Today the warmth I felt when you flattered me with your attention and the currents of excitement that charged through my body as you smiled engagingly as we made plans for dinner have faded like the words on the park sign, weathered by the harsh exposure to the sun's intensity and the pounding of the rain.

Today as I begin my walk, the black granite rocks that protect the path from the tide look particularly jagged. Today their uneven sharp peaks glisten in the sun from the salt water that sprays upward as the waves slam against the fortress of their layers, reminiscent of the truths I have encountered during our relationship.

Today I think of the conversation we had a month ago driving back from the coffeehouse when I told you, nervously stumbling over my words, I couldn't be your lover anymore. The beam of light that shone through your window from the lamppost overhead exposed, for a second or two, the stunned expression on your face. Your mouth hung open in disbelief. When you inquired impatiently why I had arrived at this decision, I answered firmly, "I just need to do this for myself." You pushed for details, yet my silence was unrelenting as you turned the car towards my apartment realizing that I wasn't going with you to help warm your down covers.

Today I am writing from my path to finally tell you why I can't be your lover anymore. As I sit in the cool grass, my back resting against the sturdy trunk of a poplar tree, one of many in a long row that lines the park, my eyes cannot help but meet the snow-capped mountains that gently crisscross one another in the distance appearing to caress. I close my eyes and try to feel the seductiveness of your touch. But I remember the hours I spent, more hours than I care to admit, staring into the distance, as I tried to make sense of your behavior. Over a period of weeks we could spend many evenings together enjoying dinner at our favorite restaurants or conversation over espresso. As we walked to your car under the sheer yellow blanket of the moon's light, your passionate embraces would soon have me tight against the car door, and in the morning, our bodies would be warmly entangled under your sheets. I had even grown accustomed to your late night phone calls rousing me to come out.

Then suddenly weeks would go by, and I wouldn't hear from you at all.

Today, my body aches with a sadness. The evening you asked me to explore my feelings to see if there was anything for us to build on, you asked for more from this relationship than you are capable of delivering. I know I want something different in my life than what you can offer. How I long to hear the pledge of affection you whispered in my ear from someone I can trust.

With you there have been too many questions. The hour-long phone conversations in the middle of the night in which you confessed your addiction to women have been too numerous. I have been foolish to think I heard sincerity in your repentant tone. I wanted to believe that your recovery was close at hand, but the engaging looks you'd continue to give the beautiful women we'd pass walking into the theater or the flirtatious manner you would use ordering dinner from our waitress, say it isn't so. At night when I'd climb into your bed and catch sight of three used condoms left carelessly next to a pile of books, how could I not help counting back and realizing that I had only spent two nights with you during the week? I don't want to be part of your ongoing slumber party anymore.

As I watch the waves breaking on the beach, their repetition recalls for me the hours I have spent listening patiently to your problems or the frustrations you have encountered trying to hustle freelance work as a photographer. I feel exhausted like the flowers that wilt along the path, starved of proper nourishment. Rarely have you inquired about my interests and work. The times you did take the time to ask, your interest waned quickly. The distracted look on your face as you began to glance around the room or the immediacy with which you changed the subject always gave you away. How could I ever trust you with my fears or dreams when your inattention made me feel so hollow?

Lately, you have left messages on my answering machine just to tell me that you are thinking about me. What were your thoughts nights when you dropped me off at my apartment in the darkness, and I heard the screech of your tires pulling away before I reached the safety of my door? I'd watch your red taillights vanishing and wonder.

Today, as I finish writing you from the path, my thoughts are clear like the crystal blue sky victorious after a long heavy rain. I have come to trust myself and the inner feelings that guide me. The colors of the landscape where I have been sitting are brighter than ever as I rise to leave and walk home, choosing a new path across the park.

Elizabeth's decision "to finally tell you why I can't be your lover anymore" creates in her a stronger, more assertive, more self-advocating personality. Elizabeth wrote this version in her first sitting. She used the prompting of the cause and effect cluster and the use of listing (notice how six out of nine paragraphs start with the word "today") as practiced in the earlier poetry exercises. Something bubbling around inside her came out fully formed when Elizabeth applied the craft of writing. Her practice with description and narration and the use of like constructions allowed her words to flow and make direct good sense. It is not often that writing arrives this effortlessly, but when it does, you get to see the facility you do have with structures and how that skill is there to help you when you are ready to say something important.

Michael Dorris ends "Fetal Alcohol Syndrome, A Parent's Perspective" with the sentence: "To be best known for one's saddest story is not the road to notoriety anyone would willingly choose." When you write cause and effect essays, you must not judge yourself too harshly. Whatever you choose to write about will ultimately put you in the good light of being honest and capable of self-reflection.

KEEP DRAFTING

Go back to your draft now and get the responses you need. Write again from beginning to end. If you are not satisfied with your second draft, get new response as needed and write another draft. Remember, you are trying to discover the ways in which you are different today as a consequence of the decision or life circumstance you are writing about.

CHAPTER EIGHT

The Definition Essay
Writing to Understand the Roles You Play

By itself, nothing "out there" has any definition without a perceiver.
—*Deepak Chopra, M.D.*, Unconditional Life: Discovering the Power to Fulfill Your Dreams

Hearing-impaired, diabetic, daughter, mother, wife, husband, father, son, teacher, student, refugee, head of household, adoptee, caregiver for an Alzheimer's patient, construction worker, office temp, the "good" one, the black sheep, "them." If one of those words describes you, you are in a position to more fully understand its meaning using the definition essay. This fuller meaning is what essayists call doing an "extended" definition.

In a definition essay, a writer explores a subject by describing the qualities that distinguish it from any other subject. Division and classification is inherent in definition because to define something we must identify what classification it belongs to and how it is alike or different (comparison and contrast) from other divisions. Writers often define a subject by listing what qualities it does not have. This is a way of showing the boundaries, the uniqueness of the subject under discussion. Writers usually offer examples to clarify their definitions. Sometimes, these are in the form of anecdotes or short narrations and always include description. Ultimately, even how-to and cause and effect can help a writer create an extended definition essay. How something functions, for instance, can be part of defining it. The cause and effect style helps a writer with definition when the writer explores what happens as a result of having or being something.

Here are some more examples of how the cause and effect and how-to styles of essay writing can help in writing a personal extended definition essay: A definition of "bus driver" can be made by showing how one learns to be a bus driver. Defining what it means to be a daughter can include the effect a daughter's behavior has on her parents. Defining what it means to be a mother or father can include the effects of mothering or fathering on children's lives. What it means to be a diabetic can include how diabetics consider their diet.

I have officially been a teacher since 1970 when I received my B.A. in English from the University of Wisconsin and became a middle school classroom reading and English teacher in Matawan, New Jersey. Twenty-four years and two degrees later I have taught senior citizens, pre-schoolers, parent volunteers, adult learners, teachers-in-training, high school and college students, as well as my own two children and my husband's office staff. I might decide it's finally time to define the role of teacher. I would include as my list of distinguishing characteristics an absolute respect for the intelligence of others, a perception that the job of teaching requires patient demonstration of what is being taught (Marshall McLuhan's "The medium is the message") and a willingness to laugh at oneself to avoid communicating perfectionism which blocks learning. These characteristics could be contrasted with the qualities I believe have no place in teaching: believing that you are smartest because you are older or the teacher, believing that saying something equals doing it, and believing that stern seriousness and hiding one's own mistakes help maintain standards necessary for learning. I could further define my idea of what constitutes a teacher with stories from my classrooms. I could compare how I was taught to teach with how I have learned to teach. I could show the effects of my teaching on students and I could show the effects of my students on my teaching.

You can ask the "write" question for your definition style personal essay this way: "For what situation in my life do I want to describe what lies beneath the label?" You might begin by thinking about what people call you — a grandfather, a widow, a transactional analyst, a biker, a golfer, a pool shark, a professional volunteer.

If you have a writing area in mind, you can insert it into the question like this, "What am I called as a consequence of (to use our examples from before once again) divorcing, parenting, visiting a new country, fighting in a war or coping with an illness? What do I want to describe about what lies beneath this label of divorcee, single parent, tourist, veteran or Parkinsonian?"

Before you work on answering the "write" question, though, look ahead to the example definition essays.

EXAMPLE: DEFINITION ESSAY

In the following example essay, Michael Shurgot defines the modern baseball fan. He starts by letting us know the modern baseball fan is not like the one of yesteryear. As you read, think about what other techniques he uses to define the modern baseball fan. Note where you see comparison and contrast, cause and effect and how-to at work in addition to description and narration.

When you have finished reading the essay, do you know how Michael would know this modern fan so thoroughly? Why does he define this fan?

CAESAR'S "STUFF;" OR, THE MODERN BASEBALL FAN

In the old days, say thirty years ago, being a baseball fan was simple. Those were the days of the Polo Grounds and Ebbets Field, before free agency, before the designated hitter obliterated strategy from half of major league baseball, and before anyone even contemplated (horrors!) lights in Wrigley Field. I recall vividly my days as a bleacher bum in Offerman Stadium, home of the Triple A Buffalo Bisons of the old International League. My dad started taking me to games when I was six, and by my tenth birthday, he allowed me to go with just the other kids on the block. We took only the bare essentials: $1.50 or $1.00 for general admission seats and $.50 for a hot dog, and our tattered mitts with which we hoped, nay prayed, to snag an errant foul ball in the stands along the third-base line. We were unsupervised thieves, scurrying from the bleachers to the reserved seats in the top of the fifth when the ushers ceased caring about who sat where. Devoted fans, we cheered lustily for our minor league heroes: Bill Sernea, Joe Caffie, and the great Luke Easter, who finished his career with the Bisons and hit some tremendous home runs that remain in orbit somewhere over the western New York skies.

But like nearly everything in baseball, except the magic of the game itself, the baseball fan has changed. The modern fan, adapting consciously to our increasingly technological world and to the creature comforts of contemporary fandom, no longer attends with just his ticket money and glove. The modern baseball fan arrives at the park schlepping a bizarre collection of *impedimenta*, a word Caesar used to describe the vast assortment of material he and his troops lugged across the Alps during the Gallic Wars of 53 B.C. *Impedimenta* derives from the Latin *im*, a negative prefix, and *pes, pedis*, a noun meaning *foot*. Hence, "impedimenta," like our verb *impede*, is that which "bars or hinders progress; obstructs or retards." In a word, stuff. A scrutiny of modern baseball fans reveals just how sophisticated and technological they have become, and suggests also that they believe their "stuff" is as vital to appreciating ball games as Caesar believed his "stuff" was to bashing the Gauls.

As he approaches his seat along the third-base line, the modern baseball fan is heavily laden. In one hand he carries his brightly colored, foam rubber, inflatable seat cushion. Bearing the logo and colors of his home team, this cushion protects its owner's haunches from the rigors of the metal seats or benches where he will spend the next three hours. What a godsend this invention is! Oh, to have had a seat cushion to insulate my derriere from the slivers of the decaying wooden benches in Offerman Stadium! I wonder only if they would have impeded our theft of reserved seats in the fifth, becoming, as it were, brightly colored flags signaling our chicanery.

In his other hand, the modern fan carries a large, canvas bag jammed with gadgets designed to increase his appreciation and enjoyment of the game. Sitting on his now-inflated cushion, he opens his sack and gingerly removes its contents, resembling an impromptu peddler about to set up shop on the town square. The first object removed is a small, portable radio, complete with earphone, which enables the fan to supplement what he sees with the radio announcer's expert commentary. This additional, expert knowledge often makes the modern fan an authority on controversial plays, even though by the time he has synthesized the announcer's remarks with the numerous instant replays on the electronic scoreboard in center field, the game may have progressed to the next inning. Undaunted by this possibility, however, the modern fan inserts the radio into his breast pocket, carefully maneuvering it around the collection of pens adorning the same pocket. Once the radio is carefully ensconced, the fan then inserts the earphone and listens to the pre-game show while he completes his preparations.

The second object removed is a stat sheet, cut out from the sports pages of the evening paper. If the fan is lucky, he will have two sheets, the second provided at the entrance gate, usually by a local bank. If he has only one sheet, he can quickly scan its figures,

assuring himself that he will know the batting averages and win-
loss records of all players on both teams. If he has two sheets, he
must then compare them, assuring himself that he has the latest
statistics, since one or the other sheet may not include information
from last night's games on the coast. This comparing can consume
several minutes, during which the managers have chatted with the
umpires, promising not to kick dirt on home plate, and the national
anthem has been sonorously sung. To all of this the modern fan is,
of course, oblivious, his mind entirely consumed by his stat sheets.

Next out of the bag is another marvel of technology: a minicom-
puter. With eyes riveted to the sheet(s), and fingers running nimbly
over the tiny buttons, the fan computes how many hits so-and-so
needs to raise his average to .300, and how many Ks what's-his-
name needs to regain the league lead in strikeouts per innings
pitched. All of this information must be dutifully recorded on the
pad of paper super-glued to the back of the computer. Once these
calculations are finished, the fan takes from his breast pocket—
careful not to disturb the radio—a red pen with which he under-
lines the calculations crucial to tonight's game. This process completed, the fan can now attend to the game itself, by now well
under way.

Suddenly the fan hears from the earphone thunderous noises,
and he must ask his less well-equipped neighbor what all the cheering is about. He learns that his team's clean-up hitter has just
belted a three-run shot into the right field seats. Dismayed, the
modern fan reaches frantically into his bag, removes his binoculars,
and strains them towards home plate just as the slugger heads for
the dugout. As he gazes at the huge electronic scoreboard, he realizes it is already the bottom of the third inning.

Irked that he has missed nearly one-third of the game, the modern fan asks his neighbors what happened during the previous 2½
innings, and then quickly begins filling in his score sheet, only to
realize after several mistakes, caused by confusing his neighbors'
reports with radio commentary, that he has forgotten to use his
erasable ink pen. As he reaches into his pocket to find it, he knocks
his radio onto his lap, taking the earphone with it, and thus misses
the announcer's saying that the slugger has now recaptured the
league lead in RBIs. Flustered, the fan sits back, gazing at his
messy, illegible scorecard, hoping desperately that the radio announcer will recap the previous innings, pitch by pitch, hit by hit.

Later in the game, the opposing team's shortstop slices a foul line drive towards him. Realizing suddenly that he has a chance for this coveted souvenir, the fan dives into his bag, takes out his brand new glove, and lunges for the ball. It lands squarely in the middle of his glove, pops out, and rolls down two rows where a scruffy kid snags it with his tattered mitt and triumphantly waves his prize above his head. Staring at his spiffy glove, the modern fan realizes it had no pocket, and, as fellow fans cheer the wily youngster, he vaguely recalls the oldest ritual in baseball: soaking a glove's center in neatsfoot oil; slamming a ball into it; tying it securely with string and rubber bands; and waiting three days for a pocket miraculously to be born. Bereft of his souvenir, the fan sits down, realizing only two innings later that his cushion has fallen under his feet, upside down.

As he trudges from the ballpark, impedimenta in hand, the modern fan contemplates the night's epic battle, trying vainly to recall who hit what when and for how many runs. His team having won on the slugger's second homer of the game in the bottom of the ninth, he realizes he had recorded the homer in the eighth inning on his scorecard. A scruffy kid behind him rattles off stats on the slugger's RBI production, the winning pitcher's earned run average, and the league standings. Hoping to get the latest scores, the fan stops, takes out his radio, implants the earphones, and then discovers the radio isn't working. The batteries had been lost during the lunge for the line drive.

The modern fan is a fixture in baseball today, a microcosm of the technological advances in ballparks and in the game itself: domed stadiums, huge electronic scoreboards which flash instant replays on mammoth screens; TV sets under the grandstand; artificial surfaces; pitching "machines"; managers' own computers and two-way radios; and what George Will calls "talking fences" which "bleep" when an outfielder approaches.

But one wonders. There is a world of meaning in Caesar's word "impedimenta," suggesting perhaps that he wished he had not needed, or thought he needed, all that stuff when he crossed the Alps. Perhaps, had he traveled more lightly, he might have enjoyed the scenery much more, which must have been spectacular before all those chalets and ski resorts were built. Perhaps, too, the modern baseball fan, were he to schlep less of his own impedimenta to the ballpark, would appreciate more thoroughly the magic of the game being played before him.

The Discovery in "Caesar's 'Stuff;' or, The Modern Baseball Fan"

After describing, through images gleaned in childhood, how an old-fashioned baseball fan behaved, Michael introduces the word "but" at the start of paragraph two. Every characteristic he points out in the modern fan will be contrasted to what came first — the relatively unencumbered fans with the worn mitts and the voices for cheering.

To have us understand one of the basic characteristics of the modern fan which separates him from the old-time fan, Michael gives us the word *impedimenta* and a dictionary definition for it. After thinking about the effect of the stuff the modern fan carries to the game, Michael narrates the time the modern fan enters the stadium to the time the game ends and he leaves. Inside this narration, there is a step-by-step how-to-be-a-modern-baseball-fan as the author shows the fan using his technology in the stadium. Unlike the old-time fans, some of whom appear to be in the stadium, the modern fan is always a play or more behind. The characteristics that make up the modern fan are his reliance on personal technology and his ensuing clumsiness as it keeps him from getting the information he seeks.

The game over, the fans headed for home, the author still needs an ending to his essay. He moves the camera of his mind back for a wider view — this modern fan is, it turns out, just a mere microcosm of all the new technologically oriented ballparks in the country. "But one wonders," the author opens his final paragraph. This allows him to return to thinking about impedimenta and Caesar. Using a comparison, the author asks what the new baseball fan has in common with Caesar besides stuff. Not surprisingly, it turns out to be the unused opportunity to appreciate what spectacles are before him.

EXAMPLE: DEFINITION ESSAY

Following is an essay I wrote. I had been reading through a manuscripts-wanted listing in an arts commission newsletter. One magazine wanted short essays by women on work. Clustering around the word "work" was for me like clustering around the word "role." What work roles did I have? How did I feel about them? Which one would I really like to define more fully than usual? It turned out the one I wanted to write about was the one I wanted to define for myself, the one I wished I could have on an ongoing, paying basis.

As you read, notice my use of narration to describe the role I am defining. Notice, too, the characteristics of the role and the how-to inherent in my description of performing it. The effects of having such a job are useful to my ending. My beginning utilizes a small comparison.

DREAM JOB: A DAY IN THE LIFE OF A RESIDENT POET

I administered a poem to my husband this week much as a nurse administers medicine. He was out of town for two and one-half weeks, working hard and missing being home. When he is on the road teaching all-day seminars, he fills some of his nights going to places listed in his guide to the best billiard halls in the country. He says the nonverbal activity focuses his mind. When he gets back to his hotel, though, he is lonely. I sent him a poem this time. "The Poet at Seventeen," by Larry Levis, about playing pool. It begins:

> My youth? I hear it mostly in the long, volleying
> Echoes of billiards in the pool halls where
> I spent it all, extravagantly, believing
> My delicate touch on a cue would last for years.

After meandering through tilled fields, teen boy fantasies about girls, reading poems in school, and driving a tractor before more billiards in the autumn nights, the poem ends:

> And then the first dark entering the trees —
> And inside, the adults with their cocktails before
>   dinner,
> The way they always seemed afraid of something,
> And sat so rigidly, although the land was theirs.

How hard it is for my husband sometimes to be the teacher, the expert in the subject, the one who "owns" the day, when inside he remembers a way without words, a stick to touch, the bond of those who play. My husband was happier for having read the poem, he told me. He sounded warm and more connected to his experience.

I was reminded when he thanked me for the poem of a dream I had years ago. In it, I'd hung a shingle outside my house. Sheila Bender, R.P., it said, in black calligraphic letters on a white board. R.P. meant Resident Poet. On the second story of my house, at my desk under the eaves, I would work on my poetry. The many books of poems I knew and loved would surround me on shelves. From time to time, I'd hear my doorbell ring.

I'd descend the stairs and let the person in. We would enter my writing room and sit at a small round table having tea. The caller would describe why he or she had come to see me. It might be the grief of losing someone dear, the uncertainty of parenting, the concentration-breaking joy of newfound love, the awkwardness of wanting to talk to an old lover, the loneliness of perceiving differently than one's family. I would go to my bookshelves, my pharmacy of poems, and I would pull a book down, open it to where I knew the right poem lay. I'd watch my caller read the poem and, watching the muscles of his or her face, I would know the poem was right. I would hand my client a pen and sheets of paper with instructions to copy the poem and the author's name from the book, word for word. After that, we'd read the work together once and sit a moment more.

My caller would take the poem home to memorize. To whisper at night, to belt out under the sun, to recite while driving. Poems require looking past anger and hate and irritation, loneliness and grief. Though many a poem is planted in the soil of such emotions, a poem bursts through that soil and flowers. It is, to paraphrase William Wordsworth, one person's insides speaking to another's, and so it provides the intimate contact we need for healing and for growth, for knowing what is human in our lives.

There are feelings and longings we understand and accept in ourselves only when we recognize them in someone else's words, words that would never have been ours to speak until we saw them written out of someone else's life. Words come from another's experience in a place and in a time that miraculously match our experience in our own place and time.

As my callers would leave, they would place payment in a white porcelain bowl on the post at the bottom of my staircase. With the money, I'd buy more poetry books and the time to read them.

The Meaning in "Dream Job: A Day in the Life of a Resident Poet"

I compare being a resident poet to being a nurse in the administration of a "pharmaceutical" for the patient's relief. I give an example in the form of short narration of administering this pharmaceutical to a person in emotional stress. I see that my action fits with an old dream I had of actually doing this sort of work as an occupation. I describe the steps in performing this work. I discuss the function of this kind of work: "There are feelings and longings we understand and accept in ourselves only when we recognize them in someone else's words."

Having made my most important point, the discovered articulation of why I love poetry, I end my definition of the Resident Poet's job with the ending of the narration: the client pays. What is the result of this job for me? More poetry books, more time to read them.

When I was finished writing, I reread the submission request in the arts commission newsletter and realized I'd missed the deadline. Then I remembered another publication that was interested in essays about work, so I sent my essay to that publication. I was pleased when it was accepted for publication, but most of all, I enjoyed using the definition style to write a personal essay about a favorite role, one I wish I could have on a more consistent basis.

EXERCISE FOR DEVELOPING YOUR MATERIAL

Now let's go on to an exercise that will facilitate your extended definition writing.

A Dictionary Game Look-Alike

To find out how much you already know about definition as a structure, play the following game with your family or a group of four or five people. It is fun for everyone, even those who are not going to write a definition essay.

Each person needs a scrap of paper to begin. They must write one word on this scrap, a word they believe no one in the room has heard. The word can be a nickname or a word coined by friends. It can be an esoteric term from a hobby or course of study. It can be a foreign word. The word, however, mustn't be spelled exactly like some other word someone would already know the meaning of. For instance, the word *crunchy* meant embarrassing in school-age slang for a while, but it also means what it always has meant about texture. This word would not be a good candidate for the game because the person defining "crunchy" would already have a meaning in mind even if he or she didn't know the slang meaning.

When all have written down words, they fold up their papers and drop them into a hat or bowl. All now draw a paper out of the hat or bowl. When all have selected words for which they do not know the meaning, they must write for five minutes making up definitions for these words.

For instance, if I had picked the word "hoila hoila," I might write:

> This is a phrase a community of descendants of explorers from the South Pacific use to express their shock and surprise when a member of their community marries outside of the clan. For example, one might hear: Hoila Hoila Marie has not called her mother in ten years, or her grandson went hoila hoila on her and lives in California.

When everyone in the group has written a "definition," the more outrageous the better, the group should listen one by one to each word and its "definition." After each person reads, the person who contributed the word can explain its "real" meaning. I might find out, for instance, that "hoila hoila" is the sound a group member's children made whenever she served them food they thought was too fancy.

After you have heard all the words and their new and original meanings, think about all the techniques that were used in defining them. I am sure that the people in your group wrote, just as I did, about the class of activities, events, people or objects to which their word belonged. I am sure they described how the activity, event, person or object could be distinguished by its main characteristics or functions. Some people probably included examples. Some probably compared or contrasted their object, event or activity to other objects, events or activities. Others may have told what characteristic their word did not include as a way of honing in on a meaning.

We use these techniques of defining quite naturally and noticing them in the examples from the game will help you feel confident in your ability to write an extended definition essay.

If you can't do this exercise with a group of people, go to a library or newsstand and pick up reading material in Italian, French or Spanish. Jot down some words and take them home. One by one, put the foreign words at the top of a page. Next, write a few paragraphs for each word, "defining" it based on how it sounds to you and what you associate with the sound. You can also do this exercise by taking words from law books, medical books, or technical manuals, as long as the words you choose don't have synonyms or exact homonyms in everyday speech.

LOCATING YOUR DEFINITION MATERIAL

Put the word "role" in the middle of a piece of paper. Then cluster from that word all the roles you can think of, those you like, dislike, envy in other people's lives and regret in your life or in another person's life. You may come up with employee of the year, youngest sibling, non-custodial parent, rock band leader, aspiring musician, neighborhood gossip.

You may not have a name yet for a role you could write about, just a feeling. You can write that feeling and then cluster labels around it. For instance, perhaps you felt "out of it" in high school. Write that down and circle it. Then think up labels that suited you in high school that could have contributed to that feeling: class valedictorian, class clown, nerd, slower learner, pot-head, member of the "wrong side of the tracks" crowd.

When you find a role to write about that interests you, do another cluster starting with that word in the middle of your paper. You might want to write about a condition you have or someone close to you has that requires special care. If you are diabetic, for instance, you might see that many people think that it only means taking insulin and not eating sugar. You would know, though, that having and managing diabetes entails far more. Ask yourself five questions: "What are the characteristics of this role I (used to) play?" "What are the things this role is not?" "How does one perform this role?" "How is this role different than other roles or different than other people may think?" "Why do I call it what I do?" If it helps, you can cluster answers for each of the questions.

If the word "role" doesn't grab you, use the word "situation," and think of all the situations you or people close to you find themselves in — homelessness, having chemotherapy, living with a cancer patient, being an "ex." When you have decided on one situation that interests you, do another cluster using that word in the middle to start. Ask yourself: "What are the characteristics of this situation?" "What is missing in this situation?" "How does one behave in this situation?" "How is one restricted from behaving in this situation?"

If you already have a writing area in mind remember to ask the "write" question this way: "What am I called as a consequence of _____ (insert your writing area)?" If, for instance, your area is fighting in a war, you may have come up with veteran, hero, coward, sergeant, private, general, etc. Choose the role that interests you. Then use the questions from above and cluster around the word you have selected.

WRITING YOUR ESSAY

When you are finished clustering all the images and phrases you associate with the word you have decided upon, do a freewrite. Remember the way definitions worked in the group game. Feel free to go from one definition technique to another: listing characteristics involved to listing what characteristics are not involved, comparing and contrasting characteristics or using narratives as examples. This will help you extend your definition of the role you are exploring. Put the freewrite away for a bit. Look at it again. Read over it and see what interests you in the writing.

When you feel ready, start a first draft of your definition personal essay. You might start with an anecdote that places you or someone you know in the role or situation you are defining. You might start with a dictionary definition to which you will add or with which you might disagree. You might plunge right into the classification and characteristics you have distinguished and want to discuss.

Michael Shurgot starts with a statement of how simple it used to be to be a baseball fan. I start with a narration of my action toward my husband. Elizabeth, as you'll read in her essay, starts with her physical reaction to statements about her adoption, which for her is the most distinguishing characteristic of being a daughter. Essayist Daniel Harris begins a definition essay titled "Cuteness," which appeared in *Salmagundi* in 1992 and in *The Best American Essays 1993* with description: "She stands in maroon bloomers and a pink dress that flares tantalizingly above two acrylic legs that descend, unvaried in diameter, all the way down to her gout-stricken ankles crammed in her booties."

Whether you make a statement, start a narration, or supply a vivid description, it is never long in a definition essay before distinguishing characteristics come to the fore. Trust yourself. Begin where it feels right and keep going until you feel you have come to an ending.

DEVELOPING THE DRAFT

As you probably picked up in many of Elizabeth's essays, her late twenties have been a time of finishing the business of separating from her family and their image of what she should be and what she should do in her adult life. She is fashioning a door through which to walk into her adult life. It is not a surprise, then, that Elizabeth would chose the role of daughter for her extended definition. As you read this essay, look for categories of characteristics. Look for strategies Elizabeth uses to create the categories of characteristics and to skip from one group of them to another. Notice how she uses narration several times to keep on telling her story about what a daughter is. Note your responses to the images she uses and to her method of stringing them together. Can you state the subtext in this draft? Why is Elizabeth defining the role of daughter?

HANGING OUT STARS — A DAUGHTER'S JOURNEY

To this day, I get goose bumps listening to my mother's account of my adoption twenty-nine years ago.

I was the easiest and fastest pregnancy she ever had. In fact, she didn't gain a pound. At thirty-nine, after giving birth to my brother, Bill, five years earlier, she found herself unable to conceive. As each visit to the fertility specialist had no result, she and my father began to discuss adoption with increasing frequency.

As my mother would have it, I was just "hanging out stars," waiting for the right loving family to come along and scoop me up. Imagine, me up there in the ethers, wand in hand, propelled by tiny wings, fluttering about directing star patterns. Until I was about six, I bought the story, wings and all. What a disappointment when I learned I was a womb baby just like everyone else.

The local adoption agency was very encouraging about the possibility for a placement—an administrative term for a baby. My parents filled out the necessary paperwork and endured endless interviews that they felt to be as thorough as an employment screening for the CIA.

About a month later, my parents were rewarded with a call from

Virginia Warren, who was my caseworker. My days of hanging out stars were about to come to an end. As Ms. Warren described my personal history, my mother savored each detail of information about how well I was doing on formula and what my nap schedules were. After all, this was her daughter they were talking about.

What did having a daughter mean to my mother? Could she feel the wave of pride that would wash over her as she introduced me to her friends as "her daughter"? Did she think about the heart-to-heart talks we would have over periods, acne, boys and sex? Did she have any sense of the hell I would put her through over my frustration with not having the "right" clothes to wear to school?

We met at Virginia's house on March 7, 1962. I wasn't quite three months old. I was dressed in a mint green outfit with tiny pink rosettes woven throughout the soft cotton fabric.

History tells it that I took to my father right away. He was dressed in his officer's uniform bedecked with sparkling brass buttons that invited me to touch. He held me for over an hour as my mother and Virginia discussed my diet of formula. What could he have been thinking as he held me to his breast? Did he have any sense of what daughters were all about?

What does it mean to be a daughter? What are those qualities parents identify with little girls? Do they think we're always soft, like our flannel jumpers? Just a little mischievous like not wanting to nap? If my parents thought they were taking home sugar and spice twenty-nine years ago, I am afraid that what they got was a little baking powder thrown in.

As far as sugar, I have been caring and sensitive. I have never forgotten a family birthday, anniversary or holiday. Graciously, I have worn outfits my mother has given me that I would rather have died than been seen in. I have endured many a field hockey game running up and down the field to the tempo of my father's voice yelling, "That a girl, Lizzie. Go for her shin." Pop and I have danced the box step every time the band struck up "Daddy's Little Girl" at a family wedding even though I was bursting with embarrassment.

In school, I have always gotten "outstanding" for my willingness to help others. Daughters are supposed to be helpful, especially around the house. I imagine in my life I have probably dusted the furniture, vacuumed the carpets and scoured the bathrooms thousands of times.

If being a daughter means playing the game of "I'd like to see you get involved," after seven years of ballet, two years of violin, four years of swim team and three years of girl scouts, I'd say I was acceptable on the chessboard of parental desire.

A daughter is thought to be obedient. For the most part, I did what I was told. I ate all my vegetables, said my prayers before bed and was home typically ten minutes before my curfew.

As I grew older, though, the properties of baking powder began to manifest in my behavior. When mixed with other ingredients and heated, baking powder begins to catalyze the foundation of a recipe, the flour, sugar and eggs. Baking powder liberates a recipe. The other ingredients can't grow without it. Growth involves challenging boundaries even if it means you might come out a tad misshapen. This powder made me sometimes burst beyond the boundaries. I began to challenge authority just to see what it was made of.

But a daughter is more. She is like a bridge. She stretches between the past and future and crosses the present. She reflects for her parents, like a mirror, the look of their expectations. She invites them to see that daughters are not people who only live for others' desires.

A daughter is not predictable. Just when parents think they have a sense of who she is, she alters her direction. A daughter is like a fresh plant cutting eager to root herself in the soil of new experiences and opportunities. A daughter is versatile and she knows how to survive. As I change, the image of survival I have of myself is one of hanging out stars.

THE THREE-STEP RESPONSE:
Step One: Velcro Words

This draft has words and phrases that appeal to my senses. I am willing to not only imagine Elizabeth believing her mother's story, I can see tiny Elizabeth angel-like in the ethers, then baby-like in her parents arms. The words and images that stick with me are: "goose bumps," "fast pregnancy," "hanging out stars," wand in hand, tiny wings, "bought the story," "placement," "special families," "periods, acne, boys and sex," "not having the 'right' clothes," "mint green outfit with tiny pink rosettes," her father's officer's uniform with shiny buttons, endured field hockey games, "That a girl, Lizzie. Go for her shin," danced the box step to "Daddy's Little Girl" at family weddings, "willingness to help others," getting involved, "obedient," "parental desire," "baking powder," "tad misshapen," "catalyze," beyond boundaries, "bridge," "mirror," "plant cutting," "practice."

Step Two: Feelings

I feel the agitation Elizabeth is feeling to move out of her cocoon. I feel her desire to show herself and her readers that underneath the obedient girl was a different person with her own tastes and desires. I feel the wish for a smooth break, one that will not leave a big rift despite the force it will require on Elizabeth's part.

Sentence by sentence, my feeling responses are these: I like starting with goose bumps. I feel Elizabeth's connection and distress over this topic. I enjoy the retelling of the family stories about her meeting her parents. I feel informed with the "hanging out stars" story about the people she is joining and their desire for her to be happy. I feel the poignancy of her collecting the details of her early meetings with her parents—what she wore, how she played. I feel the strangeness of having these details but not the others most of us have about our births. Elizabeth asks, "What does it mean to be a daughter?" and I feel the particular sensitivity she would have to this question. I feel her ambiguity about the idea of having been a chosen baby.

I was eager when I read the list of sugar characteristics because I knew there would be a contrast coming with the baking powder characteristics. When I hear the analogy between how baking powder works when heated and how the heat of adolescence caused Elizabeth to push her boundaries, I feel set up to see her do that the way I have seen her be sugar and spice. But I feel disappointed when she doesn't show images of herself in that stage of life. And I feel disappointed not to see her parents' reactions to that stage.

Next, I feel I am racing around from metaphor to metaphor— bridge, mirror, plant cutting—I want to linger with each. I want to have a way to move between the different landscapes they represent.

Step Three: Curiosity

I want to see how a daughter is like a bridge, mirror, plant cutting. I want to know what this daughter has survived and what she has transplanted. I want to know the unpredictable qualities in her, and I want to know the images and details of her adolescent period.

I want to know the circumstances from which Elizabeth learned she contained baking powder characteristics.

♦ ♦ ♦

Get the response you need to the draft you did. Then look ahead to Elizabeth's developed draft before you rework your draft.

THE SECOND DRAFT

HANGING OUT STARS — A DAUGHTER'S JOURNEY

To this day, I get goose bumps listening to my mother's account of my adoption twenty-nine years ago.

I was the easiest and fastest pregnancy she ever had. In fact, she didn't gain a pound. At thirty-nine, after giving birth to my brother, Bill, five years earlier, she found herself unable to conceive. As each visit to the fertility specialist had no result, she and my father began to discuss adoption with increasing frequency.

As my mother would have it, I was just "hanging out stars," waiting for the right loving family to come along and scoop me up. Imagine, me up there in the ethers, wand in hand, propelled by tiny wings, fluttering about directing star patterns. Until I was about six, I bought the story, wings and all. What a disappointment when I learned I was a womb baby just like everyone else.

The local adoption agency was very encouraging about the possibility for a placement—an administrative term for a baby. My parents filled out the necessary paperwork and endured endless interviews that they felt to be as thorough as an employment screening for the CIA.

About a month later, my parents were rewarded with a call from Virginia Warren, who was my caseworker. My days of hanging out stars were about to come to an end. As Ms. Warren described my personal history, my mother savored each detail of information about how well I was doing on formula and what my nap schedules were. After all, this was her daughter they were talking about.

What did having a daughter mean to my mother? Could she feel the wave of pride that would wash over her as she introduced me to her friends as "her daughter"? Did she think about the heart-to-heart talks we would have over periods, acne, boys and sex? Did she have any sense of the hell I would put her through over my frustration with not having the "right" clothes to wear to school?

We met at Virginia's house on March 7, 1962. I wasn't quite

three months old. I was dressed in a mint green outfit with tiny pink rosettes woven throughout the soft cotton fabric.

History tells it that I took to my father right away. He was dressed in his officer's uniform bedecked with sparkling brass buttons that invited me touch. He held me for over an hour as my mother and Virginia discussed my diet of formula. What could he have been thinking as he held me to his breast? Did he have any sense of what daughters were all about?

What does it mean to be a daughter? What are those qualities parents identify with little girls? Do they think we're always soft, like our flannel jumpers? Just a little mischievous in not wanting to nap? If my parents thought they were taking home sugar and spice twenty-nine years ago, I am afraid that what they got was a little baking powder thrown in.

As far as sugar, I have been caring and sensitive. I have never forgotten a family birthday, anniversary or holiday. Graciously, I have worn outfits my mother has given me that I would rather have died than been seen in. I have endured many a field hockey game running up and down the field to the tempo of my father's voice yelling,"That a girl, Lizzie. Go for her shin." Pop and I have danced the box step every time the band struck up "Daddy's Little Girl" at a family wedding even though I was bursting with embarrassment.

In school, I have always gotten "outstanding" for my willingness to help others. Daughters are supposed to be helpful, especially around the house. I imagine in my life I have probably dusted the furniture, vacuumed the carpets and scoured the bathrooms thousands of times.

If being a daughter means playing the game of "I'd like to see you get involved," after seven years of ballet, two years of violin, four years of swim team and three years of girl scouts, I'd say I was acceptable on the chessboard of parental desire.

A daughter is thought to be obedient. For the most part, I did what I was told. I ate all my vegetables, said my prayers before bed and was home typically ten minutes before my curfew.

Now as I grow older, the properties of baking powder have begun to manifest in my behavior. When mixed with other ingredients and heated, baking powder begins to catalyze the foundation of a recipe. Baking powder liberates a recipe. The other ingredients can't grow without it. Growth involves challenging boundaries even if it means you might come out a tad misshapen. My baking powder is my autonomy. I am fascinated with it as much as I am reluctant to heat up and see where my boundaries reach to.

I want to quit my job and travel in Europe. I want to leave behind the disappointment of not having the husband and three kids I imagined by thirty. Who knows, maybe I want to teach English in Prague, move to an organic farming community in Port Townsend, or take up photography instead of merely admiring my ex-lover's work.

A daughter is hardly predictable, however much her parents would wish that she were. My parents may have to revise their sense of who I am and what I am doing now that I am raising the temperature of my life, bubbling at high temperature, free of the old boundaries of pleasing them. When I was a teenager I saw a road I didn't really have the wherewithal to start down. "Why?" and "How come?" were not questions I could find my own answers to during those times that my parents "laid down the law."

Now I can go where I please as long as I can allow myself the freedom. I am grateful for the image of those tiny wings, that wand, the stars I'd been given to hang in the sky. It may look to my parents that I am flying away to the ethers, but I am confident that, ultimately, I am a bridge stretching from the past, over the present to the future. I am my parents' daughter. They found me once. They will find me again.

Notice how some of Elizabeth's metaphors have slipped away in the service of making the remaining one (the bridge) stronger. In considering my response about wanting to see the baking powder behavior, Elizabeth realized it was her behavior now, not her teenage behavior that had baking powder characteristics. Defining daughter as she has come to know the role in childhood and in her twenties, Elizabeth has evoked the journey of her essay's title—the journey back to the ability to hang out stars. And of course this brings with it the power to believe her parents will once again find her, but this time as the woman she wants to be.

Elizabeth has relied on the analogy form of comparison and contrast quite a bit to define what being a daughter has meant and does mean to her. Her strength is now like the fairy girl's who hangs out stars. Her personality has gone from having the expected characteristics of sugar and spice to having unexpected baking powder-like characteristics. Her narration of her adoption and her rhetorical questions to her parents show their expectations and desires for a daughter. We even get to see part of the process of how an adoption is made.

Elizabeth describes growing up as wearing outfits that her mother gave her which she didn't like and playing hockey to please her father. These descriptions offer a continuing sense of how a daughter, especially an adopted one, can believe she is here mostly to please her parents. It also draws a portrait of a daughter who has been loved, but who, of course, must still seek her own adulthood. So with the help of description, comparison and contrast, and how-to, this definition essay is a personal manifesto, a declaration of independence, a statement of faith both in herself and her parents.

KEEP DRAFTING

Michael Shurgot was put off by the modern fan; I realized in sending my husband a poem, I was getting to be what I had dreamed of being; Elizabeth saw there is more to being a daughter than her mother and father would let on and only she can live that part. When you write your developed drafts, you, too, will be searching out the reason you are writing your definition as you write it.

Your first-hand experience with a subject puts you in a better position than most to define it as it really is. If you have recently been in a hospital, you know what the role "patient" is like better than those who haven't been one. If you have just seen your last child off to college, you know what "an empty nest" is better than those who haven't yet experienced it. If you are a community activist or a welfare mother, a plumber or a survivor of Epstein-Barr Syndrome, you know more about these roles and situations than others do. Define them and learn the truth of your experience.

CHAPTER NINE

The Argument and Persuasion Essay

Writing to Change People's Minds

... reason works better when emotions are present. ...
— *Rollo May*, The Courage to Create

There are times in our lives when we desire to persuade others to take action or change their thinking. Letters to the editor and op-ed sections of newspapers and magazines contain writings from personal experience motivated in this way.

How does one write persuasively? How does one move others to read and stay interested in an argument and perhaps even to change their thinking and behavior? There is a recipe. It includes:

1. making an assertion
2. providing at least three supports
3. ordering that support toward a crescendo
4. giving time to the opposing position
5. using images and details to persuade the reader instead of relying on emotionally loaded words that tell, rather than show

It probably will not surprise you that the ingredients you'll use in the above recipe for an argument and persuasion style essay are any and all of the previous seven essay styles.

In the seventies, I was directing a day care center and raising babies of my own. I read the work of Edna La Shan, an early childhood specialist in Washington State. She said something about dealing with children that I remember when writing argument and persuasion essays. She said that people are most alike in their feelings and least alike in their thinking.

How often we tell children to calm down and behave without finding out what the feeling is that is causing them to fidget or to whine as if they already understood that controlled behavior is valuable sometimes. If we start first with identifying feelings (What is troubling you?), and we address those feelings (Yes, it must be uncomfortable to sit here when your feet don't reach the floor), then we can probably "fix" the situation (Here, I'll move over and why don't you put your legs up on the seat for a while?).

In essay writing, this truism about people translates into two ideas: First, in order to write effective argument and persuasion pieces, you must understand something of the feelings behind what is making your opponents behave as they do and you must express that understanding. Second, you must understand that revealing your own feelings will be most instrumental in making connection with your readers — although they may not think like you do, they do have the same repertoire of feelings. An adult understands discomfort even if the situations that make an adult uncomfortable are very different than the ones that make children uncomfortable.

In writing about the twenty-fifth anniversary of the Peace Corps, Alan Guskin, President of Antioch University, said in the Fall 1991 issue of *The Antiochian*, "Growing up in the U.S. makes one predisposed to cultural arrogance, a sense that our culture is not only different but better than others, a belief that everyone else should speak English but that it is not necessary for us to speak their languages." This very predisposition is so internalized, that even inside our country, inside our own families, we are unaware of how this "cultural snobbism" plays a role in blocking effective communication. It diminishes our ability to consider other points of view and their validity and historical roots. We might not even recognize there is room for these differences. In addition, often we don't consider whether our point of view is our own, obtained through our own experience, or whether it is merely an untested, unverified, soaked-in-by-osmosis piece of cultural snobbism.

The points of view you can most authentically persuade others to hold are points of view that come directly from your experience. If you have lived something, you are an authority. But you must examine your experience closely to find out what you have really come to believe. The argument and persuasion essay style provides a strategy for accomplishing this. First you come to see your beliefs, and then you can open the door for another to go your way if they are willing.

Examining your experience according to the argument and persuasion essay style, you get to learn not only your own point of view, but how you formed it. However, if you begin by believing unquestion-ingly that everyone (including yourself) should think like you do and value what you value, you will short-circuit your own ability to find out what it is you really believe and what it is you truly value. In working the steps and exercises I am about to describe, you will have the opportunity to learn about your own thinking and how you formed it. You will get to see if it still fits you.

The "write" question for this style essay is, "In what area do I have experience that can inform others and change their thinking or actions?" If you have a writing area in mind, you can insert it into the "write" question, "In what area of (to use our trusty examples) divorcing, parenting, visiting, fighting wars, or coping with illness do I have experience that can inform others and change their thinking or actions?" After the sample essays, I will share a way of finding more areas in your experience than you might think of at first.

EXAMPLE: ARGUMENT AND PERSUASION ESSAY

Kim Morrow used her practicum experience in dental hygiene to con-vince others to change their behavior and thinking about their teeth. As you read her essay, pay attention to what is most effective in swaying your opinion. Pay attention, too, to which of the previous seven essay styles the author employs. Do you see the strength of the description, narration, comparison and contrast, how-to and cause and effect styles in making the argument?

DENTURES: YES OR NO

Give me a dollar for every time I have heard a patient say, "Just pull my teeth and give me dentures!" and I would be wealthy. But if people only knew the effects dentures would have on their lives, they wouldn't even joke.

Run your tongue along the gums under your lower front teeth. That bone you are feeling is called the mandibular ridge. Now imagine it gone. You need to understand that your jaw bone is there to hold your teeth in place. Take away the teeth and the bone will slowly begin to reabsorb at a rate of approximately a half a millime-ter a year. I'm sure everyone has seen a little old man or woman whose chin and nose look like they are almost touching. Believe me, they did not look like that before they had their teeth pulled. That is the result of the years without teeth and loss of the bone.

Next take a bite of food. Now, gracefully so no one will notice, divide that bite in half and place half of the bite on the right side of your mouth and half on the left. Now chew. Get used to eating that way, for with a denture, chewing has gone from an unconscious act to a task you must learn. When you first get your denture you will probably have enough bone to hold it in, but you will lose bone in those first few months. In twenty years, your lower ridge (the bone you feel right in front of your tongue) will probably be flat. Then you will have to learn to balance your denture to keep it in one spot. Placing equal amounts of food on both sides of your mouth while you chew helps you do this.

Now I would like you to become aware of your tongue. When it's resting, is it touching the roof of your mouth? How about when you eat? With your tongue against the roof of your mouth, I would like you to imagine PLASTIC. This plastic on the roof of your mouth will not only affect speech, but also your sense of taste. Although most people with a denture do learn to talk just fine, and most people listening to them don't notice any change in their speech, the majority of people receiving dentures do comment on the fact that their speech is altered. Down the road after your bone on the top has started to reabsorb, you will need to increase the length of the pink plastic that represents your gums. This is so that when you smile you will see teeth. The added plastic adds weight to your denture, however. The added weight can make the front teeth drop when the wearer of the denture coughs, sneezes, or eats.

Scientific studies have shown that because of problems with chewing, the digestion of denture wearers is affected. Premature loss of your teeth can shorten your life span by five years.

One remote problem, but one definitely worth mentioning, is the possibility of allergic reaction. If you have ever had an itchy or burning allergic reaction, imagine having it in your mouth — forever. I have only run into one woman who was allergic to her denture, but she has been trying for twenty years to find a way to relieve her pain.

Lastly, no matter what Aunt Martha says about how she can eat anything she wants, you will not easily be able to eat all foods. Lettuce can be hard to tear, apples hard to bite into, and sticky things just plain hard. These people who believe Aunt Martha's denture tales must ask themselves this: If dentures fit so well and nobody has trouble keeping them in, how do all the denture adhesive companies stay in business?

Now that you have most of the information on the effects dentures can have on your health, you can make a more educated choice.

Thinking About How This Essay Works

Clearly, Kim is trained about the difficulties and health risks of dentures. She uses that knowledge to describe for us (via description and narration) scenarios we would find very unpleasant, unpleasant enough to force us to take care of our teeth and get proper dental attention rather than just thinking we can replace our teeth when they fall out. Her experience with denture wearers contrasts with the ideas of people who request them as an easy solution to bad teeth. She shows the contrast to us via a short how-to: Run your tongue along the gums, take a bite of food, become aware of your tongue. Following these steps, we do become aware of how our mouths are constructed and of the relationship between our teeth and the rest of our face. Finally, we are shown a few of the effects of wearing dentures. Kim exits her essay with an assertion that summarizes our need to make a more educated choice about our future: Take care of your teeth; they are not as replaceable as you think!

Now that you've looked at how she uses different essay forms to make her argument vivid, look at how she starts her essay. She says she'd be wealthy if she had a dollar for each time she's heard someone say, "Just give me false teeth." Her next sentence starts with a "but," and she compares this bad joke with the ones we may play on ourselves if we don't heed her advice.

SECOND EXAMPLE: ARGUMENT AND PERSUASION ESSAY

In another argument essay, Teresa Knowles wishes to persuade children of alcoholics to speak up and look for help. Notice that she begins with a narration of events in her own childhood. Notice, also, that after narrating events and giving descriptive examples of her father's behavior, Teresa opens a paragraph with the sentence, "We learned many things," introducing the cause and effect style. This style helps Teresa travel from past to present. Next, pay attention to how Teresa employs the definition style to show her reader the grown child of an alcoholic. What are the characteristics inherent in this person? Lastly, look for the how-to style which Teresa employs at the essay's end to motivate her targeted audience to take action.

REVEALING THE SECRET

That morning my brothers and I went out the door to catch the school bus just as we did every other weekday morning. Fortunately, our school bus was a small van and there were only five or six other kids on it, because on that particular morning there was a red Ford pickup truck in the ditch across from our house. Slumped over the wheel of the truck, bleeding from a cut on the head, was our dad. The bus driver made some comment about him only having a few feet further to go before he'd have reached the house. The other kids laughed; so did my brother and I. I don't know if they knew why we were so unconcerned over a seemingly serious accident. I do remember that my brother and I did not look at each other, or exchange a single word that morning. I also remember the fleeting thought that passed through my mind—I hoped he was dead. What my brother and I both knew, but did not say, was that Dad was drunk. As usual.

That drunken incident was just one more in a long succession of many. It evoked no more, or no less, of a reaction from us than any other episode. It was simply one more.

I have many memories, when I care to recall them, of events that occurred in my home, that I, until recently, believed to be normal occurrences in a normal family situation. One night our whole household was in an uproar; Daddy came home and decided to set the house on fire while we slept in our beds. Mom said he got tired of her involvement with the Girl Scouts because it kept her away from home too much "running the roads." We accepted that explanation and felt thankful that he'd made so much noise strewing papers around the basement and swearing when he couldn't get the match to light. I have forgotten the number of nights my younger brothers and I sat at the top of the stairs and listened to the violent arguing going on below us. I can see us sitting there, each of us crying silently, not touching or speaking, taking in the accusations, the name-calling, the excuses. When it all started to wind down, we would get up and silently make our way back to bed. Many nights Mom would get us up and, still in our pajamas, we would file into the car, where we would wait while she made the endless round of bars, searching for him, pleading or bullying him to come home when she found him.

Our entire home centered around my father. Many meals were eaten late and cold after Mom finally admitted that he wasn't going to make it. Family excursions were cancelled on a moment's notice. We spent our evenings holding our breath, each silently wondering the same things. Would he come home? Would he be drunk or sober? Ugly drunk or friendly drunk? Who would he single out to harass tonight?

We learned many things. To tiptoe around when he was there, because we did not want to arouse his anger or even his attention. Not to count on him for anything. That we would seldom receive Mom's complete attention; she was always preoccupied with Dad, keeping him from drinking if he hadn't started yet and stopping him if he had. To live with inconsistency and broken promises. To scream and yell when we were angry, which was most of the time. To count on no one but yourself. We learned never to discuss the real reason for the problems in our home, and above all, never ever to tell anyone about them. They were a family secret.

The lessons I learned as a child are still with me today.

It is extremely difficult, impossible at times, for me to express my true feelings. When I was sixteen, I came home from work one night and was informed by my parents that they were moving to another state a great distance away. I was not invited to join them. Rather, I was told to find a friend's family to live with while I finished high school. The next couple of weeks they spent selling all the furniture and household items I'd grown up with. I spent as little time as possible at home during their preparations prior to leaving. When the moment came to say goodbye, I couldn't cry. I couldn't even say, "Goodbye." I said, "See ya," and went out for breakfast. I told all my friends how much fun I would have—wasn't I lucky to not have my parents around? In the next four months I lost twenty pounds I couldn't afford to lose. I stopped menstruating. I was sick for the better part of the next year; strep throats, lots of infections, internal bleeding. The anger, betrayal, and loneliness I was feeling were literally eating away at me. Yet I told no one that I missed my parents. I acted as though everything was just grand.

I need to be in absolute control of my life, but am always fighting the pervasive sense of losing control and being totally overwhelmed. I create consistency in my life with small, daily routines which I stick to religiously. I have fussy, little habits (my clothes must hang facing right; the opening of my pillowcase must be to the outside of the bed) that give me a sense of control over my life when I am anxious. Recently, my very best friend, with her husband and children, stopped by to visit me for an afternoon on their way from New York to Alaska. I had not seen them for six months; their second child was six weeks old. Their visit, rather than filling me with joy and happiness, caused me to become uptight and nervous. Although I eventually did, I was unwilling to vary my routine to spend time with them. I had a severe headache during their entire visit. I could not relax and simply enjoy being with them again. It took me three days after their departure to calm down and regain my equilibrium. The disturbance of my ordered life threw me into a tailspin.

Many times the thought has crossed my mind that I may be a very shallow person incapable of feeling deep, true feelings. Not long ago, I shared with a close friend a memory of an incident in my childhood. It was not a pretty story, yet, he noted, I recalled it in a voice devoid of emotion. When I finished, he asked me how I felt about what had happened. After thinking about it for a moment I replied that I really didn't feel anything, good or bad. It felt to me like telling a story about a girl I once knew but didn't have any particular feelings for. My friend asked if that was a normal response to such a terrible situation. I could not answer him. What would the normal response be? My response was the only one I knew. My true reaction, my true emotional response to that situation is buried deep inside me. It is easier, and safer, not to face it.

I now realize that if I had revealed the secret and sought professional help, my mental and emotional health could be better today. Discussing my situation with a professional trained in dealing with the special problems of a child of an alcoholic would have allowed me to realize that my family situation was not the "normal" family situation. I would have been reassured that the fear and anger I felt were well-founded. Today I would know how to express my true feelings; I wouldn't have this hard knot in my stomach day after day. I would realize that I no longer have to keep such a tight rein on the circumstances of my life for fear of losing control. I would not have guilt and fear pervading my every action, my every thought, every day. I would know how to relax, how to enjoy, and how to like myself and others. I would be a happier and healthier person.

Speaking with a professional, first and foremost, gives the opportunity to discuss the situation. Thus begins the healing, a halt in the denial process. You must recognize that you have the right to discuss the real issues and the right to feel.

I know how difficult it is to break the unwritten law of silence. I know about the feelings of guilt and betrayal. I know that it is easier to keep to yourself, to pretend that you don't feel anything, that everything is just fine. But those feelings, although they seem to be buried deep within you, affect every aspect of your life. If you don't seek help, the only person you are betraying is yourself. You will rob yourself of the basic right that every individual has. Seeing a professional does not mean that you are crazy or sick or unable to help yourself. It does mean that you realize that you are not living in an atmosphere conducive to good mental health and that you care enough about yourself to discover what it is you are missing as a result.

Begin the healing process slowly. First recognize that there is a problem. There are several books available written by professionals in the field of recovery for the children of alcoholics and co-dependents. *It Will Never Happen to Me* by Claudia Black and *Children of Alcoholism, A Survivor's Manual,* by Judith S. Seixas and Geraldine Youcha are good ones. These books contain questionnaires that will help you to identify whether or not you are the child of an alcoholic and, if so, how your mental health has suffered as a result.

Once you have admitted to yourself that, yes, you are the child of an alcoholic and are suffering the effects of that relationship, the next step will be to seek outside help. You will ask yourself, "Where do I find such help? Can I afford it?" Al-Anon has groups available specifically for children, as well as adult children, of alcoholics, and they are free of charge and do not document a person's involvement. The individuals in these groups all share the same problem. They meet to help themselves and each other. Other options available are special councils or centers, such as the National Council on Alcoholism (NCA), which can be found listed in the Yellow Pages. Councils and Information and Referral (I&R) Centers can also provide assistance in finding a resource available in your area. Private therapists who specialize in this field most likely can be found in the Yellow Pages.

I don't know which is harder to do—admit to yourself that there is a problem or admit it to someone else. I do know that these were the two biggest obstacles I ever had to face. It took all my courage to reveal what I had kept hidden for so long. And it isn't getting easier. But the knowledge that I am helping, really helping, myself and that when I get through this I will be the person I always wanted to be gives me the strength to keep going.

Every child of an alcoholic parent possesses strength; it is being used to suppress emotions, to create order in a disordered life, and to perpetuate the myth that life is just fine. Draw upon that strength, that courage deep within yourself. Tell the secret—seek professional help.

Thinking About How This Essay Works

Teresa's childhood story convinces us of the severe effects an alcoholic parent has on a child. Her short how-to on healing the damage is invaluable for someone in her situation. Experience has informed Teresa about her topic, and passion born of the hurt she endured has led her to make the following assertion: Keeping the family secret about an alcoholic parent damages a child's emotional and mental health; therefore, children of alcoholics must gather the courage to seek professional help and direct their energy toward their own betterment.

In writing this, she is moving upstream against an opposing current of denial in her targeted audience: Children of alcoholics may put off receiving help because of their own denial that anything is wrong and the difficulty of overriding years of keeping the family secret. The courage the author displays, though, in describing her home situation and her scars is in itself persuasive.

If I were to meet a person who revealed she had kept the family secret of alcoholism for years, I would find the right time to share Teresa's essay with her.

A SHORT SERMON TO GIVE YOU CONFIDENCE

In an essay entitled, "The Distance Between a Hero and a Human Being" columnist Ellen Goodman argues that we in the United States need a new understanding of what a hero is. When she wrote her essay, papers had just been published verifying Martin Luther King's extramarital affairs and graduate school plagiarism. She wished for Martin Luther King still to be admired for his leadership despite the recent publication. In her argument essay, she quotes Clayborn

Carson, the head of the King-paper project, "I don't think it's healthy in a democracy to believe that there are some people who were born great and not without human flaws and limitations." She quotes King himself in a sermon, "I want you to know this morning that I am a sinner like all of God's children, but I want to be a good man, and I want to hear a voice saying to me one day, 'I take you in and I bless you because you tried.' " Herein lies Goodman's assertion: It is valuable for Americans to use this new information about King's adultery and plagiarism not just for a revisionist view of King, but for a revisionist definition of what constitutes a hero. We must change, she says, from thinking heroes are saint-like versions of people, versions we create and can never ourselves match. We must begin to see heroes are human beings, flaws and all, who serve humanity by finding the greatness within themselves when the times demand it.

We can find the greatness inside ourselves when we are called to. That call sometimes comes in the form of a deep desire to write what we have witnessed or lived through in order to persuade others in our own small way to take steps or adopt thinking that will lead toward their own better health and the better health of our larger humanity.

EXERCISES FOR DEVELOPING YOUR MATERIAL

Your experience has informed you. It has taught you to do something differently than you had done it in the past or than other people do it. It has taught you to think differently than you used to or than others think. Here is a procedure to help you get at that material and answer the "write" question.

Conducting a Survey

Divide a sheet of paper into three columns. One column should be labeled "personal" experience, one "social" experience and the last, "educational/vocational" experience. Jot down any and all experiences that come to you under these headings.

Elizabeth's three columns looked like this:

PERSONAL	EDUCATIONAL/ VOCATIONAL	SOCIAL
Dating	Going to college	Being part of the
Being single	Trying grad school	local arts
Family Council	Learning dance	community

Only daughter/ adopted	Social work	Growing up middle class
Being in debt	Writing Courses	Being part of a neighborhood
Youngest child		Fundraising
Breaking up		Event Planning
Renting apartments		Festival Production
Being a friend		Waitressing
Deciding on college		Recuiting and Training
Deciding career		Personnel
Being childless		Hotel Management
Living miles from family		
Losing friends		
Making new friends		
Dabbling with Tarot		

Elizabeth put some experiences I would have thought of as educational in her column headed "social" experiences. Her personal experience of them must have been more social than vocational. That is fine. It is not so much that you place the experiences in the right columns, but that you find a way to list and come up with the extraordinary number of experiences you have had.

After you make your lists in columns, ask yourself which items in the columns generate some passion for you right now.

Here are the passion items Elizabeth identified:

PASSION ITEMS:
Being single
Being adopted
Losing friends/making new ones
Being childless
Being well versed in several professional areas

Making Assertions

After you have picked out your passion items, you can make assertions concerning them. My passion area is raising children after a divorce. I assert, "A divorce can be the opportunity for parents to enrich their children's emotional development." As soon as I write this assertion, I hear a chorus of voices disagreeing or getting upset or saying, "How can you say that?"

"Good!" I say to myself and the chorus of voices. I have something to convince you of! I know what my work is.

According to my assertion, I have to show you how divorce can offer the divorced parents an opportunity to raise emotionally enriched children.

Using Assertions as Blueprints for the Essay

Unlike in the other essay styles, in argument and persuasion essays you know ahead of time what insight you will reach. Assertions are *required* in writing argument and persuasion essays and they help you write them; they are your blueprints.

According to my blueprints, I can support my assertion by using several styles of essay writing. I'll narrate anecdotes from the lives of my own children. I'll distinguish the characteristics necessary for good emotional development and show how they are present in the divorce situation. I'll contrast my family when I was a single mother with the two-parent household we had to show the opportunity for the children's emotional growth.

Stay Out of the Fog

Assertions are always *statements*, never incomplete sentences, never a question. I could not write a strong argument if I said to myself merely the phrase, "Raising children when you divorce." I could not write a strong argument if I merely asked, "Can a divorce be the opportunity for raising emotionally enriched children?" My *answer* to that question is yes, but the word "yes" is not a blueprint—it doesn't tell me that I must show cause and effect, that I must define emotional enrichment. The answer to that question in full sentence form is an assertion. I need my assertion to keep me focused on what I am going to say to support it and on what order best helps me support it. The assertion is not only a blueprint, it is a lighthouse guiding you away from the rocks of illogic and incoherence.

Here are the assertions Elizabeth wrote from her passion items:

1. Being single can cause one to be insensitive and impatient with the routines and schedules of friends who are part of a couple and/or have families.

2. Being single affords one a freedom that sometimes isn't appreciated until compared with the time constraints of friends who are juggling time with partners and families.
3. Being single is just as much of a challenge as being married.
4. It is important for people who are adopted not to be ashamed of their background and to share their experience with others.
5. An adopted child's search to uncover her history is an opportunity for deep self-discovery.
6. Dating can teach you as much about what you like in a partner as it can about what you don't.
7. Dating is more of a challenge the older you get as people tend to be more settled in their own routines and less willing to be flexible.

Notice that assertion number four has the word "important" in it. This judgement word tells how Elizabeth feels about revealing she is adopted but not what the value of doing so is. The assertion is too general for use as a blueprint in building her argument essay. Why is it important for people who are adopted not to be ashamed of their background and to share their experience with others? The answer to that question, in statement form, is an assertion that a writer can use to shape an argument essay. Here is the assertion I think underlies the word "important": Revealing to others your history of adoption and as much as you know about your background helps build self-esteem because it keeps you from hiding, denying and feeling that you have a secret self.

From an assertion like this one, Elizabeth could show the effects on her self-esteem of not revealing her history and of revealing it. She could describe how self-esteem is built and how it is eroded. She could persuade me that there is a link between revealing her history and building her self-esteem.

Now write the assertions you can think of concerning your passion items. Select the assertion that most interests you. There are two more exercises ahead before you start writing.

Supporting the Assertion

What can you use to support your assertion? Here is a list:

1. The testimony of experts, authorities and other people who should know
2. Statistics

3. Comparisons that show essential nature (an essay I read once compared all of us on the planet using up its resources to airplane mechanics popping rivets off a plane and saying it doesn't matter there are plenty more)
4. History of how something happened
5. Effects of something that happened
6. Solutions to correct something
7. Statement of the opposition's argument (the chorus of voices I spoke about earlier) and way of thinking before countering that point of view

By reporting the opposing point of view you show your astuteness, your respect for differences of opinion. Your willingness to see differences invites your readers to look at your opinions and experience without being defensive. Displaying the opposition's point of view credits you; it shows you have looked deeply into your situation.

Make a list now of all the evidence and supports you can think of that further your assertion. Start by writing your assertion across the top of a blank page. Then list the supports and evidences you can think of or know you can find out about.

Sometimes you make an assertion you really feel you believe in, but when it comes to supporting it, you find you have more support for the opposite side. Well, switch sides then!

Organizing the Argument and Persuasion Essay

Now that you have written your assertion and thought of supports for it, you must decide in which order you will present the supports to build a powerful argument. Put your strongest support first; next squeeze in the weakest. Put your third strongest next and then the second strongest. You want to get the reader's attention and keep it. You don't want your argument to wind down or fizzle out.

Here is Elizabeth's list of supports in the order she decided would be strongest:

ASSERTION, REASONS AND EVIDENCE

Assertion: An adopted child's search for her natural parents is an opportunity for self-discovery.

Reasons why this is an opportunity for self-discovery:
1. Adopted children are born with secrets; any journey to unveil them is an opportunity for self-discovery.

2. The rewards of this journey are not always so great; there is pain. However, what you discover if you are willing to risk the pain is how to stand up for yourself in this world and how the natural parents' decision may have benefitted you.
3. Many people say looking for and finding natural parents shows an adoptee's ungratefulness to her adoptive parents, but the help of the adoptive parents in the search can add to the adoptee's gratefulness.
4. The search for information presents the adoptee with choices to pursue and in making the choices the adoptee discovers her own thinking.

WRITING YOUR ESSAY

In "Dentures: Yes or No," Kim Morrow starts with a statement she hears a lot from people that couldn't be further from what she knows to be the truth. Teresa Knowles starts "Revealing the Secret" with a story of one of her father's drunken episodes as seen from her eyes as a child. This narration draws us to her as a speaker and ultimately to her subject. We want to hear what she has to tell us. How will you begin your argument? If you can't think of a snappy start at first, write your assertion and go from there. Next, flow from one support to the next until you come to a just conclusion.

DEVELOPING THE DRAFT

Put your essay aside while you read Elizabeth's first draft. As you read the draft think about whether the information supports her earlier assertion.

UNTITLED

The first time I ever was confronted with revealing my adoption to a stranger I was left with the most hollow feeling. I had been suffering with a typical case of teen acne and after I complained endlessly, my mother took me to see her dermatologist. Mother and I sat across from one another in the doctor's office while he leaned against the wall, the same one that displayed his credentials, asking questions about my medical background. At first, he asked me about my history of allergies or any particular rashes I encountered from medications. Soon he began to inquire about my parents' medical history and as I tensed up I could sense my mother's concerned eyes move towards me. I met them with a look of help-lessness. Waiting for my response, he peered over the top of his glasses as I summoned the courage to explain that I didn't know the answers. As I uttered my reason, "I'm adopted," he looked back down at the white pad where he had been recording my answers and drew a line with his pen, which sounded very long to me, through the remainder of the questions. I felt as blank as the sheet that now lay before him.

Years ago, when I was first told of my adoption, my mother presented me with a thin green fabric book called "The Chosen Baby." As we sat together in my bedroom, mother cradled me in one arm and the book in the other as she told me the story of a mother and father who couldn't have any more children and how they went about finding a baby to love. After mother finished read-ing, she explained with great care that my adoption was a very special experience. I can still remember how excited I was by the word "special." Her words indicated that there was something slightly different and unique about me. I had a secret perhaps, that not many others shared.

Well, adopted children are born with secrets. They exist in every aspect of our lives. Unlike biological children, we have no mirrors to look at in our parents or relatives to determine the origin of our freckles, our eye color or our height. When my mother suffered from two bouts of cancer she confided in me that this was the only time in her life she was ever thankful that I wasn't biologically related as the disease had taken her mother and two cousins. What unforeseen condition could be lurking in my future as a result of not knowing my medical history as my adoption files lay in the stomach of a vault in a county building in North Carolina, their contents sealed by a wax emblem?

In the past I always dreaded the question of my nationality. Sometimes I would make up an exotic medley like Polish, Russian and Swedish hoping my blonde hair and fair skin would pull off my impersonation. I have gotten tired of the charade.

The process of self-discovery is a hunger to gain knowledge of oneself through observation or in my case through a search. My exploration has been fed by a passionate desire for insight into my very being. When adopted children search for their natural parents, they are engaging in a deep opportunity for self-discovery.

There are those outsiders who discredit an adoptee's curiosity and need to search as nothing more than signs of ungratefulness towards the parents who have loved and raised them. In my case, it has been my parent's love and support that has encouraged me to strike out and ask questions about where I really came from.

An adoptee's journey can be initiated in many ways. I started with numerous conversations with my mother, many of which took place at night after my father had gone to bed or was walking the dog.

That isn't to say that my journey hasn't been filled with that sharp pain of rejection when my letters to the state's judicial office have gone unanswered.

Elizabeth stopped here, as she had done in the how-to essay, knowing she wasn't finished and unable to help herself continue. Let's run through the three-step response method and see how Velcro words, feelings and reader curiosity helped her to continue.

THE THREE-STEP RESPONSE
Step One: Velcro Words

I am struck by the doctor's pen drawing a line through Elizabeth's medical history form, the story "The Chosen Baby" and the child Elizabeth liking the feeling of having a secret. I am struck by the idea that adopted children have secrets in their lives, from explanations about why they look as they do to what medical problems lurk in their genetics. I am struck by Elizabeth's dread of telling her nationality and by her made-up story of being Polish, Swedish and Russian. I am struck with the words, "I have gotten tired of the charade."

Other phrases that stick are: "Insight into my very being," "parents' love and support encouraged me," "my father had gone to bed or was walking the dog," "rejection when my letters to the state's judicial office have gone unanswered."

Step Two: Feelings

Overall, I hear passion and need. Elizabeth has a hunger to know who she is, and part of knowing that is knowing where she came from. To me, this passion and need to know are stirring.

Here are my feeling responses sentence by sentence: I feel lured into the drama of the first time Elizabeth had to tell she was adopted, a secret it seems she kept into her adolescence. I feel the chill in the room that she felt as the doctor looked back down to his paper and drew a line on it.

I feel the warmth in the next paragraph of her mother doing her best to help Elizabeth with the truth. I feel the little girl Elizabeth's excitement about having a secret.

Then I feel the shift from excitement to feeling burdened with the words, "adopted children are born with secrets. They exist in every aspect of their lives." I feel informed about her lack of knowledge about herself. Then with the talk about ethnic background I feel the immediacy with which these secrets lie in her.

Then I feel jarred. I go from being inside Elizabeth to a dictum: "The process of self-discovery is a hunger to gain knowledge of oneself through observation or, in my case, through a search." Here, I miss Elizabeth and her feelings. I do feel more comfortable, though, with her assertion, "When adopted children search for their natural parents, they are engaging in a deep opportunity for self-discovery," because I know she wants to discover more about herself and this belief buoys her up.

I appreciate her statement about the opposing view, that some people think adoptees who search for natural parents are ungrateful. I know some people, and even some adoptees, do think this way. When she says that in her case her parents' love and support encouraged her, I am interested. When she begins to explain her journey, I get a little put off. "An adoptee's journey can be initiated in many ways," doesn't inform me of the ways. Starting with "numerous" conversations doesn't sound loving and encouraging to me; it sounds long and drawn out and hard. The father going out or to bed when the mother and daughter talked conflicts with the idea of both parents encouraging Elizabeth.

Just because she had good conversations with her mother doesn't mean, she says, that she hasn't felt pain when her letters to the state's judicial office go unanswered. I feel the wires crossing in my brain— why would one cancel out the other?

And so we are on to the next of the three steps in response.

Step Three: Curiosity

I think the reason Elizabeth is having difficulty continuing in her essay is captured in the phrase, "That isn't to say." From whom is she defending herself? Why would we think that just because she is capable of getting information and support from her mother that the dead ends of the legal system wouldn't be hard to bear?

I would like more details about her search. How is the father supportive if the talks take place when he is not there? What has her mother told her? What do you write to the state judiciary office and why? Who else does she talk to on her search? How long has it been? What has she found out? What does she know about herself now that deepens her sense of self?

Now get the response you need to your first draft and go on to read Elizabeth's developed draft.

THE SECOND DRAFT

FOR ME

The first time I ever was confronted with revealing my adoption to a stranger, I was left with the most hollow feeling. I had been suffering with a typical case of teen acne and after I had complained endlessly, my mother took me to see her dermatologist. Mother and I sat across from one another in the doctor's office while he leaned against the wall, the same one that displayed his credentials, asking questions about my medical background. At first he asked me about my history of allergies and rashes from medications. Soon he began to inquire about my parents' medical history, and as I tensed up, I could feel my mother's eyes move toward me. I met her eyes with a look of helplessness. Waiting for my response, the doctor peered over the top of his glasses. I summoned the courage to explain that I didn't know the answers. As I uttered my reason, "I'm adopted," he looked back down at the white pad where he had been recording my answers and drew a line with his pen, which made a very long sound, through the remainder of the questions.

Years ago, when I was first told of my adoption, my mother presented me with a thin green fabric book called "The Chosen Baby." As we sat together in my bedroom, mother cradled me in one arm and the book in the other as she told me the story of a mother and father who couldn't have any more children and how they went about finding a baby to love. After Mother finished reading, she explained with great care that my adoption was a very special experience. I can still remember how excited I was by the world "special." Her words indicated that there was something slightly different and unique about me. I had a secret that not many others shared.

Well, I have found that the secret affects my life at its very foundation. Unlike biological children, adoptees have no mirrors to look at in our parents or relatives to determine the origin of our freckles, our eye color or our height. When my mother suffered from two bouts of cancer, she confided in me that this was the only time in her life she was ever thankful that I wasn't biologically related as the disease had taken her mother and two cousins. What unforeseen condition could be lurking in my future as a result of not knowing my medical history as my adoption files lay in the stomach of a vault in a county building in North Carolina, their contents sealed by a wax emblem?

In the past, I always dreaded the question of my nationality. Sometimes I would make up an exotic medley like Polish, Russian, and Swedish hoping my blonde hair and fair skin would convince everyone. I have grown tired of the charade.

In August of 1990, I began to look for my biological parents, and although I have yet to locate them, this search has provided me with a deep opportunity for self-discovery. There are those outsiders who discredit an adoptee's curiosity and need to search as nothing more than signs of ungratefulness towards the parents who have loved and raised them. In my case, it has been my parents' love and support that has encouraged me to strike out and ask questions about where I really did come from.

My research has included everything from detailed conversations with my parents to written requests petitioning the county where I was adopted for my records. Although I have had to struggle against a backdrop of frustration caused by obstacles in trying to access information about myself, the rewards in terms of insight gained about myself are immeasurable.

My search has involved asking a great many questions. I began questioning my mother, who, knowing how very much my history means to me, has always shared any detail she can recall. When I think about her unselfishness, I think also about the young woman who became pregnant in 1960 at age eighteen, and determined to finish college and have a career, still carried me to term and a life with a family who desperately wanted a baby. I think of both women and recognize with great joy the probable origins of my commitment towards family and friends.

I have been successful in unveiling some secrets like the physical description of my parents as listed in the prenatal records. I will never forget the sensation that filled me when I read about their fair skin, strawberry blonde hair and blue eyes.

I have made numerous telephone calls to lawyers in North Carolina trying to locate some assistance on how best to approach the bureaucracy to access my adoption files. Each inquiry rarely gets beyond the secretary who informs me in her polite southern drawl that it is impossible to open my records. Left feeling deflated and always next to tears, I am, however, finding other ways and I have begun to work even harder.

I realize now how in the past I would allow others to take advantage of me. I used to let others at work take credit for my efforts. When I worked at a hotel and had original ideas about how things could be done differently, I didn't have the confidence to think that the manager would listen to me. After all, I would rationalize, he must like things the way they are. But I would share my ideas with co-workers, who then went to the manager and got credit for them. In my search for my natural parents, my motivation to find them has made me overcome hesitancy about asserting myself.

One of the most fulfilling aspects of my journey has been sharing experiences with other adoptees. Hearing common stories of insecurity and fear of not living up to expectations, I have examined my own deep sense of not belonging, of profound feelings of separation, despite my adoptive parents' love and strong desire to raise me. Sometimes I feel guilty to have such feelings in the face of all their acceptance, but knowing I share this emotional situation with other adoptees allows me to feel more accepting of this part of myself.

Just as I have had to accept the duality of feeling lonely despite the complete acceptance of my parents, so I have discovered another duality. It is not the answer to my question, "where did I come from?" that provides me with the sense of myself. It is the process I have engaged to answer that question. I started my search out of a deep sense of insecurity, and I have found that it isn't necessarily finding an answer that makes everything OK, but what is gleaned from the process. If someday I should find and meet my natural parents, it won't be for them to make me whole. It will be for me to show them the gift of who I am.

Do the three-step response process again on this developed draft if you'd like, then go on to writing your own revision.

KEEP DRAFTING

Think about the response you received to your draft. Go back to developing your argument essay and get more response until you feel like you have created a fully persuasive piece of writing. Leave this piece alone for many days. Come back to it. Are you still persuaded? Is this what you believe? Can you see the importance of what you have lived now that you have written it in this style?

CHAPTER TEN

Continuing the Journey You Have Begun

A writer is not so much someone who has something to say as he is someone who has found a process that will bring about new things he would not have thought of if he had not started to say them.
— *William Stafford, "A Way of Writing"*

Now you've learned and practiced all eight essay styles. Using the "write" questions and the essay styles paired with them, you've probably surprised yourself by writing about experiences you didn't previously think were worth writing about. You were probably also surprised to find out why these experiences turned out to be important. If you explored experiences you already knew you wanted to write about, you were probably struck by what you had learned, deep inside, from those experiences. You were probably struck by how both seemingly insignificant memories and events and undeniably overwhelming ones are important to writing.

To continue writing essays, you can start from the beginning of this book again and use the same questions to conjure material on different subjects, or you can choose chapters randomly and create additional essays from personal experience. You have a built-in guide when you start with a "write" question because the structure that goes with it helps you journey toward the answer. When you have a burning subject in mind or when an editor or teacher gives you a subject to write on, peruse the questions in this book. Put your subject or assignment into the questions. For example, if I suddenly wanted to write about what kind of music I liked when I was my daughter's age, and I needed a way into my subject, I could try on the "write" questions to explore possible ways of approaching my subject.

I could ask myself, "When I was in college, for what music teacher, piece of music, musical instrument, or activity to do with music did I have strong feelings of love or of hate?" Judy Collins' "Both Sides Now" comes crooning again from my college roommate's stereo. The Beatles' "Sgt. Pepper's Lonely Hearts Club Band" drifts in from a remembered college friend's apartment, its windows covered with tie-dyed scarves and its rooms filled with people partying sixties' style. I can see myself strumming "Norwegian Wood" in an upper-classman's room having hired him to teach me guitar. All of these images interest me as ways of describing what music I listened to and why.

Next I could ask myself, "When I was in college, when did I lose someone or something or find someone or something connected to music?" "Did I gain an opportunity or lose one because of music?" The images don't appear as quickly for me with this question. Perhaps this question is not the best for me on the subject. That is not to say it couldn't work. Let's see. I can remember times I lost and found opportunities connected to books but not to music. I could write about those times someday. For now, sticking to my subject, I'll go onto the next question.

"What would I want to tell my daughter about something I learned to do or to make connected with music?" I could tell her about my guitar lessons and how to fail at guitar lessons since that is what I did. I could tell her about learning to feel comfortable in record shops which is something I learned to do in college.

"What about the music I liked then was not the way it was supposed to be?" Well, that makes me think of watching the Beatles on the Ed Sullivan show while I was in high school. I remember how my parents could not understand at all what their sensational impact was about. I remember when I was in grade school, how songs by "Elvis the Pelvis," as our mothers used to call him, blared from new transistor radios on beach blankets in summer, and I remember how parents didn't think that was music. It makes me think how I hear the Seattle grunge sound now that I am a parent, and I cannot easily accept it. It seems parents never find music to be what it is supposed to be.

"What kinds of music did I listen to when I was my daughter's age?" After Elvis there was the Beatles, then Peter, Paul and Mary; and Judy Collins; and Simon and Garfunkel; and The Mamas and The Papas. There were show tunes I wouldn't admit I listened to. I could continue listing, and I bet I could come up with some fun classifications—music to accompany dreaming of unrequited love, music to accompany the hope for love, music to accompany being with boyfriends, music to worry parents, and music to enjoy which was music I wouldn't admit listening to.

"What effects did music have on my life when I was in college?" It set the mood for studying, demonstrating, despairing. It brought friends together. It kept us focused as a group separate and different than the generation in power. I guess I could explore the effects of certain songs on my thinking and feeling and actions. I would have to cluster on songs and what they make me remember.

"What role did music play in my life during my college years? How can I describe this role?" Here I am stumped again. Was music a mother? A flirtatious girl? A bloodstream and circulatory system? I probably could do a better definition paper on the topic of what a student was in the sixties than I could on music. So for me, onto the next question.

"In what areas am I so well-trained concerning music that I believe some action or rethinking on the part of others is imperative or worth considering?" This isn't my forte concerning music. I think I'd stick with either the description essay, the comparison and contrast essay or the division and classification essay. I'd go back and do the exercises for one of those essay styles because I'd be able to create a spirited and moving essay

Whenever you are given a topic or have one you want to stick with, you can run through the questions as I did in my example. After you consider them all, ask yourself which question makes you want to explore your subject the most; then go for it! Remember, the subject you bring to the writing or the one that is assigned by another person is only the beginning of your journey toward discovering your deepest knowledge.

READ PUBLISHED ESSAYS

Now that you are sensitive to essay styles, another way to keep in practice and contribute to the development of dexterity in your own writing is to read published essays and notice how the eight styles are woven in. The authors themselves may not have consciously thought about which styles they were using as they wrote. However, when you observe their writing and name the styles you see and follow the weave in the fabric the authors made by using them, you are learning a great deal that will help you.

Athletes learn moves from their coaches, practice them and study the way other athletes make those moves. When they play, all of their previous practice and observation flow together into brilliant moves of their own. It is this way with writing as well.

In the following pages I will excerpt from four published essays to point out how professional writers answer the "write" questions and weave styles together to do it. The writers whose work I have selected for discussion are Andre Dubus, fiction writer and essayist; Faye Moskowitz, essayist and director of George Washington University's Creative Writing Department; David Reich, editor and journalist for the Unitarian-Universalist's magazine *The World*; and Brenda Peterson, novelist and essayist. Each of the four essayists uses a different essay style as a basic form of organization and inquiry. Andre Dubus narrates the story of the time he lost something. Faye Moskowitz defines the role of caregiver in a unique way. David Reich persuades his readers that U.S. media accounts didn't accurately report the thinking and spirit of the people of Nicaragua whom he met in Estelí, a provincial capital of about 50,000 people in the northwest region of the country. Brenda Peterson shows how to swim with dolphins and how that helps her become more fully human.

"Out Like a Lamb" is the first essay in Andre Dubus' book *Broken Vessels*. It is a narrative about the time the author and his family care for a flock of sheep in exchange for low rent and lose some of the sheep. The author introduces his narrative about that year:

> When I was a boy, sheep had certain meanings: in the Western movies, sheepherders interfered with the hero's cattle; or the villain's idea about his grazing rights interfered with the hero's struggle to raise his sheep. And Christ had called up his flock, his sheep; there were pictures of him holding a lamb in his arms. His face was tender and loving, and I grew up with a sense of those feelings, of being a source of them; we were sweet and lovable sheep. But after a few weeks in that New Hampshire house, I saw that Christ's analogy meant something entirely different. We were stupid helpless brutes, and without constant watching we would foolishly destroy ourselves.

This is an unusual opening for a narration because it tells the insight gained from the story before the story is told. Dubus reports his insight through a comparison and contrast (things are not what they are supposed to be) style. The definitions Dubus had held of sheep and their symbolism contrast with his personal experience of them. Dubus is about to relate the story of how he changed his definitions, not only of sheep but of humans.

The story of that year of sheep tending begins with sheep merely getting out of their pen and not seeing the way back in. It continues with sheep killed by a fox in the pen, sheep eating the roses and the lawn, and Dubus himself inadvertently killing a sheep from the herd. But most importantly, he describes his own and his family's behavior as they grow increasingly violent and aggressive against the sheep who are in their charge:

> We looked from the dinner table and saw them eating the roses, and tenant-fear hurried us outside, to kick and push and pull at those woolly hulks, to shout: No no not her *roses*. They ran around the lawn while we dived at them, missed them, caught them, pulled them kicking toward the fence, and always they got away.

The sheep moved from the roses to the lawn and Dubus reports:

> I went to my den where a twelve gauge double-barreled shotgun hung on the wall. I loaded one barrel with bird shot, stepped outside, and aimed at the rump of the rose-eater. When I fired she stopped eating and looked at me. Then she looked at her rump. Then she started eating again. The other sheep had looked up too, and were grazing now. I put up the gun and went back to the table, muttering about sheep not even having the sense to know when they're being shot at. After dinner, a child said: "Something's wrong with the one you shot."

Dubus' essay ends with the burial of this sheep, his pondering how much he'll owe his landlord, and his surprise over what number seven bird shot "can do to such a big animal with all that wool on her flesh." This story is Dubus' explanation of the way he learned that humans are "stupid, helpless brutes" who, without constant watching, begin foolishly to destroy themselves.

Faye Moskowitz opens her book *And the Bridge Is Love* with an untitled essay that begins with a description, moves briefly through comparison and contrast and then goes into classification and division in order, ultimately, to define the role of caregiver. She begins writing with a simple description of where she is the moment she is writing:

> Outside the window of my daughter's old room where I lie in bed alone, the homely night scenes of my street play themselves out. The aftermath of a spring shower drips from leaf to leaf, slides down the trunks of stately trees; night birds chirp their silver chain of melody and couples coming home anticipate in easy whispers a last drink, a page or two, or the familiar comfort of making love before calling it an evening. No such closure for me, my bones intimate terminal diseases, and my heart loses time.

In comparison and contrast style, something is not the way it is supposed to be. The couples she speculates about contrast with her insomnia and her aloneness in a room apart from her husband. She writes that because of sciatica, "he hurts so much my picking up the newspapers in our room makes him wince." Moskowitz sets the reader in this night of her being awake and skips to remembering and classifying other times she has been nighttime caregiver. As a first-time grandmother she stayed at her daughter's house to care for the new grandchild so the parents could get sleep:

> Getting up in the middle of the night is nothing to me. But that thin little wail, blue as skim milk, brought it all back, ripping through my sleep with the insistence of heavy muslin sheets tearing. I felt for a moment as if I were once again bent over in the rocker, cradling my own baby, and she, rooting, head bobbing, then mouth fastening onto my nipple cracked and sore, my whole body recoiling from those blind blue eyes, that first searing suck, and then my womb contracting in empathy and relief. I used to have fantasies about bombing La Leche headquarters; those smug women suckling away, while I could never get the hang of nursing at all.

She classifies caregiving according to her relationship to the person she is caring for—mothering her first newborn, grandmothering her first grandchild. These nights she feels guilty because she is a wife deserting her husband in his pain. She needs to hear his appreciation for her though he is weak and preoccupied with his own condition. She remembers nights she cared for her friend Jenny, who was dying of cancer and needed company. Moskowitz would go over and do her friend's nails or brush her hair. When her friend asked for help in the shower, Moskowitz fretted at having helped her friend overexert herself. Caring as daughter for her dying father, she remembers how she had refused him the cigarette "that had become his final shame-faced request."

> "They're bad for you, Daddy," I had told him, still pre-tending to the very end. I wish now I had given him that smoke; what difference would it have made to anyone but him?

In describing each classification of caregiver, Moskowitz learns about the insecurity she felt on each occasion. But she learns also she has received from the experience of caregiver: "After the refusal to believe, after the wrenching leave-takings and the resignation, come the small gifts freshly seen." Ultimately, her definition for a caregiver is one of learner and recipient of both insights and love.

Moskowitz most fully comes to this definition as she closes her essay with a short narration of the ending to the following day:

> This afternoon, when I brought him lunch, Jack said, "What would I do without you? What do sick people do who are all alone?" This is the way he tells me he loves me, and remembering that now, I go back to our own room and crawl gingerly into bed beside him, where I lie very still, my knees grazing his back, trying not to cause him any more pain.

David Reich published his argument and persuasion style personal essay entitled "Quiet Days in Estelí" in the literary and political journal *North American Review*. In it, he persuades his readers that the people in Estelí, Nicaragua, do not support the U.S. idea that the *contras* are the party upholding democracy. Reich describes the town he experienced while volunteering to help build a health clinic there. As he moves from his work at the construction site to the houses, church school and business district he visits, he describes the people and their lives:

> Doña Luz María sees me on the patio outside the bath-house, holding my towel and my bar of soap. If I want to go up the street, she says, I can fill up a pail at the water tower. She shrugs her small shoulders. Her face looks tired. "The lack of necessities is hard," she tells me. "But here one gets accustomed to this manner of problem."

Another woman he often talks with is Dora, a twenty-five-year-old teacher at a Catholic school which once charged very high tuition fees and therefore only the children of the wealthy could attend. Under the Sandinista government, the school has become free for any child to attend. "We still have two hours of religious teaching each week, the principal is still a nun, and nine of the twelve original nuns continue teaching here," says Dora.

Reich comments to Dora contrasting what U.S. media had been reporting to what he is experiencing himself:

> "It's a strange thing," I say. "Many of the papers back home in the States say that your government is attacking the church, and yet this town is full of churches and people attend the services and no one seems to bother them. The priest in El Calvario is described by the people as 'a good Sandinista.' And now I see this school. . . . Is there any truth at all to the stories I've read?"
>
> Dora gives a slow smile. "What would your conclusion be?"

Sitting in a wealthy businessman's kitchen, Reich assumes this man Rolando will have something to say against the Sandinistas and in support of the Somoza government that preceded it and for which the U.S.-funded *contras* are fighting:

> . . . he talks to me instead about the *campesinos*, how under Somoza they had no land and couldn't exist off their pitiful wages, how their children had no schools to go to, how many went through life without seeing a doctor and many lacked housing and lived in the road, while now, on the

other hand, everyone eats and has a roof over his head, education and health care are free of charge. . . .

"These achievements are very beautiful, very important," I tell Rolando. "But, of course, you're not a *campesino*."

He looks in my eyes with his large green eyes. "Obviously. But, *mira*. My children can attend the university, a *campesino's* children can attend the university, the children of a worker can attend the university. This is called equality. Now I am proud of my government. In Somoza's time I never voted, knowing who there was to vote for."

And Reich continues with his description and the dialogues that evoke the nature of the people and the social climate of Estelí differently than the way he hears about Nicaragua back in the U.S. In a front room where chickens roam the dirt floor, Reich hears Rolando's conversation with some farmers:

The conversation turns to the city of Masaya, where recently the government, after weeks of demonstrations and demands by landless *campesinos*, redistributed some large plots of idle land. Everybody in the room agrees it was a good decision. Rolando: "How are we supposed to feed ourselves? So much of the land has been out of production. A rich man will say, 'I am saving this farm for my son to work,' and then the son will go off and become an engineer or lawyer."

One morning Reich and a companion walk toward a fruit and vegetable stand. A bomb, the work of the *contra*, had just exploded in a doorway severely injuring a young boy. The lack of emotion in the boy's uncle as he tells Reich that the boy has been taken for brain surgery reminds Reich of a conversation he had earlier in his stay. Doña Estela, the mother of the construction site's manager, had said matter of factly while holding a baby in her lap, "This little girl's father was killed in an ambush fifteen days ago."

After sharing these two images, which contrast with the openhearted and productive people Reich has seen, he moves to cast his description and comparison and contrast in the service of an argument:

... I thought her attitude was the product of shock or fatalism or possibly even callousness, but thinking of the people I've gotten to know here and considering their lives, I lose the desire and confidence to label it or judge it. The experience of colonialism, especially the Somoza years, has turned the Nicaraguans into experts on death, the gradations of death, the many ways of dying—death at the hands of the National Guard, death by addiction and forced prostitution, death by starvation, polio, tuberculosis. Couple this with the fact that most Nicaraguans, unlike Ronald Reagan, believe that a *contra* victory would inevitably mean a return to Somoza-style government, and you can see why they'd be so willing to lay down their lives and the lives of those they love. According to the hard equations that people in their circumstances have to live by, death as a martyr of the revolution may have more to recommend it than death for the lack of a pound of beans or a dose of penicillin.

Reich knows from his own first-hand experience that Estelí under the Sandinistas, contrary to reports back home in the U.S., encourages lives and livelihood among a group of united people. Why they are willing to fight the *contras* is, according to Reich, apparent when you examine their history and the choices they have. The description works in the service of argument because it is a first-hand account by a man willing to serve people by helping them build what they need for themselves, a man willing to listen to the people and to observe who they are.

"Animals as Brothers and Sisters" is the third essay in Brenda Peterson's collection entitled *Living By Water*. She opens her essay with a brief description of a game she played with her brothers and sisters as a child:

> *What country are you? What body of water? What war? What animal?*
>
> My sister was Ireland, the South Seas, the War of Independence, and a white stallion. My brother was Timbuktu, the Amazon River, the One Hundred Years War, and a cobra. I was South America, the Gulf of Mexico, the Civil War, and a dolphin.

Peterson narrates that her siblings would call upon their animals: her sister galloped away from adults, her brother hissed fiercely to ward off his pesty sisters, and Peterson soared through sea and air. Now as an adult she is swimming with dolphins and learning their lessons of acceptance, communication and healing. She describes her swim at the Dolphins Plus Marine Mammal Research & Education Center in Key Largo where the dolphins are free to swim back to the ocean if they want and where humans are their playmates. In order to make the dolphins want to play with her, Peterson tells us, she will have to swim creatively, not just bob and gawk like a float toy. She swims "snorkel mask down, arms at my side to signal that I would wait for them to choose to play with me...." While she swims to interest them, her mind wanders to viewing humans as dolphins must. "We are the only creatures in the sea who splash at both ends of our bodies. Our appendages don't move in sync with the sea as do the long arms of anemones.

"The dolphins always come when I'm most distracted, when my mind is not on them at all, but drifting, perhaps dreaming." This, Peterson tells us is the second step in swimming with dolphins. She feels in her "floating reverie" the "sensuous skin stroking my legs ... the silken, clean, elegant feel of dolphin belly...." Then all three young dolphins swim toward her.

"Choose one!" the researcher shouts. Peterson remembers his earlier instructions that dolphins are possessive and the swimmer must bond with only one or the dolphins will squabble among themselves. Peterson chooses and swims with a dolphin's dorsal fin tucked under her arm, her world sky and bubbles and the sound of "dolphins' dialogue."

Next, she imagines ways of swimming with the dolphin, and whatever swimming she imagines her dolphin enacts. Suddenly the author gets too close to another dolphin and the child with whom that dolphin is swimming. She receives a wallop to her shoulder. When her body goes vertical the researcher shouts to her to get horizontal or the dolphins will think she is drowning and try to raise her above water. She pictures herself surrendering to all three dolphins and they come to her. She thinks words to them, "*I am small ... I am just a human being—afraid and fragile in your element. Be careful with me?*" Suddenly they are gentle with her and Peterson loses track of time.

"You'll all have to link arms to signal the dolphins that you're serious about getting out. They'll respect your tribe. But they'll protest!" the researcher says firmly.

Now that she has swum with the dolphins, Peterson thinks of them as guides out of water as well as in and she shows how they guide her. "For example," she writes, "I'll often find myself in some situation thinking: '*What would a dolphin do?*' In my own life, the flexibility and adaptability of a dolphin mind, their sense of tribe and play, guides me. I can call upon the dolphin inside me for counsel as well as companionship."

Finally, Peterson proposes that we might all use animal guides to help us make the greatest of all crossings:

> Each of us has an animal totem, some are blessed with many. We can all summon our animals and they will come. They will be our brothers and sisters and live alongside us — even swim upstream to die with us so we will not be without a guide through that greatest change of worlds.

In this essay, one how-to led to another, and then that one led to one more. By the essay's end, we are thinking not only about how it is swimming with dolphins, but how it is when we let animals into our consciousness.

CONTINUE YOUR JOURNEY

Whether you are trying a "write" question to help you think your way to an essay, trusting your images and style preferences to take you there, or examining another writer's work for practice in absorbing how styles integrate, you are learning and practicing the powers of description, narration, how-to, comparison and contrast, cause and effect, division and classification, definition, and argument and persuasion. When you write, you explore these powers from the inside out. When you look into another writer's work you recognize them from the outside in.

All of this is important to your work. But remember, you are always in your own court, and the ball is always in your hands. Admire another's moves, and move on. You have much to discover, evoke and share.

CHAPTER ELEVEN

Publishing Your Personal Essay

If you want a record of what happened today, you pick up a newspaper; if you're interested in a timely or trendy topic, you read a magazine article; but if you want to get closer to the dynamics of a culture's thinking, you need essays.

— *Robert Atwan*, Foreword, The Best American Essays 1993

Personal essays are often written because authors have a need to answer a life question. Sometimes, though, they are written specifically for a particular market. And, either way, there is a growing market for personal essays. It is composed of literary magazines, newspapers, popular magazines, trade and professional journals, thematic anthologies with writings by selected authors and book-length collections by individual authors. Most authors of essay collections and most authors of work included in anthologies have first published their work widely in periodic publications. For instance, the 1994 essay collection *Paper Trail* by Michael Dorris includes essays that first appeared in a range of publications: *Family Circle, TV Guide, Ladies Home Journal, Parents,* the *New York Times,* the *Los Angeles Times, Center for Disease Control, College English, Booklist, Hungry Mind Review,* and *Three Penny Review* among others.

Focusing on publishing essay by essay pays off. Concentrating on three areas helps you do this.

1. Read publications that use personal essays to get a first-hand feel for what editors like, where essayists are finding publishers, and how essays are used in periodic literature.
2. Learn to use market directories available at libraries or for purchase to expand your idea of the market.

3. Create an organized, continuous submission process to keep your work in the mail to editors.

You may want to consider building your publication credits by publishing in local small press and specialized publications first, then in regional or wider circulation ones, and then in national publications. Since well-known publications get thousands of submissions from which they must select only a very few essays, even after publishing in well-known national venues, many authors continue to publish personal essays in the smaller literary journals.

Remember, the value in publishing your personal essay is in sharing your work with people who might be moved by your words and by your experience. If you want to see your essays published without delay, you must be creative and thorough in your search for places to submit your work. The closer to home you submit your work, the more chance there is of seeing it in print. Your work may actually be of particular interest because it is locally written. Local neighborhood newspaper editors and editors of local literary journals may be more receptive to your work and more willing to offer guidance if you are a new writer. Having published locally helps you introduce yourself and your work to editors of publications further from your home base.

FIND PUBLICATIONS THAT INCLUDE PERSONAL ESSAYS

The best way to find markets for your work is to read as widely as possible, noting which publications regularly feature personal essays. Such publications range from tiny, local newsletters to large-circulation, nationally distributed magazines.

Local and Special Interest Publications

Cafes and delis in large towns and cities of all sizes have become distribution points for many free specialty publications. Every week there are new ones and better and better issues of the ones that have been out for a while. The interest areas of these publications range widely. They may cover the local music scene, women in local businesses, the arts, theater, drug dependency recovery, alternative health care, spirituality, retirement, raising families, being gay, motorcycling, eco-wisdom, ethnic news, RV-ing, computing, employment, vacationing and buying or renting homes. I've come across a free literary magazine subtitled "a journal of imaginative trouble." Each of these publications will most likely have a personal essay or two by authors whose experiences are in line with the publication's interests. Think about the life experience essays you have written and about why one or more could be of interest to the editors of one of these publications. You may get paid only in copies, but you will get a chance to build up your publication history.

Form the habit of being continually aware of publications. For instance, when I go to my health clinic, I see an in-house magazine with the personal stories of patients and their doctors. Several times a year, the alumnus magazine from the college I attended as an undergraduate arrives in my mailbox with personal stories by alumni and professors and students. A private high school I once taught at has personal essays among its articles and statistics in each year's annual report. When I work out in a gym, I find industry magazines that might feature someone's story about how exercise paid off in their lives. When I go to the paint store, I find little publications about home repair with do-it-yourself first-person accounts. The college that I teach at has several newsletters for staff and faculty in addition to the student published newspaper which sometimes uses work by staff and faculty.

Be sure to read editions of your local town, city, and neighborhood newspapers and see if they solicit and/or publish first-person essays for their living or local scene sections. Weekly or monthly tabloid format newspapers may use personal essays for their back page.

Small Press Literary Publications

Many small press literary publications are produced by universities or by groups of writers supported by endowments and grants. Many of them are famous and long established. Some are very new. Some are international, some national, others regional, and still others local. You will certainly want to find many samples of small press literary magazines.

Browse them in your library, at a large bookstore or in a well-stocked newsstand. You can also find out about them by reading directories (see my heading "Learn to Use the Market Directories"). Sometimes one distributor may be involved helping a number of small press publications get to market. You may be able to find out the distributor's name from a newsstand owner, and then you can talk directly to the distributor about small press titles and where to find them in your area.

In addition, many of these publications have taken to advertising in magazines like *Poets and Writers* and the *New York Times Book Review*. Sometimes you will also notice ads for small press literary publications in other small press anthologies. Don't forget to call the English departments of local universities, colleges and community colleges to find out if creative writing journals seeking submissions from writers are published in your area.

If some of the people you know are writers, be sure to ask to see any small press publications in which they have published their work and publications to which they subscribe. When I was handed a copy of the *Georgia Review* in which a friend of mine had published an essay, the publication made a stronger impact on me than it had ever done before. Reading the published work of someone you know brings the possibility of your own publication nearer to home. It can happen!

The Mainstream Popular Press

Browse through news magazines, women's and men's magazines, teen magazines, sports magazines, house magazines, hobby magazines, electronics magazines and so on to see if they publish personal essays from people outside their own staffs. Pay attention to the topics and experiences portrayed in these essays. How do the essays seem to fit the publication's focus? Would one of your essays be suitable for that focus?

Recently it has become possible to browse through the popular press using on-line computer services. A computer user can find titles and download sample articles from the bulletin boards. There are also services that have files from special interest magazines, business publications, and major newspapers as well as directories of these publications. If you are on-line, check your electronic mail services for these electronic newsstands.

It is not particularly easy to get your essays published in these national venues, but with a publication history and a close tie-in between your essay topic and the magazine's focus, you may succeed.

Essay Collections

Ask booksellers to direct you to collections by well-known essayists. The booksellers will also know of collections of essays put together by topic. For instance, there are essay collections featuring writers on writing, writers on cross-cultural experiences, Irish writers on the experience of being Irish, and daughters on the experience of having literary mothers. These books are not necessarily shelved under the subject "essays" — they may be in ethnic studies or women's studies or men's movement literature or in the writing section or in the travel section or even in literary criticism. Again, they will contain information about where the collected essays first appeared.

University and college bookstores will have excellent collections of essays put out by the college text divisions of major publishers. These will be shelved with the texts required for students' English course work. Since professors order these books in just the right numbers for their classes, you should use the shelves for browsing and then ask the bookseller to order you a copy of any you might want to buy. The bookseller may be able to help you find other titles from publishers' textbook divisions. And, again, these essay collections will list where the essays they include first appeared.

Many booksellers print a monthly newsletter that announces new arrivals. Sign up to receive these newsletters. Many new collections of essays are being published and advertised. By reading the newsletters, you can add to your knowledge of presses publishing personal essay collections, and, by scanning the books, you can learn more about where the authors first published their personal essays.

Be sure also to scan book reviews. Small press magazines often contain reviews of anthologies or collections of essays by smaller regional presses. Although you shouldn't overlook the *New York Review of Books* and the *New York Times Book Review* section for reviews of collections of essays, state or special interest magazines such as *Alaska Magazine* and *Sierra Magazine*, for example, may review books of essays not mentioned other places. Writers on nature and ecology, for example, usually write essays and more often their collections are reviewed in magazines concerned with those topics.

Some presses publish a compilation of each year's best essays. An important one is *The Best American Essays* put out each year by Ticknor and Fields. Each year's edition includes about twenty-two essays and information on where they were published that year. It also includes a list of other notable essays and where they were published as well as biographical notes on the authors published in the current edition. Those notes often include the names of other books and presses.

Another yearly anthology is *The Pushcart Prize: Best of the Small Presses* published by The Pushcart Press in Wainscott, New York. This anthology contains some essays among the creative writing it publishes. In addition to publication information about the essays and biographical notes about the authors, this anthology also includes a list of all the presses featured in past *The Pushcart Prize Editions.* Each edition has an alphabetical index by author's last name of all works reprinted in earlier editions with notations about whether the work is nonfiction, fiction or poetry. Another collection, *Creative Nonfiction* is a new twice-yearly anthology from the Department of English at the University of Pittsburgh.

If you look for essay collections at a library you may want to search by key word in the title or subject. Try key words like *first-person writing*, *personal narrative*, *personal experience*, and *personal essay*, in addition to *essays*.

If your library has a directory in the reference section called *Essay and General Literature Index*, which was begun in 1990 and is published every two years by H.W. Wilson, you can use it to help locate places to submit your essays by looking up subject headings. For instance, if you look up "trees," you will find some listings about essays concerning trees in publications you might not have heard of such as *American Forests.*

The *Reader's Guide to Periodical Literature*, also published by H.W. Wilson, is in every library's reference section. Here, too, you can use a subject head. However, it is hard to tell an essay from an article by this index's descriptions.

Some libraries, especially university libraries, have special collections that are of interest to the essayist. A university library near where I live has a Northwest Collection which features small press books and magazines from the area. Perusing these books and magazines and taking down information about the editors is useful for finding local markets.

LEARN TO USE THE MARKET DIRECTORIES

A directory you will want to use in the library or purchase yourself is the *Writer's Market* from Writer's Digest Books. In this directory, you'll find market information about publishers of books and trade and consumer magazines, as well as information about contests. You'll learn what they publish, how often they publish, how many manuscripts they buy in a year, how long they take to report back, what their payment structures are, and whether to query or send a manuscript. Look for "nonfiction" and "essay" as the keys words here when looking for places to publish your personal essays. You will find hundreds of places from *Looking Fit, The Magazine for Health Conscious Tanning and Toning Centers,* which accepts operational how-to about selecting locations and buying equipment to the Dog Writer's Association of America Annual Writing Contest which accepts previously published writing about the rearing, training, care and companionship of dogs.

Another treasure is the *Writers Northwest Handbook, the Market Guide to the Pacific Northwest 3,000 Publishers and Resources, Essays, How-to Articles, Tips.* You don't have to be from the Northwest to publish in the region's magazines. *The International Directory of Little Magazines and Small Presses,* edited by Len Fulton and *The Writer's Handbook,* edited by Sylvia K. Burack are also helpful with long lists of publications. Ulrich's *International Periodical Directory* lists addresses and phone numbers for publications. *Gale Directory of Publications and Broadcast Media* (formerly called the *Ayers Guide*) lists all magazines and newspapers in the United States and is particularly useful if you have published an essay and want to find places to reprint it. This guide has addresses for Sunday supplements which regularly use reprints.

Another reference book helpful for writers is *Magazines for Libraries* which lists major and small press magazines and describes them in terms of who puts them out, what points of view they support, who has published in them previously, and who will enjoy using them and why. A perusal of the three-page table of contents is rewarding— periodicals are categorized as literary reviews, literature and little magazines, among other headings like news and opinion, real estate, singles, hiking and climbing, and consumer education. The short entries for each publication are precisely and lovingly written to encourage the adoption of subscriptions by libraries but they tell you what genres are represented.

Check the appendix of this book for more information on the directories mentioned and for the titles of additional market directories.

In addition, ask your librarian to help you find indexes for foundations and associations to learn about specialized newsletters that might be interested in your work. Don't forget to ask the librarian for suggestions about which magazines to look at for personal essays. Librarians know periodicals, and they may introduce you to some you might otherwise have overlooked.

Your reference librarian will also know how to find a good listing of writer's organizations and arts commissions. Their newsletters contain announcements of publications seeking manuscripts. The International Women's Writing Guild based in New York, PEN, Poets and Writers, Inc., and the National Writer's Club should be on your list as well as any local literary centers. Call these centers and your local arts commission to get on their mailing lists for information about local, state, national or international publications about writing, publishing, and writing conferences where you can meet publishers and small press representatives.

Subscription magazines such as *Writer's Digest* publish monthly listings of publishers seeking manuscripts. In addition, if you live near a university, college, or community college visit the creative writing offices and professors. They receive information from journals all over the country that are looking for material. The offices usually have a bulletin board where the fliers and brochures are posted. And, if you haven't already, find out whether the college produces publications to which you could submit your work.

SUBMIT YOUR WORK

Anytime you find a publication or a listing about a publication that seems like a potential home for one of your essays, note the editor's name, the publication's name and address, and information on whether the magazine accepts unsolicited manuscripts, has a specific reading period, or requires you to query the editor before you send your manuscript. Add a note in your records about which essay you are thinking is appropriate for that magazine. Keep this information in one notebook. You will find it easier to make your submissions if you do this.

If submission requirements are not clear from the magazines and directories or you want more information, write the publications for guidelines about their submission processes. You might also inquire about the cost of sample copies if you need one to see what their material looks like. Enclose a legal size self-addressed stamped envelope for their reply. Keep a three-ring loose-leaf binder for all the printed sheets of guidelines you get, and in it, place them in alphabetical order by publication name.

A typical guidelines sheet will tell the background and purpose of a publication, its format, what kinds of writing its editors seek, how long that writing can be, what the publication pays, what its rights agreements are, any deadlines an author must meet, and to whom to address the submission. One guidelines sheet I saw listed the distributors who handle the publication along with a list of what other small presses those distributors handle! Now I had more presses I could query about publication!

Here is how one author, Christi Killien, starts her process and keeps records:

When she reads an essay she likes, she learns about the place it was published to see if that place might be interested in one of her essays. She finds the address of the publication in one of the directories or calls the reference section of her downtown library and asks for the address. She dashes off a request for guidelines on a Post-it note affixed to a self-addressed stamped envelope (SASE). The guidelines come back quickly. She uses a three-hole punch and then inserts the sheets in alphabetical order by publication title.

In this notebook, Christi also keeps a master sheet of where she has sent which essay in which version since sometimes even after she has sent one out, she continues revising it. Or sometimes she may have revised an essay to meet certain length restrictions as noted on the guidelines. She also lists on her master sheet possible places to send the essay should it be rejected. Some publications do not like authors to make simultaneous submissions because their editors don't want to be reading a piece that may get accepted somewhere else before they accept it. Some authors make simultaneous submissions anyway thinking that they can always withdraw their submission from one editor if the work gets accepted somewhere else. Most writers dealing with small press publications don't do this, however, because most of those publications still frown on it. Even when you are submitting a piece for reprint, you need to recognize editors' needs for exclusivity. Submit your piece for reprint to one editor in a geographic region at a time.

Christi keeps one notebook for each essay with all of her versions in chronological order. At the beginning of each of these notebooks she will keep any correspondence she has had with editors or publishers about the piece. For tax purposes this proves that even in monetary dry spells she is engaged in the business of writing. Her system also allows her to keep track of where each version was read and to review what various editors have said. This information can be useful for figuring out what to send certain editors in the future.

The Submission Package

Most of the time, guidelines say to send the whole manuscript when it is something as short as an essay. This is to be sent not only with an SASE but with a cover letter that includes biographical information. Christi also includes a sheet about her published books.

Here are two examples, one of a cover letter and one of a query letter that she has written. For her cover letter, after the inside addresses she wrote:

> Dear (Editor's Name):
>
> Enclosed is my personal experience essay entitled "The Curse" for consideration for *Left Bank #5: Borders and Boundaries*.
>
> "The Curse" is part of a collection of essays I'm currently working on entitled *Breast in the Bone*. It is a memoir of sorts, although I'm writing thematically about both my family's past and the present. When I read your guidelines for the December, 1993 issue, I thought that "The Curse" described the boundaries that exist between generations in a family, and attempts to answer your question, "How do we create change, both in ourselves and in the society?"
>
> I have also enclosed my resume of published books and an SASE for your response. Thank you for considering my work.
>
> Sincerely,

Her work was accepted for the publication, and you can find "The Curse" by Christi Killien in *Left Bank #5: Borders and Boundaries* published in 1993 by Blue Heron Publishing, Inc., Hillsboro, Oregon.

Although literary magazines don't usually require query letters, Christi queried the editor of a Montana magazine before sending her essay. After the inside addresses, she wrote:

> Dear (Editor's name):
>
> My grandfather was a Montana homesteader and butcher who, as a hobby, made beautiful canes out of bull penises. He gave the canes to nursing home patients and told them that they were made of wood, and thought it a great joke. To me, those canes were a strange mix of the brutishness of Grandpa's hard life, his silliness, and art.
>
> My personal experience essay "Grandpa's Canes" is approximately 850 words, and is part of a collection of essays I am currently working on entitled *Breast in the Bone*. Would you be interested in seeing it?
>
> Six of my intermediate level novels have been pub-

lished by Houghton Mifflin and Scholastic Books. One of my essays has appeared in *Publisher's Weekly*, one in *Writer's Digest Magazine*, and one is in *Left Bank #5: Borders and Boundaries* from Blue Heron Press in Oregon.

I have enclosed an SASE for your response. I look forward to hearing from you.

Sincerely,

The editor she wrote to responded with interest, but after reviewing the essay decided to pass. This one has been resubmitted elsewhere with the correspondence duly entered into that essay's notebook. Also entered into the notebook now is a clipping from a catalog of western gear. The husband of a woman in Christi's writer's group happened across an item listed and described as canes from bull genitals. Perhaps Christi might send her essay to the publishers of the catalog!

Be sure the essay you submit to a publisher is a freshly typed copy, computer printout or clear photocopy. Always keep a copy for your own records. Things get lost in the mail and editors cannot be responsible for the return of unsolicited manuscripts. Even if they request to see a manuscript, there are many opportunities for one to get lost.

The type on the copy you send must be dark. Worn out ribbons on typewriters and printers must be replaced. Editors want to be able to read your submission easily. The essay should be double-spaced and labeled at the top right of each page with a heading including the author's last name and the name of the essay because pages can get separated on an editor's desk. The pages should be numbered and the margins should be standard. There should be no spelling, punctuation, capitalization or grammatical errors. It is wise to have several people proofread your essay before you send it off. It is very hard to find small errors yourself because you are so familiar with the work.

Acceptances

When one of your essays is accepted for publication, be sure you understand the copyright situation. Most small magazines and journals state that the copyright reverts to the author after the first publication. That means in the future the author is free to have the work reprinted in an anthology or other publication. Occasionally, a small press publisher doesn't grant that the copyright reverts back to the author. In this case, it may be because that publisher wants to put out an anthology in the future without repaying the authors who they have already published or they hope to make some money down the line from magazines or book editors who want the rights to republish the work.

Usually, a press that published the essay first but had the copyright revert back to the author still desires an acknowledgement that the essay appeared there first. In the case of major magazines, the author has to negotiate reprint and future publication rights. Sometimes the word "licensed" is used — is the author or the magazine licensed to reprint or otherwise reuse the essay? Make sure you understand and accept the terms of publication or modify them to meet your needs. The time to do this is after an editor wants your piece and before you sign a contract agreeing to the publication.

Keep several copies of the magazine or journal in which any of your work is published. Long after your flurry of activity about that particular essay ends, an editor or grant panel might like to see your work and the context in which it was published. Photocopied printed pages make a nicer sample than manuscript pages. Also, long after you've retired your notebook on particular essays, you may be asked to make up a bibliography of your published work with information about where and when it appeared! You might need the information in the magazine for assuring reprint rights. You can certainly keep that information in records, but seeing the whole magazine can be helpful. In addition, you might want to make a gift of the publication in which your work appears to someone you care about or to an editor interested in your work.

Rejections

Don't despair. Don't throw your work away. Don't even throw the rejection notice away. File everything. When you can bear to, take it all out and reread your work and the rejection. If the editor has written any kind of personal note, try to make sense of it. Try to decide whether your piece was rejected because it didn't suit the publication's needs or the editor's taste, whether there merely wasn't enough room for it, or whether it needs work. If you believe it was rejected for one of the first two reasons, get the piece out in the mail to another magazine. That handy list of where you want to send next kept in your essay notebook helps you handle rejection and keep your work out there.

Sometimes mailing your piece away and having it read by a stranger who then mails it back to you with a rejection letter helps you see the piece with new eyes. You might slow down between submissions and rework the piece. Find your trusted readers or run the three-step response method yourself now that you have more distance from the work.

Someday you will be used to rejections slips—when you are actively circulating your work you can expect them. Some have wallpapered their bathrooms with the slips. Others have published them. They are certainly a part of every writer's life.

CONTINUING

Sending essays out for publication, reading sample essays and publications, and working on your own essays is a back-and-forth process. Therefore, in addition to the notebooks of records about where and what and to whom you have sent, you may end up with a box of publications to read and reread as you find the time. You may keep one notebook in which you copy passages from essays you admire and jot down notes to yourself about how you might use a similar technique. You might keep a notebook of jottings about topics you know about that are related to ones in essays you are reading. You might keep a notebook of essays cut from magazines and newspapers to reread. Filing them by style—description, narration, how-to, comparison and contrast, cause and effect, division and classification, definition, and argument and persuasion—helps you fine-tune your own abilities with the essay styles. It helps you realize these styles are used by the professionals to good end. Pretty soon you will have a few essays of your own in print to put into this notebook!

EPILOGUE

Letter to My Readers

Dear Readers,

The Centrum Arts Foundation has provided me a cottage at Fort Worden State Park this September to live and write for a month. Maintained as non-commissioned officers' housing while the park was an army base, it is still institutional green inside and out. Rust shows through the enamel of the refrigerator, and my bed slants, but I am happy. I have moved the large mahogany office desk from against a back wall to the middle of the living room. That way when I open the door in the warm afternoons, I can see Mt. Rainier looming white over the blue waters of Admiralty Bay. I can even hear the lapping of waves against the shore.

Nice as it is, I am restless for activity after twelve days of writing, and I note an announcement in the local paper about an annual wooden boat festival. As many as 20,000 people will visit Point Hudson in downtown Port Townsend. I can get to this gathering of dories and sea kayaks, canoes and three-masters by walking the beach.

As I walk, I think of another morning (twenty years ago) when I was reading the paper just after I'd moved to Seattle. An article said Julie Nixon would be in the city to officiate at an army ceremony to give an installation back to the people. I went.

A crowd waited by a plywood platform. Soon a helicopter hovered over our heads. It dropped a rope ladder and Julie climbed down, her white dress billowing in the wind, and her blond hair flowing. She walked to the platform to sit beside Seattle activist Bernie Eagle Bear, whose long black hair was tied tight behind his head. After the army personnel gave a short introduction, Julie went to the lectern. She said her father had taken a walk near San Clemente on a beautiful sunny California day and wondered why people weren't out enjoying the beach when his advisors told him the beach was army property and, therefore, not accessible to the public. According to Julie, it was then her father hatched his idea of returning the properties. Soon Bernie Eagle Bear rose to accept a parchment certificate designating much of the grounds, now to be called Discovery Park, for a Native American cultural center.

Discovery Park. The name of a park I love and a good name, it seems, for the state I feel I am in when I write. On the bluffs of Discovery Park, I see further out over the water than I ever thought I could. When developing my drafts, I see more and more about my life and the situations in it. In late summer, when vines of blackberries hang over the trails of the park, I don't mind the pricks I get picking the sweet fruit. In writing, I twinge many times, but I enjoy the sweet nectar of the truth inside my stories. When I walk to the top of the dunes in the park, I welcome sun-warmed sand in my hands. When I write, I welcome insights from the trail of my images, from the words on paper. At the ceremonial ponds by the Native American Cultural Center, spirits in the shade seem to whisper secrets, just like my unconscious sometimes whispers unexpected words and sounds. Summers at Discovery Park, I might find a waterfall near the beach and stand under it as long as I can stand the cold of the water. From such a waterfall, I watched as two of my friends left their clothes on the beach and walked in rhythm with each other into the cold waters of Puget Sound. I watched until they dipped under the water, their two heads bobbing like sea birds, like memories that come to shore when I am writing.

And each memory links to another and each new experience enters the house of another experience. The village of my experience is there, sometimes ten, sometimes forty minutes away. I can get there. I have the questions; I have the tools. I am like a president with the power to take land back from the austere uses of defense and open it up for the revitalization that comes with re-creating.

I am many minutes into my walk now. The hard sand has given way to seaweed-draped rocks. My feet tip them sometimes and I am slowed. When I look up from my feet at the beach, I see a great blue heron standing very still amidst seagulls and crows, cousins of ravens, harbingers of journeys. When I look at the heron straight on, I see the slender neck but there hardly seems to be a head housing the two eyes that glisten against the sun. Curious, I walk a little further down the beach and look back at him. In profile, his head is very thin and very long. I know his wingspan is wider than any gull's. He has flown in from somewhere, and he is giving me as long a time as I need to watch him.

Our writing is like this. We find our wisdom by walking down the beach from our experience and looking back. Like the heron, we have wingspan to get us to and back from somewhere we may not have known we were going, though those large wings working to get airborne can look awkward at first. Does it take courage to be a heron among ravens and gulls? Perhaps. I don't know. But it does take courage for us to stand as still inside as this heron stands now for me. That is the real courage of writing. Slowing down, sitting down, taking pen in hand, discovering the paths and stones in our lives.

This is the burden of writing, I think, as I begin to gather rocks of remarkable color, unexpected greens, blues, pinks, ambers, roses, and buffs. They will be heavy when I carry them in my backpack, but when I get to my cottage, my perch on the top of the bluff, I will set them on the long cement ramp to my front door. Carrying them is temporary. I will lift them off my back. Like images in essays, I will set the rocks out in patterns. In writing, patterns become a house for my experience, and I am free, like my two friends, naked and heading for the water.

That day, two female park rangers caught my friends sunning themselves on the beach and told them bathing suits were required. My friends walked back to their clothes, and the rangers walked on. Seeking response to my writing-in-progress is like getting comfortable walking naked on a beach when everyone, all of my life, was a park ranger telling me not to reveal myself or my mistakes in public.

A little more of Port Townsend's beach left to walk, but the smell of food and coffee draws me up inland. There are food vendors outside selling to the Wooden Boat Festival crowd—burritos, bratwurst, Maryland crabcakes, baked potatoes, local corn, espresso and cheesecake. Picnic tables are set inside the circle of vendors. I stop for some coffee and crabcakes—it is noon and I haven't had anything yet to eat. That's how it is some days writing, looking out over the water.

I make my way past the craftsman's booths and the vessels they have built. Cedar and pine, doweled and varnished and waxed. There is cabin furniture with drop leaves and narrow shelves. Boat bumpers and deck mats and ladders all made of cotton rope. The corn vendor hands customers steamed and buttered cobs on husks instead of plates. Here is a festival of natural materials and little waste.

If there were a Personal Essay Foundation, its festival would draw people who know an essay is a small boat on a big journey with only essentials on board. Personal Essay Foundation members would celebrate the natural materials of writing: what they see, hear, taste, touch and smell. They would love to work and rework words, cutting and polishing, until their function is doweled to their form. Most of all, the Personal Essay Foundation members would know there are like-minded people with whom to learn and to share.

You know this now that you have begun, essay by essay, to set down the images of your experience, to glean the insights of your lives. You will never forget how.

Godspeed and right winds,
Sheila

CONTRIBUTORS

Elizabeth Bamber has stopped working for the community outreach department of a large cooperative health care organization. She has recently married and travelled to eastern Europe, and she is now enrolled in a certification program for teaching English as a second language.

F. Jeffrey Calvert majored in business at the University of Puget Sound where he was president of Beta Theta Pi fraternity and captain of the Men's Lacrosse Team. He keeps a journal of short stories and hopes to write a book.

Yvonne Crain has worked for years in the broadcast industry and looks forward to starting a family with her new husband and continuing her education.

Andre Dubus lives in Massachusetts. He has published nine books of fiction and essays, including the recent *Broken Vessels* and *Selected Stories*. He has been a Guggenheim Fellow and been awarded a MacArthur Fellowship.

Michael Kuntz is a Northwest native who decided to pursue a college education at age 36. At age 41, he received a B.A. in English. He works in the publications field.

Robert W. Lowery manages the customer service (read complaint) department for a broadcast and recording studio equipment manufacturer. Now married, he returned to college in 1992 to finish a degree he had abandoned twenty-five years before while pursuing the sowing of wild oats and a career in broadcasting.

Mary Meza's son is now in college. She works as a school librarian and as a piano teacher. She is interested in returning to school.

Kim Morrow studied to be a dental hygienist in the state of Washington. With her husband, she is now raising their two children.

Faye Moskowitz lives in Washington, D.C., where she directs the

Creative Writing Program at George Washington University. Her books of personal essays and fiction include *A Leak in the Heart, Whoever Finds This: I Love You,* and *And The Bridge Is Love.* Recently, she has edited an anthology for Beacon Press entitled *Her Face in the Mirror: Jewish Women on Mothers and Daughters.*

Teresa Nettleton has a degree in Computer Application and Information Management and has worked for a small software company writing accounting software and reference manuals. The mother of two, she now helps her husband in managing their own business.

Tri Nguyen was born in Vietnam and lived under communist rule for five years before escaping. After living in America for over twelve years, he sometimes misses the simple life in Vietnam where you only had to worry about the government. He is studying to be an electrical engineer to return and help rebuild Vietnam.

Roy Nims has "a lengthy record of assaulting various musical instruments and film medium." His recorded works are used on radio segues and throughout PBS's "Bill Nye the Science Guy." His videos of the "Tiny Hot Orchestra" may soon hit MTV.

Brenda Peterson lives in Seattle, Washington, and is a contributing editor to *New Age Journal.* Her novels and collections of essays include *Duck and Cover, Becoming the Enemy, Living By Water, Nature and Other Mothers,* and the forthcoming *Living By the Word.*

Suzanne K. Pitré writes essays, plays and short fiction. Her work has appeared in the literary anthology *Spindrift* and one of her plays has been produced by The Playwrights in Seattle. She enjoys cooking, skiing and photography.

The late Charles Procter served in the U.S. Navy as a lieutenant from 1942-1946. He received a Bachelor of Arts in physics at Berea, Kentucky, a Masters Degree in biology at the University of Utah, and a Ph.D. in oceanography at Texas A&M. At the age of fifty-five, after years of technical writing, he began writing poetry as if a faucet had been turned on.

Michelle Ramsey wrote essays about being a single parent when she enrolled in college to pursue a degree in Medical Records Technology. She received her degree with honors in June, 1994 and published several of her essays in the new *Single Mother's Companion* published by Seal Press in Seattle.

David Reich is editor of *The World*, the award-winning national magazine of the Unitarian Universalist Association. His fiction, essays and journalism have appeared in *The North American Review*, *Transatlantic Review*, and *The Smith* among others. He lives in Quincy, Massachusetts, where he enjoys walking the beach and lifting weights.

Robert Roden is the father of two teenagers. He works full-time and attends college at night because he likes learning. He spends as much time as he can having outdoor adventures.

Michael Shurgot teaches writing and literature at South Puget Sound Community College. He has published scholarly essays about Shakespeare and essays and poetry. He fervently believes being a baseball fan keeps one eternally young. "Caesar's Stuff; Or, The Modern Baseball Fan" appeared in the July, 1990 issue of *Hardball*.

Gary Snyder is a world-renowned poet and essayist from California whose work is closely allied with ecology and eco-awareness.

Rizwana Firdous Syeda-Kazmi was born in Gujrat, Pakistan. She came to the United States after graduation and is now taking a degree in philosophy and pre-engineering.

Kate Wright graduated from Dartmouth in 1991 with a B.A. in biology and environmental studies. She pursues a freelance degree in western perspectives and has cooked for elk hunters, worked with the Aleuts on environmental issues, been a field biologist in North Dakota's badlands, and instructed nordic skiing in Montana.

APPENDIX

SUGGESTED READINGS
Essays, Collections, How-Tos:

Aaron, Jane E. *The Compact Reader: Short Essays by Theme and Form* (Boston, 1991). This is a strong collection of essays that demonstrate the various essay styles.

Applebaum, Judith. *How to Get Happily Published*, 4th Edition (New York, 1992). This book covers everything from what editors want to how to self-publish your work, and it includes over seventy pages of resource listings for writers.

Atwan, Robert, ed. *The Best American Essays* (New York, yearly since 1986). Series editor Robert Atwan chooses a guest editor to compile the twenty-plus essays selected each year from hundreds that have appeared in print in American major and small press magazines. Forewords to each volume by Atwan are informative about the history of the essay and the place and evolution of the personal essay. Introductions by the guest editors are equally valuable reading.

Cahill, Susan, ed. *Writing Women's Lives* (New York, 1994). From the introduction: "The vitality of these life histories comes from their power and variety on two levels: that of primary lived experiences . . . and that of narrative made about such experience." This book contains writing by fifty famous women authors.

Conway, Jill Ker, ed. *Written By Herself: An Anthology of Autobiographical Writing by American Women* (New York, 1992). This book includes works by many famous women writers including Maya Angelou, Louise Bogan, Zora Neale Hurston, Maxine Hong Kingston, Margaret Mead and Gloria Steinem.

Deford, Frank. *The Best American Sports Writing* (Boston, 1993). Each year the series editor and his guest editor glean the best of sports writing from over 350 magazines, newspapers and other publications. Many of the essays are personal ones written by reporters who love sports, athletes and the events they are sent to cover.

Dubus, Andre. *Broken Vessels* (Boston, 1991). Twenty-two wise and moving essays from this fiction writer's life both before and after a freak accident and his recovery and adjustment to life in a wheelchair.

Edelman, Marian Wright. *The Measure of Our Success, A Letter to My Children and Yours* (Boston, 1992). In ninety-seven pages, Ms. Edelman, founder and president of the Children's Defense Fund and first African-American woman admitted to the Mississippi Bar, writes twenty-five lessons for life.

Fulwiler, Toby. *College Writing, A Personal Approach to Academic Writing* (Portsmouth, NH, 1991). A college text, this one lends itself to the essay writer who writes to learn.

Gutkind, Lee, ed. *Creative Nonfiction* (Pittsburgh, yearly since 1993). This journal is the only one in the world devoted to this genre. According to the editor, "the word 'creative' refers to the unique and subjective focus, concept, context and point of view in which the information is presented and defined, which may be partially obtained through the writer's own voice, as in a personal essay."

Hall, Donald. *Writing Well*, 6th edition (Glenview, IL 1988). A fine college text that covers the elements of strong writing and revision.

Hamilton, Indiana Congressman. Closing remarks to Lt. Col. Oliver North on Iran-Contra affair during hearings in Congress. Available by contacting Room 2187, Rayburn House Office Building, Washington, D.C. 20515-0001 or calling (202) 225-5315 and requesting the section of the Congressional Record that contains the hearing transcriptions for July 21, 1987. This speech addressed to Lt. Col. Oliver North is a sterling example of the well-constructed argument essay.

Henderson, Bill, ed. *The Pushcart Prize* (Wainscott, NY, yearly since 1975). Each edition contains poems, essays, and fiction reprinted from small presses and little magazines anywhere in the world.

Hoagland, Edward. "To the Point, Truths Only Essays Can Tell," *Harper's Magazine*, March 1993. This narrative about the author's writing serves to argue the nature and purpose of personal essays and discusses which material is useful for them.

————*Walking the Dead Diamond River* (New York, 1993). The author was hailed by John Updike as "the best essayist of my generation." This book, which reprints two earlier collections of essays, contains nineteen essays from the author's perspective.

Junker, Howard, ed. *Roots and Branches, Contemporary Essays by West Coast Writers* (San Francisco, 1991). Among these essays collected from the pages of literary review *Zyzzyva* is "The Savings Book" by Gary Soto in which he narrates his handling of his first bank account and the way in which his life eventually changes when he loses some of his fear of impeding disaster.

Kirschenbaum, Carol. *How to Write and Sell Your Personal Essays* (Austin, TX, 1994). Ninety-minute audio of expert advice on how to transform your personal experiences into this highly salable writing form. Available through Writer's Digest Book Club.

Killien, Christi and Bender, Sheila. *Writing in a Convertible With the Top Down: A Unique Guide for Writers* (New York, 1992). Christi and I compressed years of writing experience into this book that helps writers use metaphors from their own lives to get started and keep going.

Lopate, Philip, ed. *The Art of the Personal Essay: An Anthology From the Classical Era to the Present* (New York, 1994). The volume contains over seventy-five personal essays ranging from influential forerunners in Rome and the Far East to Montaigne's groundbreaking work in the sixteenth century to current-day varieties from Africa, Asia, Europe, Latin America, and North America. The editor's introduction is a splendid essay about the personal essay.

Metzger, Deena. *Writing for Your Life* (San Francisco, 1992). Each chapter gives thought-provoking anecdotes and challenging exercises to help readers tune up their sensibilities in the continuous struggle between passion and intellect.

Moskowitz, Faye. *And the Bridge Is Love* (Boston, 1991). Seventeen personal essays that utilize the various essay-writing styles to expertly evoke the author's childhood and adult experiences as a Jew, wife, daughter, mother and teacher.

Murray, Donald M. *Write to Learn* (Austin, TX, 1984). This book is a useful look at the writing process including collecting material, focusing the material, ordering it, drafting and clarifying.

Nerburn, Kent. *Letters to My Son* (San Rafael, CA, 1993). A series of personal essays that use all the essay styles to share life lessons and impart knowledge about love, marriage, strength, and other issues in a man's life.

Pennebaker, James W., Ph.D. *Opening Up: The Healing Power of Confiding in Others* (New York, 1990). Chapter 7, "Understanding the Value of Writing," is a cause and effect inquiry into the reason writing about trauma helps people heal. "People reach an understanding of the events and, once this is accomplished, they no longer need to inhibit their talking any further."

Peterson, Brenda. *Living By Water* (Seattle, 1990). Thirteen personal essays that weave the author's deep connection with the world's ecosystem, her family, and the larger community of humankind.

Sherline, Reid. *Letters Home: Celebrated Authors Write to Their Mothers* (New York, 1993). Mark Twain's letter to his mother from Carson City, Nevada on October 26, 1861 is full of description aimed to horrify her. Wallace Stegner's "Letter—Much Too Late" appears here as it does in his book, *Family Portraits*.

Simonson, Rick and Walker, Scott, eds. *The Graywolf Annual* (St. Paul, MN, yearly since 1984). Not every edition is entirely essays but there are many which include personal ones. Number 5 contains thirteen personal essays addressed to multi-cultural concerns and interests. Number 3 contains essays, memoirs and reflections. Number 10 contains essays on community.

Trimmer and Hairston, eds. *The Riverside Reader*, 4th edition (Boston, 1993). A wonderful culturally diverse and current selection of essays grouped by style. Writing by Shelby Steele, Charles Johnson, Lely Hayslip and Hong-Kingston are included. The out-of-print volumes 1 and 2, 1st and 2nd editions (1981, 1983, 1985) remain my favorites, however. Among particular essays I enjoyed are a narration essay by Langston Hughes and one by Richard Wright, a description essay by

Eudora Welty, a classification and division essay by William Golding, a definition essay by John Ciardi and another by Dorothy Parker, a cause and effect essay by E. M. Forster, an argument essay by Anne and Paul Ehrlich, and a hilarious how-to by H. Allen Smith.

Uland, Brenda. *If You Want to Write: A Book About Art, Independence, and Spirit* (St. Paul, MN, 1987). This book coaches the writing spirit with integrity and encouragement.

————*Strength to Your Sword Arm* (Duluth, MN, 1993). In this collection of selected short personal essays from Uland's career, you'll find each of the essay styles well-used. "Tell me more, On the fine art of listening" (also printed in *The Utne Reader*, November/December, 1992) is a definition of listening that includes the forms of how-to, narration, comparison and contrast, and cause and effect.

Willis, Sue Meredith. *Deep Revision: A Guide for Teachers, Students, and Other Writers* (New York, 1993). A text on revision, this book offers practice in revision by using others' comments and revising others' work.

White, E. B. *Essays of E.B. White* (New York, 1992). As Joan Frank, reviewing in the July/August 1990 *Utne Reader*, said, White was a near guru of the form.

————*Writings From the New Yorker 1927-1976* (New York, 1990). These were the essays that made E. B. White famous.

Zinsser, William, ed. *Inventing the Truth: The Art and Craft of Memoir* (Boston, 1987). Six essays by famous people inspired by their lives. Lewis Thomas' essay about the history of cells, language acquisition and our lives is a knockout.

Zinsser, William. *On Writing Well, An Informal Guide to Writing Nonfiction* (New York, 1990). A chapter on writing about yourself among other chapters with sage advice.

More Essayists and Autobiographical Writers:
Paula Gunn Allen, Maya Angelou, Russell Baker, Saul Bellow, Wendell Berry, Joan Didion, Stephen Dunn, Carlos Fuentes, Ellen

Goodman, Judy Grahn, Donald Hall, Patricia Hampl, William Hazlett, Charlayne Hunter-Gault, Denise Levertov, Barry Lopaz, Nancy Mairs, William Matthews, W.S. Merwin, John McPhee, James Merrill, George Orwell, Reynolds Price, Anna Quindlan, David Rain, Adrienne Rich, Gary Snyder, Susan Sontag, Kim Stafford, Calvin Trilling, Terry Tempest Williams, Geoffrey Wolff, Tom Wolfe.

Directories:

Bacon's Magazine Directory. (Bacon's Information, Inc., 332 S. Michigan Avenue, Chicago, IL 60604. 312/922-2400.) A guide to more than 9,500 business, trade, professional and consumer publications in the U.S. and Canada by theme such as Horse and Horse Breeding, Insurance, Hunting and Fishing.

Directory of Literary Magazines and Presses, 1993-94. (Council of Literary Magazines and Presses. Moyer Bell: Wakefield, RI and London.) 500 magazines in 49 states, the Virgin Islands, and Washington, DC. Entries address questions readers, writers, libraries and publishers often ask.

Gale Directory of Publications and Broadcast Media (formerly *Ayer Directory of Publications*). (Troshynski-Thomas and Burck, eds. Gale Research, Inc., 835 Penobscot Building, Detroit, MI 48226-4094.) Published annually since 1869, this directory lists publications by state and city in which they are published. It also includes the population of each city listed.

The International Directory of Little Magazines and Small Presses, 29th ed., 1993-94, Len Fulton, ed. (Dustbooks, P.O. Box 100, Paradise, CA 95967.) 5,500 markets for writers.

Internet World's On Internet '94, An International Guide to Electronic Journals, Newsletters, Texts, Discussion Lists and Other Resources on the Internet, from *Internet World Magazine*, 1994. (Meckler Media, Westport, CT.) The subtitle says it all.

The Internet Yellow Pages by Hahn Harley. (Osborne McGraw-Hill, Berkeley, CA, 1994.) A great guide to listservs and news groups on the internet including ones about and with writers.

Magazines for Libraries. (R.R. Bowker, P.O. Box 31, New Providence, NJ 07974-9904.) Since 1969, this directory has been a source of information on periodic literature from national, regional and small independent presses.

Network, The International Women's Writing Guild Newsletter. (IWWG, Caller Box 810, Gracie Station, New York, NY 10028. 212/737-7536.) The IWWG is a network for the empowerment of women through writing. Write or call about membership. The newsletter contains a section on markets in each issue.

Oxbridge Directory of Newsletters. (Oxbridge Communications, Inc. 150 5th Avenue, New York, NY 10011. 212/741-0231.) This directory offers a comprehensive guide to U.S. and Canadian newsletters listed by subject such as botany, college students, and genealogy.

Poets & Writers Magazine. (Poets and Writers, Inc., 72 Spring St., New York, NY 10012. 212/226-3586.) Published six times a year, this magazine contains information on markets, grants, and the issues writers face.

Religious Writer's Marketplace, 4th edition, William H. Gentz and Sandra H. Brooks, eds. (Abingdon Press, Nashville, 1993.) This guide to the opportunities in religious publishing lists Christian and Jewish periodicals, books, newspapers, syndicates, contests and more.

Small Press, The Magazine of Independent Publishing. (Small Press, Kymbolde Way, Dept. NW, Wakefield, RI 02879. 401/789-0074.) A listing of small press publications, many of which are interested in essays.

Small Press Review. (Dustbooks, P.O. Box 100, Paradise, CA 95967.) Monthly subscriptions are available.

Ulrich's International Periodicals Directory. (The Bowker International Serials Database, R.R. Bowker, P.O. Box 31, New Providence, NJ 1/800/346-6049.) This yearly index includes listings of periodicals (even irregular serials and annuals) and daily and weekly newspapers by title, by geographical area, and by subject. There is an index to publications of international organizations.

Working Press of the Nation: Magazines and Internal Publications Directory. (National Register Publishing, 121 Chanlon Road, New Providence, NJ 07974.) This one has more than 5,500 magazines in over 200 categories including 2,500 corporate, government, association and club publications.

Writer's Digest Magazine. (F&W Publications, 1507 Dana Avenue, Cincinnati, OH 45207-9965.) Each issue contains a listing of markets as well as how-to articles and advice for writers.

The Writer's Handbook, Sylvia K. Burack, ed. (The Writer's Inc., Boston, 1994.) For over 50 years this book has offered tips for writers from essayists to feature reporters, and it offers information on rates and requirements in over 3,000 markets.

Writer's Market, Mark Garvey, ed. (Writer's Digest Books, 1507 Dana Avenue, Cincinnati, OH 45207.) This extensive directory is updated every year and of interest to essay writers are the listings on book publishers, trade and consumer magazines and contests.

Writer's Northwest Handbook, The Market Guide to the Pacific Northwest 3,000 Publishers and Resources, Essays, How-to Articles, Tips, 5th edition. (Media Weavers, 1738 NE 24th, Portland, OR 97212. 503/771-5166.) An up-to-date guide to markets and author activities in Northwest publications.

Writer's NW, News & Reviews for the Community of the Printed Word. (Media Weavers, 1738 NE 24th, Portland, OR 97212. 503/771-5166.) More information on what is going on for writers and the NW markets.

INDEX

More Great Books
for Writers!